MEMOIRS OF A JEWISH PRISONER OF THE GULAG

MEMOIRS OF A JEWISH PRISONER OF THE GULAG

ZVI PREIGERZON

**Edited & Translated
by Alex Lahav**

BOSTON
2022

Library of Congress Cataloging-in-Publication Data

Names: Preigerzon, Zvi, 1900-1969, author. | Lahav, Alex, 1952- translator, editor.
Title: Memoirs of a Jewish prisoner of the Gulag / Zvi Preigerzon ;
    translated and edited by Alex Lahav.
Other titles: Yoman ha-zikhronot, 1949–1955. English
Description: Boston : Cherry Orchard Books, 2022.
Identifiers: LCCN 2022017345 (print) | LCCN 2022017346 (ebook) | ISBN
    9781644699034 (hardback) | ISBN 9781644699041 (paperback) | ISBN
    9781644699058 (adobe pdf) | ISBN 9781644699065 (epub)
Subjects: LCSH: Preigerzon, Zvi, 1900–1969. | Political prisoners–Soviet
    Union–Biography. | Jews–Soviet Union–Biography. | Authors,
    Hebrew–Soviet Union–Biography.
Classification: LCC HV8959.R9 P6813 2022 (print) | LCC HV8959.R9 (ebook)
    | DDC 365/.450947–dc23/eng/20220625
LC record available at https://lccn.loc.gov/2022017345
LC ebook record available at https://lccn.loc.gov/2022017346

Book design by Kryon Publishing Services
www.kryonpublishing.com
Cover design by Ivan Grave

Published by Academic Studies Press
1577 Beacon St.
Brookline, MA 02446
press@academicstudiespress.com
www.academicstudiespress.com

Contents

Introduction

Zvi Preigerzon wrote his memoirs in 1957-1958, a year and a half after his release from the Gulag, where he was held in 1949-1955. He was arrested during the period of brutal antisemitic campaign unleashed by Joseph Stalin in the last years of his rule. The campaign started in 1948 with the murder of Solomon Mikhoels, the chairman of the Jewish Anti-Fascist Committee, and the arrest and execution of all the committee members—well-known Jewish writers, poets, and actors. During the campaign against "rootless cosmopolitans," all Jewish newspapers, magazines, and theaters in the Soviet Union were shut down. Many innocent Jewish government officials, scientists, engineers, and just simple Jewish people were arrested. They were accused of anti-government nationalistic activity, using the infamous article 58 of the penal code, and were sent to the Gulag with sentences ranging from five to twenty-five years. The antisemitic campaign culminated in 1952-1953 with the "Doctors' Plot," when thousands of Jewish physicians were publicly accused of the poisoning of Communist Party officials and ordinary Soviet citizens.

The antisemitic campaign was in full swing in the Soviet newspapers and on the radio. It was intended to conclude with a series of public trials to expose the widespread Jewish conspiracy. Public riots and pogroms against Jews were already planned. The multimillion Jewish population of the Soviet Union was intended to be deported to the eastern parts of Russia, where they would be starved and murdered far from the public eye. In short, Stalin's goal was to replicate Hitler's "Final Solution." Only Stalin's death in March 1953, which accidentally coincided with the Jewish Purim holiday, prevented this disaster from happening. Some call it "the miracle of Purim." Eventually, in 1954-1956 the Jews who survived the brutal forced labor camps, together with millions of other Soviet and foreign citizens, were released. Most of them were formally acquitted and their rights restored. Zvi Preigerzon was one of them.

Zvi Preigerzon wrote his memoirs about his time in the Gulag long before Solzhenitsyn and without any knowledge of the other publications on this subject. It was one of the first eyewitness accounts of the harsh reality of the Soviet penalty system. Even after the death of Stalin, when the Gulag forced labor camps were largely disbanded, writing about the Gulag could be regarded as an act of heroism. Preigerzon attempted to document and analyze his own prison experience, and portray the fellow Jewish prisoners he encountered in forced labor camps. Among these people, we meet scientists, engineers, famous Jewish writers and poets, young Zionists, a devoted religious man, a horse wagon driver, a Jewish singer of folk songs, and many, many others. As Preigerzon put it, "Each one with his own story, his own soul, and his own tragedy."

A well-known Russian writer and a former Gulag prisoner, Varlam Shalamov, famously wrote: "No man gets better after the camp. The prison camp corrupts everyone." However, Zvi Preigerzon managed to maintain his dignity and faith in the human soul. Despite of all the atrocities that he experienced, his writings are full of warmth and humor. Most of all, he treasured Jewish brotherhood, the care and support of each other, and the preservation of Jewish culture and the Hebrew language. He wrote: "While in prison, I swore to myself not to abandon the Hebrew language until the end of my life, and to this very day I have stood by this promise. And even if I am arrested for the second time, I will continue to worship the Hebrew language until my last breath."

Zvi Preigerzon (1900-1969) was an expert in coal enrichment, a professor at Moscow Mining University, where he invented technologies for coal processing and wrote textbooks that were used by college students all over the Soviet Union. However, his real passion was writing in Hebrew. "The Hebrew thrill has poisoned my blood forever," he wrote in one of his short stories. After the Communist Revolution, Preigerzon faced a major dilemma—the choice between studying in Moscow or emigrating to Palestine. This decision would shape the rest of his life, as he chose to acquire a profession. Soon, Stalin's regime made emigration impossible.

Preigerzon's short stories and poems were first published in the 1920s in several Hebrew language journals and magazines in Europe. Later, when Hebrew was banned in the USSR, he continued writing secretly without any hope of being published. He hid his writings even from his own family and friends. Preigerzon wrote about Jewish people trapped in the reality of revolution, war, and the destruction of their religious and cultural traditions in the Soviet Union. After World War II, the Holocaust became an important theme in Preigerzon's writings. Many of his short stories and the novel *When the Menorah Fades* are devoted to the suffering of Jews during the Nazi occupation.

In March 1949, Zvi Preigerzon was arrested, accused of anti-Soviet nationalistic activity, and sentenced to ten years in the Gulag. He went through brutal interrogations in Lefortovo Prison and inhumane conditions during the transfer of prisoners in Stolypin carriages. He experienced humiliation, hunger, and hard labor in numerous prison camps. Zvi Preigerzon became deeply involved in Jewish life in each of the prison camps where he was held—Karaganda, Inta, Abez, and Vorkuta. He spoke Hebrew with his friends and taught other Jewish prisoners the language. He enjoyed singing and reciting Jewish songs, verses, and religious psalms. He called these songs "my morning prayers." He wrote:

> What was my morning prayer? I sang Hebrew songs, Yiddish songs, and Jewish melodies without words. Throughout all my time in the prison camp, I collected Hebrew songs. Besides the songs that I knew from my childhood, I learned many other beautiful Hebrew songs from my fellow Jewish prisoners. . . . Over the years, I assembled more than a hundred songs, so I divided them between the days of the week. Every day I sang different songs.

After the renunciation of Stalin's terror, Zvi Preigerzon was released from prison, his conviction was revoked, and he was officially rehabilitated. He returned to Moscow, reunited with his family, and continued his professional work as a scientist, along with his writing in Hebrew. He was physically isolated from the Land of Israel, but his heart was always there. He always perfected his ability with Hebrew, using all the means available to him. His knowledge of the Jewish culture and history was extensive, and in his writings he often used expressions, allegories, and metaphors from the Bible.

Zvi Preigerzon died in Moscow in 1969 of a heart attack. When the repatriation of Jews was allowed in the 1970s, all of his family emigrated to Israel. In accordance with his will, his remains were buried in Israel. All Zvi Preigerzon's works were published in Israel. In recognition of his literary achievements, a street in Tel-Aviv was named after him. Later, his works were translated and published in Russian. The novel *When the Menorah Fades* was translated into English and published in 2020 by Academic Studies Press.

The first Hebrew edition of Zvi Preigerzon's *Gulag Memoirs*, "יומן הזכרונות" (The Diary), was published in Israel by the Am Oved publishing house in 1976. The Russian translation by Israel Minz, a former Gulag prisoner who personally knew Zvi Preigerzon, was published in 2005 by the Israeli publishing house Philobiblion.

This English translation is based on the second Hebrew edition "מחסגר," published in 2012 in Israel by the HaKibbutz HaMeuhad publishing house. The book was prepared and edited by Professor Hagit Halperin, an Israeli scholar who devoted a large part of her life to the preservation and publication of Zvi Preigerzon's literary heritage. This second Hebrew edition is extremely close to Zvi Preigerzon's original manuscript and contains many references to notable Jewish people, and facts about Jewish history and culture.

Zvi Preigerzon's original manuscript of the Gulag memoirs was written as daily diary notes and was not intended for publication. He noted: "My memoirs will not be polished or heavily edited—they will be just raw recollections—so that we will not forget the things that must not be forgotten." To preserve the logic and historical timeframe of the events described in the book, this English translation was edited and subdivided according to the chronology of the events, with special attention to the Jewish people Preigerzon met in the Gulag.

I can wholeheartedly identify myself with Zvi Preigerzon's wish that he expressed in his foreword: "The years will pass and maybe one of my descendants will read this book and discover something enlightening."

Alex Lahav
Translator, editor, and the grandson of Zvi Preigerzon
Zvi Preigerzon Foundation
www.zvipreigerzonfoundation.org

Author's Foreword

Beria and Abakumov arrested me, even though I was innocent.[1] I spent almost seven years in prison and forced labor camps, from the beginning of May 1949 until the end of 1955. I was a victim of lawlessness. Now I am a free man, I have returned to my family and my work. My rights as a Soviet citizen were completely restored. Nevertheless, the memories of these seven years are still vivid, and I have decided to put them in writing in the form of a diary. In these memoirs, I will reflect on my experiences during those seven years, meetings with hundreds of people, thoughts, events, hopes, and frustrations. My memoirs will not be polished or heavily edited—they will be just raw recollections—so that we will not forget the things that must not be forgotten.

I met many people during my time in the Gulag;[2] each one with his own story, his own soul, and his own tragedy. All those lost years! How many human lives were ruined by Beria and Abakumov, by their criminal organization, and by their zealous accomplices? Every one of them, from superiors to ordinary subordinates, managed to spit into the human soul in order to insult, weaken, and destroy it. Every one of them thought that he was doing it for the sake of the homeland. The slogans were lovely, the finest words in the vocabulary were used to force the system to persecute millions of people. But under the worn-out, soiled, and filthy prisoners' peacoats, the human soul still pounded. Cherished images and visions of nature, beloved spouses and children held firm in prisoners' eyes. The freedom of the human mind could not be put behind bars.

---

1   Lavrentiy Beria—head of NKVD, Soviet Ministry of Internal Affairs; Viktor Abakumov—Head of the MGB, Soviet Ministry of State Security.
2   Gulag—the Chief Directorate of Corrective Labor Camps

While in prison, I swore to myself not to abandon the Hebrew language until the end of my life, and until this very day I have stood by this promise. And even if I am arrested for a second time, I will continue to worship the Hebrew language until my last breath.

The years will pass and maybe one of my descendants will read this book and discover something enlightening.

Part 1

Arrest

On March 1, 1949, at about two at night, the doorbell sounded. Three men dressed in civilian suits entered, accompanied by a witness, a local woman janitor. The stated purpose of the visit was to check our passports. After examining my passport, they told me that I was the one they were looking for and I was ordered to get dressed. They showed me a warrant for my arrest signed by the MGB and by the Prosecutor's Office.[1] My belongings were searched and my pockets emptied. Later in prison, all the metal parts of my clothing were cut off, including the buttons and clasps. After getting dressed, I was told to be ready to leave the house.

At that time, my older daughter was twenty and the younger one was eighteen years old. Both were awake in another room. My son, twelve years old, was still asleep on the sofa.

"What can I give him?" my wife asked.

"Underwear, a blanket, and a small amount of money."

My wife packed these things.

"How long are you taking him for?" she asked.

"We do not know. He may be back in one to three days," was the answer. "Anyway, there is a well-known Russian saying: Prepare a sled in summer and a horse cart in winter."

It was around three in the morning and the city was still sleeping. The disaster was looming.

---

1   MGB—the Soviet Ministry of State Security. During 1946-1954, the KGB (Committee for State Security) was known as the MGB.

They ordered, "Say goodbye to your family and we shall depart."

My daughters came into the room. I kissed them. Tears welled in their eyes, but my wife's eyes remained dry. All at once, the responsibility for three children fell on this little woman. I was also allowed to say a brief farewell to my son. I entered the second room and kissed him. He was fast asleep.

"Let's go."

My wife accompanied me to the front door, where I kissed her. We went outside—that is how I left my house for seven years.

One of the men escorting me was carrying a weapon in his pocket. I was wearing winter clothes and holding a bag with underwear and a gray blanket in it. The car was waiting for us at Pogodin Street, a few meters from the entrance door. We took the back seat. "Get going," the man commanded. The car passed Devichie Pole Street and Zubov Square, then we dove along Kropotkin Street. The city was dark and quiet. I stared through the window and contemplated the scene, as if saying farewell. I was aware that a meticulous search was being conducted at my apartment. I knew this because it was not the first case of an arrest among the residents of our house or my Jewish friends. In October 1948, Meir Baazov had been arrested and a month before that Zvi Plotkin (Moshe Hiog). I was also aware that Yitzhak Kahanov (Kogan) had been arrested in Simferopol. Finally, the car arrived at Lubyanka Square.[2]

I got out of the car. The entry door to the building opened and immediately closed. It was a door to a different world, a world "behind the curtain." Trained hands searched me and my clothes; my hair was cut. Then I was taken to a shower and given a ridiculously small piece of soap. I was given the same piece of soap each time when I washed myself during the next seven years. After that, I was locked in a "box," a small cabinet the size of a closet or a toilet stall with a bench, on which I sat still for long hours. The door had a peephole, and a guard regularly observed me through it. I was given food—sauerkraut, salted herring, and a piece of rye bread. Being distressed, I was not able to eat.

The next day I was visited by two of the MGB men that had searched my apartment. They read me a search report, which listed the things that were confiscated: my two medals, one given to me for my actions

---

2   Lubyanka Square—the location of the MGB's (KGB) headquarters.

during World War II, and the second commemorating the eight hundredth anniversary of Moscow; a box of shot caps for my son's toy pistol; my "Senior Lecturer" and "Doctor of Technical Science" diplomas; and a savings deposit certificate for seven hundred rubles. They had also temporarily confiscated my typewriter, the piano, books, etc. I signed the search report and was given receipts for the confiscated items.

Part 2

Interrogation

Citizen Lieutenant Colonel

After being held in a box, I was transferred to a solitary cell on the third floor, where I spent several days. The cell was more comfortable. There was a jar with water on a small table and food was brought three times a day. In the morning, hot water with a lump of sugar and a daily portion of bread (six hundred grams). In the afternoon, a cup of plain prison soup and porridge. And in the evening, more porridge and hot water. The quality of food in prison depended on the level of collaboration between the prisoner and the investigator. The investigator oversaw the prisoner's food, sleep, and other living arrangements. The prisoner was entitled to a minimum food ration. Sometimes, if the prisoner was "behaving well"—meaning he had cooperated with his investigator—he was given better food and more time to sleep. On Sunday, by mistake, they brought me a cutlet with potatoes. It turned out that the cutlet was intended for another prisoner who had occupied the cell before me. So, the guard took it back immediately.

In the evening of my third or fourth day in the cell, I was taken to the interrogation room. The room was large with decent furniture and two desks. The prisoner's desk was placed next to the door, several meters from the interrogator. The interrogator was a short man dressed in a civilian suit. He was heavily built, with black hair, a pleasant face, and piercing eyes. I was sitting in the chair next to the doorway and he was sitting behind his desk. It was my destiny to struggle with this man during the next nine months. More accurately, I had to defend myself from the assaults of this man. However, in the beginning, I was not aware of that. His name was Lebedev, and he ordered me to address him as "Citizen Lieutenant Colonel" or "Citizen Investigator."[1]

In the beginning, he started to fill out a long questionnaire about me. First name, family name, my father's name, date of birth, names of my wife and children. When I mentioned the names of my children, Athaliah, Nina, and Binyamin, he commented that I had given my children names from the Bible... Being inexperienced and naive, I signed the document. In the questionnaire, I had also answered the question about my relatives, including my brothers. Later, I realized that this was a huge mistake. It was widely believed that the MGB cannot be wrong, that the very fact of my arrest was proof of my guilt and made me an "enemy of the people. And not only me—anyone close to me fell under suspicion. People should have stayed away from me, at a distance as far as an "arrow flight." As a result of my arrest, both of my brothers were fired from their jobs and had very unpleasant experiences.

My first interrogation by the Citizen Lieutenant Colonel turned out to be nonviolent. At the end of it, I was told that during future interrogations I should tell all the truth and only the truth. I had to know in whose hands I was being held, that they knew everything about me, my activities, my meetings, and, in short, all the details of my crime. I would suffer immensely if I do not voluntarily provide them with honest information. They would punish me as severely as they please. As he told me this, his dark eyes burst into flames and spittle flew out of his mouth.

Lefortovo Prison

That same evening or the next day, I was transferred to Lefortovo Prison. The guard entered my cell and ordered me to identify myself and collect my belongings. A black car, called Voronok,[2] was waiting in the prison yard. I was pushed into the tiny back compartment where an armed

---

1   Prisoners were required to use this form of address, as opposed to the more usual "comrade."
2   Voronok—a black car used for the transportation of prisoners. Named after "voron," a black crow in Russian.

guard was already waiting for me in the darkness. The gloomy building of Lefortovo Prison rose into the dark skies.

At first, I was locked again in a "box" with a floor made of stone tiles. I felt cold. The overweight lady, who turned out to be a prison doctor, ordered me to undress and quickly inspected me. It turned out that this inspection was critical for setting the methods of my interrogation. The beating of prisoners during interrogation was not allowed without proper medical permission. The prison doctor did not find any significant flaws in my health (even though I was suffering from a duodenal ulcer) and gave her permission for me to be subjected to a "comprehensive" interrogation.

I spent the night in solitary and in the morning was taken to cell number 204, which was already occupied by two other prisoners. I stayed in this cell for several months. Allegedly, the cell number was lucky—paragraph 204 in the Soviet legislation was about prisoner's release—but it turned out to be a miserable number.

High up on one of the walls, there was a small window with metal bars. It was impossible to see anything through it, not the land and not even the sky. The walls were very thick and the iron door had a peephole. Outside, day and night, the guard on duty walked his rounds in the corridor. At regular intervals, like clockwork, he opened and closed the peephole cover. To this day, I shiver when I recall the sound of the opening and closing of that peephole cover.

On March 29, I had the first encounter with my prison cell fellows, Farmakovsky, a Russian seaman from Leningrad, and Mustafa Adali, a Turkish car driver. I vividly remember both. Later, during my time behind bars, I met thousands of other prisoners. The memories of many of them have faded, but these two I will remember forever.

Farmakovsky only stayed with us for three days. His interrogation was already over, and he was about to be transferred to another location. He was very sick and, even under the strict prison conditions, was getting some special kind of diet. He was about my age, an experienced naval officer, who for many years had sailed abroad. He had served as the captain of a ship that regularly cruised to London. He had also sailed to Italy and other countries, and often told us stories about his travels. He was accused of espionage and had already signed his confession. We had the same interrogator, and to my question regarding his character

Farmakovsky just helplessly waved his hand and advised me not to feel bad about signing the questionnaire. Lebedev would not allow me to take back my signature anyway. Later, he told me a lot about the interrogation methods of the Citizen Lieutenant Colonel.

Mustafa was different. He was also about my age, short, with black hair and dark skin. When Farmakovsky was taken out of the cell, Mustafa and I were left with each other. Mustafa Adali told me many stories. He was born in Turkey and served in Kamal Pasha's cavalry, and even knew him quite well. In the '20s, he arrived in Russia as a member of a delegation sent by Kamal Pasha. He'd stayed in Russia since then, married a Russian woman, and had a daughter. He worked as a driver for various embassies in Moscow and told me a lot about the rules and regulations of the foreign embassies, about daily life in the embassies, parties, and official receptions, as if he himself had taken part in them.

During the war, he'd moved to Kuybyshev as an embassy employee and even there enjoyed a pleasant lifestyle and young women. Later, he married for a second time, and since the end of the war had worked at the Turkish embassy in Batumi, where he was arrested and brought to Moscow for interrogation. He was accused of espionage and was brutally beaten with rubber clubs. Eventually, he confessed to spying for Turkey during all his years in Russia and was sentenced to twenty-five years in a forced labor camp. I recall his stories about Turkey, about the lovely tradition of planting fruit trees on both sides of the road so that travelers could enjoy their fruit during their journeys. He also told me a lot about weddings, funerals, and birth customs, about relations between the Turks and the Armenians, Jews, and Greeks. All his stories had a positive tone. Mustafa was a decent man, deeply devoted to his country. He loved to sing the songs of his homeland with pleasant melodies. I even composed my own song by using one of his melodies. The song was named "We Are Being Buried Alive in the Prison House."

My Hebrew Writing

During the years 1925–1930, I published several poems and short stories written in Hebrew: "From the Folk Songs," "My Brother Moshke," "To a Gentile Girl," "Palestine," "In the Woods of Pashutovka," "Beila from the House of Rapaport," "Paranoia," "Between Purim and Passover," "My Mother," etc.

These works were published in several Hebrew language magazines and newspapers: *HaOlam*, *HaTkufa*, *HaDoar*, *Davar*, and *Hadim*, which were printed abroad. My works were certainly not anti-Soviet, and they did not express any Jewish nationalistic ideas. I did not contribute to *Bereshit* magazine, although since 1925 I had been familiar with Zvi Plotkin and his friends, who were published there. Later, they also became my friends.

For several years (1930-1943), I did not write in Hebrew, even though all my life I had cherished and loved the Hebrew language, will never abandon it, and will be devoted to it for the rest of my life. During the war with Hitler, and the dreadful years of the Holocaust, I began writing short stories in Hebrew again. I started my Hebrew writing in Karaganda between 1941-1943, when my family had been evacuated from Moscow, and later continued my writing in Moscow after our return in September 1943. For several years, I worked on the first part of the novel *When the Menorah Fades*, the short stories "In a Blacksmith's Alley," "Burden of the Name," "This Life," "Refuges," Galoshes," "Cameo," "Disguise," Coming to Faith," "Deaf Women," "In the Summer Camp," "In the Southern Town," and "In the Place of my Youth." All these works were "kosher" (not anti-Soviet): they were just written in Hebrew, and the MGB became suspicious of me.

The MGB Informer

The truth was that the MGB knew perfectly well what was happening in my home and the homes of Zvi Plotkin, Itzhak Kahanov, and Meir Baazov. One of our mutual friends, Sasha, was an MGB informer. He often came to my home, ate my bread, and drank my water, so my family knew him quite well. My wife even tried to matchmake between him and one of her female acquaintances. Sasha followed our every step. He became very close to Zvi Plotkin, who occasionally complained about Soviet rule, possibly even in my presence. In any case, the MGB most certainly had sizable folders on every one of us, covering many years of spying at our homes. Sasha was submitting to the MGB detailed records about every one of us. When he learned that Plotkin, Kahanov, and I were writing in

Hebrew, he told us that he also liked the Hebrew language. Once, I gave him one of my short stories, "The Burden of the Name," which he offered to show to his rebbe. Later, I learned that this "rebbe" was in fact an MGB officer. My story was translated into Russian and served as a piece of evidence in my criminal case, along with many others.

In 1946, Sasha started persuading me to send several of my short stories for publication in Israel. He claimed that he had a way to give them to Polish Jews, who after the war were allowed to leave the Soviet Union, and eventually go to Israel. He even provided me with information about some of them. After thinking about it for a long time, and because all my fiction was not political at all, I gave Sasha a notebook containing my short stories—which went straight to the MGB. Later, Sasha told me that the Polish woman, to whom he had given my notebook, had successfully arrived in Israel, and I believed him. A few months later, when Sasha told me that there was another opportunity to send my stories to Israel, I gave him another notebook. On the third and last time, the MGB, through Sasha, arranged for the work of three Hebrew writers to be sent to Israel. I will describe this matter in detail.

Zvi Plotkin and Yitzhak Kahanov also wrote in Hebrew, and Sasha was in touch with them. He'd known Plotkin for many years; and Kahanov was connected to Sasha through his work. Kahanov was a head of the philharmonic orchestra in one of the provincial towns in Central Russia. Sasha was quite greedy, and to make money he became the administrator of a makeshift concert touring company, that performed in the town where Kahanov worked. The concert flopped, and Sasha complained to me several times that Kahanov had failed his expectations.

Sasha also told us about a military doctor, who was going on a tourist trip to Bulgaria and could take our work with him and give it to a person who was going to Israel. One day, in the early spring of 1948, Sasha, Kahanov, Plotkin, and I gathered at Plotkin's place. We started by reading our stories aloud. Kahanov presented an autobiographical story, Plotkin recited a semi-mystical one, and I read one of my stories. Then we discussed and our stories; and at the end, this scoundrel Sasha again raised the issue of sending our writings to Bulgaria. It was decided that Plotkin would first meet the doctor and check him out.

Even though our literary works were unpolitical, the matter of sending them to Israel was of no particular importance to us. Without Sasha's (i.e. the MGB's) persistent urging, none of us would have even thought of sending our work abroad. And this is only one example of his relentlessness provocations. He also tried to convince Plotkin to write a letter to David Ben-Gurion on a special piece of paper using invisible chemical ink and put this letter together with the material that we were supposed to give to the doctor. As I learned during the interrogation, Plotkin gave in to Sasha provocation and wrote the letter. He met with the "doctor," trusted him, and handed him our work and the letter.

After the establishment of the State of Israel, Sasha arranged several more provocational schemes in which I was not involved. He organized the dispatch of several anonymous letters to different heads of state, urging them to help Israel, which at that time was at war with the Arabs. He set up a petition calling for the creation of a Hebrew language department at Moscow University and a Hebrew-language magazine. Several of his initiatives were met with enthusiasm. During that time, the Jewish public in Moscow was highly excited by the formation of the Israeli state. There were numerous rumors about Jewish youth signing petitions that called the Soviet government to allow them to travel to Israel, help in the war effort, and assist in organizing financial and material aid to the young Israeli state. So, at that time, Sasha's devious proposals did not sound very extraordinary, and I did not see in them any crime against the Soviet state. Meanwhile, our folders in the MGB cabinets were getting fatter and fatter.

The Interrogation

At first, my interrogator focused on one question only—I had to explain why I had been arrested. The MGB never arrests innocent people, and since I had been arrested, I must be guilty. To my reply that it was they who had arrested me and, therefore, they should tell me the reason for my arrest, my interrogator proclaimed that I was being stubborn and disloyal, that I was covering up my crimes, that I was an enemy of the people, that I had betrayed my homeland, and gave me other "very pleasant compliments." Since I was not aware of the reason for my arrest, I mostly kept silent. One day, a tall person with the rank of colonel entered the room and asked the investigator how I was behaving. He answered that I was stubborn and unwilling to admit my guilt. The colonel, a good-looking man of around forty, and with protruding eyes, looked at me in disgust. He told me that they would destroy me and that I did not understand how desperate my situation was. In his protruding eyes, I saw the angel of death. To prove his point, he graced me with two vigorous blows that caught me on the ears. I could barely stand on my feet, as I was completely stunned and deafened. Then, the colonel, as if nothing had happened, suggested to the interrogator that they go together to the cafeteria.

From then on, my interrogator beat me every day. Later, I counted more than fifteen places on my body where I'd been seriously hit. Along with beatings, he also used other punishment techniques. The interrogations were conducted only at night. In prison, the beginning of the allotted sleep time was 10:00 p.m. Typically, at 10:30, when I had just barely closed my eyes, the door of my cell would open and the guard would ask:

"Whose family name starts with P? Give me your full name."

Tired from the constant lack of sleep, I had to rise and identify myself.

"Do you wear glasses? Get dressed."

Then I'd be escorted to the second floor, room number 1, where my interrogator "worked."

The interrogator's desk was located deep inside the room, and the prisoner's desk was next to the entrance door. It was a simple small desk and a chair. At this desk and on this chair, all the interactions between the interrogator and the prisoner took place. Night after night, except Saturdays, I was "enjoying myself" in this terrible room from 11:00 at night until 5:00 in the morning. During the first stage of the inquisition, the interrogator was forcing me to put all my flaws, sins, and crimes in writing. I wasn't able to write much on the subject, since it was obvious to me that my friends and I were innocent. Then, the investigator was demonstratively tearing up the pages that I managed to write before my eyes. The second stage—endless beating and swearing—lasted until the morning. At 5:00 a.m., I was taken back to my cell and fell into a deep sleep. At six in the morning, the reveille sounded. Most nights, I slept for only one hour; some nights, even less than that.

These nine months of interrogation were the worst time of my life. A time of pain, misery, and bitterness. After about a month from the beginning of the investigation, the interrogator told me to sign the first protocol. Looking back, I realize that this was only a test of my resilience. Some prisoners were signing the interrogation protocols immediately, without any resistance. Later, in the camp, the Jewish poet Mordechai Grubian told me that he'd admitted to being an American spy at the very beginning of his interrogation. This accusation was very grave, but he signed his confession and even declared with excitement, "I could sign a hundred of such accusations, but I would never become an anti-Soviet person!"

The interrogation protocol was handwritten by the interrogator. There was only one question and one answer, both were false, like all the other protocols that followed. Even though the protocols were typically written in the form of questions and answers, they were not real questions. These protocols were the pure creation of the interrogator. His work was not easy. As I learned later, our "criminal gang" consisted of seven people and an informer. These seven people were like the actors in a stage play, and he was the playwright. He had to invent all the facts, conversations, meetings, actions, concepts, and motives. And his script had to be signed by all the actors (the gang members).

As I mentioned earlier, the first protocol was just a test. The question was about my attitude to Jewish culture, and the relation between the Jewish culture and the cultures of other nations. In the answer part of the protocol, the interrogator wrote that Hebrew literature and art were superior to those of all other nations of the Soviet Union. As I recollect, he managed to misspell the Russian word "art" several times (he wrote "Исскусмво" instead of "Искусство").

After all the suffering, beating, and torture, I assumed that the first interrogation protocol would include severe accusations of terrible crimes, but not such nonsense. I really adore Jewish culture, but I had never thought of it as superior to the cultures of other nations, especially to Russian culture. I told all this to the interrogator, but in response he gave me a rude slap in the face that usually preceded a beating. So, I signed.

That was a serious mistake on my part, the first defeat in the fight between the prisoner and the interrogator. I should not have betrayed myself so easily. A resolute refusal to sign any lies should have come at the very beginning. I should have shown the interrogator that his "victim" would not sign any of his false statements, even the insignificant ones. Yet, the beatings that I had experienced until then, was only an introduction, an educational beating. Its goal was to prepare me for signing the subsequent interrogation protocols, whatever they would claim.

One of the pressure tools of the interrogator was the money that my wife was sending me every month (around two hundred rubles). This money was for purchasing food in the prison shop. Because of my ulcer, I had acute stomach pains and could not eat the regular prison food. Every ten days I was allowed to order food that was more suitable for my stomach. White bread, butter, sugar, cheese, sausage, sweets, etc. However, the interrogator forbade me from buying food, so in addition to the beatings and lack of sleep, I was also always hungry. To the list of my troubles, I should also add my deteriorating nervous state, which was a result of the violence that I experienced, separation from my family and work, and the depressing prison conditions. I even experienced hallucinations.

I am sitting at the prisoner's desk next to the doorway, far away from the interrogator. It is late at night; very soon it will be sunrise, the birds will start their songs, bringing calm and joy to the people, and comfort and hope to the prisoners. The interrogator is sitting at his desk, smoking, and writing. He is working on my fabricated protocols, while using his wild imagination and lying informer's reports. He is taking some fictional or innocuous "facts" and stretching them to incriminate innocent people, skillfully using shrewd language to ensure a conviction. He writes as if a dangerous criminal is sitting in front of him, an enemy of the people, a traitor from birth, who already in his mother's womb was plotting evil crimes against the state.

The interrogator is smoking, drifting deep into his thoughts. Then he starts writing again. He asks me some trivial question and continues writing. I am sitting silently. Gradually, the members of my family, my wife, my two daughters, and a son appear at the window. I can clearly see their faces. They are staring at the investigator and tears are dropping from the eyes of my wife and younger daughter. I can see a plea and a prayer in the eyes of my son and my older daughter:

"Do not write such terrible things about our father! God, please turn the writing hand to good deeds, truth, and compassion."

The faces are fading, the large window is getting brighter: it is time for the sunrise. My interrogation will be soon over, and I will be able to sleep for an hour. The interrogator is pressing the bell button. A guard with red shoulder straps enters the room.

"Take him to the cell," orders the investigator.

"Go," the guard commands.

We are entering the corridor and a guard on duty hands me a form that I have to sign. The lines above and below are concealed by a special cover. The line in view shows only my name, the name of my interrogator, the date and time of the beginning and end of the session. I sign the form and continue walking under escort. We are going up the stairway. The open spaces between the stairways are protected by metal mesh, so that the prisoner will not even consider jumping down. The prisoner has to stay alive, at least until the end of the investigation. If another prisoner is in the way, they are forbidden to look at each other. The guard orders me, "Face the wall," and I have to stay facing the wall until the other prisoner passes me. "Go!" commands the guard and finally we are approaching the door of my cell number 204. The corridor guard on duty opens the door with a large key; I am entering the cell and the door shuts down behind me. The cell is small, the window recess is getting brighter. Mustafa is sleeping. Even though the smell in the cell is quite unpleasant, I enjoy all of it, as if it is a fairy tale palace. I am trying to get some sleep, even for an hour. I am lying on the bed but cannot fall asleep. After some time, I hear the steps of a corridor guard and the noise of the peephole cover opening and closing.

Night after night I was taken to interrogation; night after night my interrogator wrote the protocols of my investigation. In the silence of the room, I could hear prisoners' screams from the adjacent interrogation rooms, screams of men and women in the torture rooms, where the human souls were bitten and broken down. This scream roared inside the thick prison walls. However, only the prisoners, interrogators, and guards could hear it. The vast country, that was widely stretched to immense distances beyond the prison walls, was all quiet and well.

The Initial Protocols

One day, the interrogator ordered me to sign a pack of the interrogation protocols of my investigation, a stack of typewritten sheets of paper. This stack of papers added up to about two hundred and fifty pages. Two-thirds of it was devoted to the protocols. Obviously, I do not remember all the details, but these fabricated protocols with terrible lies were written on my behalf, and I had to sign all of this abomination. The choice was horrific. If I sign them, my fate will be dire, and if I do not sign them, I will suffer immensely. I started reading the protocols, and the light faded in my eyes. I had to sign every page. Obviously, the goal was to demonstrate the "joy and happiness" of the prisoner as he was going through each page of the interrogation protocols. In truth, every such signature was causing me enormous mental pain, as if I was spitting in my own face.

I am a son of the People of the Book.[3] All my life I felt deep esteem for the written word. During the years of my work, I had published many textbooks and scientific papers, and I habitually feel diligent respect for the freshly typed pages. The protocols were printed neatly on the sheets of heavy, top quality paper, acting as a psychological incentive for me to sign them.

Initially, I was given a broken piece of a pencil to make corrections, but when I tried to cross out a word, the pencil was immediately taken from me. At the same moment, another investigator entered the room.

"Look, he wants to make changes in the protocols given to him for signature," said my interrogator in a tone that implied it was an incredibly rude act on my part. The other investigator walked out, and we were left alone in the room. I signed the first two or three pages that referred to the days of my youth, even though they were written in an accusatory way, implying that already in my mother's womb I was a die-hard criminal and an enemy of the Soviet state. When I reached the fabricated self-confession part of the protocols, I realized that by signing it, I would be subjected to a long prison term. It looked like the interrogator was well aware of my thoughts.

"I will not sign these false pages; all this is a sheer lie," I told him.

At first, he tried to convince me, then he started shouting at me, and finally, he began beating me. His blows did not help; it is not in human nature to immediately yield to physical assault. If a person does that, it means that all his mental and physical strength is broken, and he has no right to be called a human being.

---

3   People of the Book—a term used in Judaism to refer to the Jewish people.

However, blows, especially if you don't return them, can have a subjugating effect. Physical fighting was not a part of the culture I grew up in. There were prisoners that, according to their words, fought back after the physical assault of the interrogator. They were immediately taken to the carcer,[4] but after that they were not beaten again, their interrogators used different means to break them. My response was different, so after the first beating, the interrogator kept pounding me in a gradual and systematic way.

The beatings had a psychological effect on my behavior and were gradually breaking my strength. This is probably the way wild animals are tamed in the circus. The blows themselves cause resistance, but, nevertheless, the animal's mental strength is gradually fractured, and the animal knows that if it does not follow its handler's command it will be beaten again. That is how the fear of beating unconsciously entered my mind. It would go like this:

I. "No, I will not sign this!" And I would be beaten.

INTERROGATOR. "Now, sign!"

I. "No, I will not." I am beaten again.

INTERROGATOR. "Sign!"

I. "No, I will not sign this falsehood!"

Then the interrogator pretends to give up.

INTERROGATOR. "Read further and sign the following pages!"

This command would be accompanied by a curse, but I would think that this time the interrogator had accepted defeat and my determination had won. In fact, this was as far from the truth as possible. The blows were just a part of the taming process, so that I would sign the following pages. On the next page, I would again find a falsehood, but not as serious as the previous one. I knew that if I did not sign this page, I would be beaten again. The strength of my resistance got weaker and weaker, and I would sign.

My health was getting worse, the stomach pains kept chasing me, and the despair of interrogation was affecting my mind. For a long time before my arrest, I had suffered from a duodenal ulcer. Usually, I treated the stomach pains with atropine. A few drops of atropine were enough to

---

4   Carcer—a small solitary prison cell without windows, typically in the basement, for the punishment of prisoners.

relieve my pain. I asked the prison doctor to prescribe me this medicine and the nurse gave me a tablespoon of the atropine. Medical professionals know very well that a large dose of atropine could have negative side effects.

I do not know if it was due to the atropine, the interrogation, or the permanent loss of sleep, but in the evening I started to behave strangely. I began raving, pounding the cell walls, putting my hands into the toilet sink. In short, I had lost my mind. My fellow prisoner, Mustafa, who later told me about it, called a doctor, who came and tried to measure the temperature under my arm, but the thermometer fell to the floor. I started behaving wildly again. After a while, when two guards entered the cell, I started shouting:

"Please do not beat me! Do not beat me!"

They took me downstairs to a different cell without furniture. There, I started to run around the room and shout again. They brought in a mattress and threw me on it. Finally, I managed to fall asleep.

In the morning, an overweight lady doctor entered my cell to examine me.

"How do you feel?"

"It looks like I am having hallucinations," I answered, "I am imaging that newspapers are covering the floor and I am reading them."

"It's all rubbish," replied the doctor. "You are healthy."

I was transferred back to my cell, and since then I have never experienced such loss of mind. The following evening, I was again called before the Citizen Investigator, and my "joyful" life routine resumed. The beatings continued, as well as the daily prison schedule. Every ten days, the cart from the prison shop delivered goods ordered by prisoners. Most of the time, it did not stop at our cell. Mustafa did not have money, and I was forbidden by my interrogator to get any extra food. Once a week, a guard, serving as a barber, entered the cell. He was quite clumsy, and his razor blade was always awfully dull. This shaving caused me even more suffering than the beatings. After each shave, blood dripped from my chin. There was an adage among the prisoners, which said that, instead of beatings, the interrogator should subject the prisoners to an extra shave.

Taraskin

One day, a new prisoner was ushered into our cell. His name was Valery Taraskin. He was around forty, tall and strong, and quite talkative. According to him, he was a well-known Moscow lawyer. Initially, I suspected him of being an informer. Several years later, I learned from another prisoner that Taraskin was in fact an attorney, but a reckless one, who was often involved in dubious cases.

Taraskin was quite a chatterer, he had a pleasant baritone and was a good singer. Singing was not allowed in prison, so he sang in a very low voice, almost a whisper. I still remember one of the songs, originally performed by the famous gypsy singer Leshchenko, called "The Wine of Love":

The days and years will pass,
Hundreds of years will elapse,
People and countries will vanish,
But the Wine of Love will stay forever.

Taraskin told us that his relationship with the interrogator was quite good. He was accused of spying. Once, a long time before the war, he'd had a meeting in the Metropol restaurant with his clients, German citizens. These clients owned a Chlorodent toothpaste factory in Russia. When the factory was shut down, they sued for compensation, and Taraskin represented them in court. The court decision was partially in his clients' favor, and they invited Taraskin to a restaurant for a celebration. Even though it had all happened a long time ago, Taraskin was arrested and accused of economic espionage. He told us that when the interrogator had tried to beat him, Taraskin, who was an amateur boxer, had shown him his huge fist. He had not been beaten since, and although he had spent many days in carcer, he claimed that he had not signed anything.

Taraskin told us many stories about himself, and every time he portrayed himself in the best light. He claimed to be a good tennis player, a former champion of Moscow. He told us that once he had stayed in a sanatorium in Sochi. There, he fell in love with a beautiful girl, who was there with her boyfriend, so he did not even have a chance to talk to her. To conquer the girl, Taraskin used some of his many talents. At first, he stayed in the shadows, but when the time came, he appeared on the tennis court dressed in a fashionable tennis outfit, and easily beat her boyfriend, while showing great tennis style. Later, at a party, he put on his dinner suit, made by the best Moscow's tailor, and, like a professional singer, performed an aria from an opera to the delight of the audience. In a single night, he won the girl's heart and inflicted total defeat on her boyfriend.

Taraskin's stories always culminated with his success. He delivered them in such a captivating manner that Mustafa and I listened to them with absolute attention. He was also a good chess player. We made chess figures from bread and, even though it was forbidden, we often played chess during the day. I think it was Taraskin who won most of the time.

There are no secrets in prison, and every one of us shared the details of his investigation. Mustafa was called for interrogation only a few times. He was mainly questioned about other people, as a witness. He was suffering from a shortage of tobacco and his trousers were torn. So Taraskin advised him to ask for a piece of paper to write a petition to his investigator regarding the trousers and tobacco. When the peephole cover was opened the next time, he raised his hand to get the guard's attention. The guard opened the door and Mustafa conveyed his request for a pen and a piece of paper. After a long wait, he was given a pen and paper. Taraskin wrote a petition for him in a very comical way.

"Although there are no ladies of high society present, it still is not courteous to show my naked butt, even to my fellow prisoners."

Then, he graciously requested a patch and a needle with a thread to stitch it. In such a humorous way, Taraskin also wrote about his need for tobacco. Mustafa signed the petition and raised his hand again, when the guard was looked at him, in order to submit it. After a while, a patch, needle, and pack of cheap tobacco were brought to him. After that, Mustafa regularly received his tobacco.

After many days of waiting, Taraskin was called for interrogation and informed that his accusation had been modified. Instead of spying, he was now accused under article 7-35, with a maximum prison term of five years, which was much less than he would have for spying under Article 58[5] of the Soviet penal code. He was very much relieved, but even

---

5   Article 58 of the Soviet penal code referred to anti-Soviet activity and betrayal of the homeland. This article was used to sentence most political prisoners in the Gulag system.

then, he did not sign the protocol. Evidently, Taraskin knew very well the value of his signature.

The Letter to Ben-Gurion

Meanwhile, my interrogation continued. The torment of signing the protocols arrived at a critical stage that concerned a letter to Ben-Gurion. Obviously, Sasha had succeeded in convincing Zvi Plotkin to write this letter, and the interrogator tried to accuse me of knowing about it and even taking part in writing it. All of this was a lie. It was the first time that I'd heard about the letter. I only recalled that at a meeting when we'd talked about sending our works to Israel, it was decided to attach a short accompanying note to Yaakov Fichman, who at that time was the chairman of the Israeli Writers Association. And now I had to sign a confession about taking part in writing the letter to Ben-Gurion. My dark nights began.

The pages of the confession protocol about the letter to Ben-Gurion also claimed that in this letter we urged Ben-Gurion not to trust the Soviet Union, but instead to rely on the USA. It also claimed that we had asked about establishing a regular line of communication with Israel, and other lies. Black nights, several black nights of resistance to torture, fell upon me. I had to withstand heavy blows, shouting, and swearing. The interrogator threatened to destroy me, to arrest my wife, my younger daughter, and even my son, who at that time was only twelve years old. During this period, the interrogator started to humiliate me by calling me "Brother Moshke." This was the name of a short story that I published in *HaTkufa* magazine. And again, and again, beatings, swearing, and sleepless nights.

Nevertheless, all these severe beatings and insults did not help the interrogator. The more he pressed me, the stronger my resistance to signing these terrible lies was. But I was not aware of their diabolic methods and, eventually, they broke me by relieving the pressure and allowing me to relax. It was an entirely unexpected psychological trick. After a night of torture, beating, and humiliation, the interrogator called me to his room at about 10–11 in the morning. I came prepared to fight but was greeted in an entirely different way. A second investigator was present in the room, a young and nice-looking man. They started a conversation about art, about music, especially about violin music. In my young years,

I played violin and studied at the Jewish musical conservatory in Odessa. They knew this because they had found my diploma from 1918 when searching my flat.

After terrible nights of suffering, all pressure was taken off me. We started to talk about music, and they asked me about my favorite musical pieces. In a room that, before this conversation, had served as a torture chamber sounded the names of Tchaikovsky and Bizet . . .

Then, the young man left the room and my interrogator approached me and quietly placed the pages of the protocol dealing with the letter to Ben-Gurion in front of me.

"Sign it," he asked me politely.

He went back and took a seat behind his desk. I looked at his face and saw an expression of concealed expectation. His face was a bit yellowish, and this time it did not have a contemptuous expression; it was the face of a professional, waiting for the results of an important psychological experiment.

And then, I signed the page. Now I understand quite well what happened. When the pressure was relieved, when the torture was replaced by Tchaikovsky, I gave up. However, despite being my beloved composer, Tchaikovsky had nothing to do with it. My signature was imposed on me by the dark sleepless nights of torture, the nights that crushed me.

Feelings of remorse overwhelmed me when I returned to my cell. Taraskin's opinion was that I should not have signed the protocol. Maybe he was still a snitch and just wanted to tease me? It was a Saturday night, a night without interrogation, but I was not able to sleep due to intense stress. My heart pounded every time I thought about the signature. I decided to ask the guard to bring me a piece of paper to submit a complaint to the prosecutor, who was overseeing the prisoners' investigations. I wanted to protest against the methods of coercion used by my interrogator, to state that I had nothing to do with the fabricated affair of the letter to Ben-Gurion.

But they did not give me the paper. Later, I realized that all my complaints and protests had been useless. Mustafa and Taraskin tried to comfort me and suggested that there would be other opportunities to fix things. I still had to sign the concluding protocol, which included the summaries of all the other protocols. I would also be able to submit my complaint personally, during an obligatory meeting with the prosecutor.

But despite their reassurances and consolation, I felt as if I had spit into my very soul.

After I signed the initial protocols, my investigator started preparing the concluding protocol. It was during the nights of June and July. I remember one summer night. I was sitting at the prisoner's desk, next to the door, and the investigator was sitting at his desk and writing and writing. I could even hear his pen scratching the paper. He was writing the concluding protocol in the form of questions and answers. Questions that he did not ask, and answers that I did not answer. All of this protocol was a lie. I could hear a few sounds coming through the large window; the vast world was hiding behind it. The interrogator was immersed in deep thought; then he pressed the button of the bell and asked the guard to stay with me during his absence. Then he went to the cafeteria to treat himself to food. When he came back, he was no longer able to concentrate. I could see his eyes closing as he started to doze off. Then, he woke up and continued writing. He was writing, erasing, and contemplating. And all this time I was sitting silently next to the door.

Meanwhile, the prison routine kept going on. The daily food ration was given with staggering precision. Every week, the dull shaving knives cut patches of skin from my chin. Every ten days we took a shower. We were given a tiny chunk of soap, clean bedsheets, and underwear. Then, all three of us were taken downstairs to the shower room, where we first had to undress in a small cabin and proceed to the showers. Taking a shower was the most pleasant part of prison routine. Twice a week, we were able to change library books. We were allowed to hold three books at a time. Most of the time, only one of them was more or less of interest to me, but I was reading everything, and sometimes in my mind I translated the sentences from Russian to Hebrew.

My stomach hurt a lot, and at times the prison doctors were called to the cell to attend tome. One of them was an overweight, middle-aged, unpleasant lady, and the other was a younger and better-looking woman with a modest hairdo. Neither actually treated me; they just gave me some soda powder and belladonna or salol pills, which did not really help.

Every day, we were taken outside for a walk. The duration of the walk was twenty minutes; it was a part of the firm prison schedule. The guards had to provide prisoners with a "portion of the walk" as if it was a portion of bread. First, we were ordered to prepare for the walk by a guard shouting through the peephole. After getting dressed, the door was opened, and we were descended the stairs and entered a small, enclosed prison yard designated for us. There, we walked one after the other with our hands behind our backs. All three of us enjoyed the walks immensely.

We were not allowed to talk during the walk. It was a time for thinking. I thought about many different things, and, since I was always hungry, sometimes I imagined a meal that I would order in a beachside café in Tel-Aviv. I remember ordering two boiled eggs, pita bread, and skim milk. Then I dreamed of returning to my home in Tel Aviv, sitting on the balcony, looking at the sea, and writing.

The prison yard was paved with asphalt. There were no plants, only a small piece of sky above. If the walk was during the evening hours, we were able to see stars. Sometimes, when the sky was free of clouds, precious sunlight shone on half of the yard. I would turn my face towards the sun with my eyes closed, and the sunlight gently stroked my face and whispered something in my ears. On the way back to the cell, we passed through a small patch of soil covered with stunted grass. It was weirdly crazy to see this blatantly green patch hiding in the middle of the prison; for a moment it became the center of the universe.

The Concluding Protocol

The days of torture began again; it was time to sign the concluding protocol. The interrogator used the familiar means: threats, beatings, shouting, and swearing. He was not ready to change even a single word in the neatly typed document that he had prepared. I had to sign everything that was written there. After exhausting arguing, I signed the initial pages, containing the less critical accusations. But when we arrived at the letter to Ben-Gurion, I firmly refused to sign it.

This time, my suffering reached its highest point, I was going through many nights of nightmares. I collected all my strength and was stubborn in my resistance. It was in the middle of July, my interrogator had plans for a vacation, and was required to get my signature before leaving. His anger was stunning.

One day, the interrogation nights ceased, and I was able to sleep at night. I could not believe it and assumed that my interrogator had finally gone on vacation. One, two, three, four nights, two weeks passed, and it was already the beginning of August. The life in our cell continued as usual. Sometimes we were busy communicating with the neighboring cells.

The prison cells in Lefortovo were well isolated by thick walls, so the only way to communicate with other prisoners was by knocking. The letter "A" was one knock, "Б" two knocks, and so on. Transmitting the letters at the end of the alphabet required a long time and precision. One of the prisoners in the adjacent cell told us that he was a naval captain from Odessa, the other presented himself as a singer, Vadim Kozin, who was well known for performing gypsy songs. Later, in Karaganda, I met one of the prisoners from that cell. He claimed that there was no Vadim Kozin there; maybe it was just one of the prison fantasies.

Usually, Taraskin led the conversation, and since my bed stood next to the wall, I was the one who did the knocking. One day, when we were chatting about Ruslanova, a popular singer of Russian folk songs, the door suddenly opened and an officer accompanied by a guard rushed into the cell.

"Who is knocking?" asked the officer.

"Nobody" answered Taraskin.

"No, we heard it. Who was knocking?"

Finally, I replied, "It was me."

They left the cell and Taraskin told me that I was going to be punished by carcer. Indeed, that same night I was put in carcer. It was a small cell, the size of a closet, two paces by three paces. In the corner, there was a narrow triangular bench. The bench was so small that it was hard even to sit on it. The carcer was in the half-basement, with an asphalt floor, so it was cold and dark. Most of my clothes were taken from me before they put me in the carcer. I spent two days and two nights there; it was very cold, and I felt really bad. The daily food ration was reduced to three hundred grams of bread, and a cup of hot water in the morning and in the evening. I was hungry and felt strong stomach pain. These two days were more than enough for me. At three o'clock on the third night, I was called to the interrogation room on the second floor. It was very warm there and, probably because of the sharp temperature change, I started shivering.

I was brought to a room belonging to investigator Tzvetaev. He seated me at the prisoner's desk, gave me the concluding protocol, and requested me to sign it. I refused and continued shivering so hard that my teeth started to chatter. Then, several other investigators, five or six of them, entered the room one by one. I was not sure if they had come because of me, but according to the rules, I had to rise each time somebody entered the room. I was standing and shivering, while they surrounded me, like a pack of wolves. One of them, the head of the pack, came close and asked:

"Are you going to sign?"

"Citizen Principal Investigator, the protocol contains a lot of lies, and I will not sign it," I answered while shivering.

"Why is he shivering?" asked one of the officers.

I explained that I had just been brought in from the cold carcer and that the sharp temperature rise had caused me to shiver. It was not a great pleasure to talk to them; it was truly humiliating to shiver in front of them. The principal investigator, a short, but strongly built, fair-haired man, said:

"He was sent to carcer because he was knocking on the wall. Apparently, he was trying to establish communication with other members of his gang."

Another investigator asked me again,

"Will you sign?"

"No, I will not sign," was my reply.

He hit me several times. My head began to bleed. Then, all the other wolves started to beat me. One of them dealt me a massive blow to the chin that broke one of my teeth.

"Will you sign now?"

"No, I will not sign."

Finally, I managed to compose myself. I got warm at once and the shivers ended.

"No, I will not sign what's written there. It's all lies."

Heavy blows again. The door opened and somebody whispered:

"Enough."

The officers left the room. Before leaving the room, the principal investigator told me:

"If you do not sign, we will destroy you."

I was left alone with investigator Tzvetaev. His rank was also lieutenant colonel; a tall man with a pleasant face. He moved his chair close to mine and started talking to me in a mild manner. He suggested that if I refused to sign this page, I should move to the next one. We will deal with this page later. He talked nicely to me, and I read and signed several pages which were relatively harmless. At five in the morning, the interrogation ended, and I was taken back to the carcer. I had to stay there for exactly three days, no less and no more. They were very punctual in this respect. After three days, I was given back my clothes and taken back to my cell.

Back in the cell, I was warmly welcomed by Taraskin and Mustafa. My face was heavily beaten and covered with blood and my tooth was broken. It was a custom to show respect to the suffering fellow prisoners. For instance, later in the forced labor camp, I observed that the prisoners with a twenty-five-year term were respected more than those with a ten-year term.

They did not beat me after that. Tzvetaev's approach was different from that of Lebedev. He behaved nicely. On several occasions, he even agreed to make small corrections in the text. After I had signed the rest of the pages of the concluding protocol, we started debating the pages with the letter to Ben-Gurion. As a shrewd salesman, Tzvetaev argued with me about every word and every letter. Sadly, the process of negotiations turned this awful and tragic accusation into something trivial and boring. In the end, I became apathetic and indifferent, the investigator started to threaten me again, and, finally, I agreed to sign the pages. Besides, I knew that I was going to meet a prosecutor, and then, I thought, I would be able to correct things. In short, I signed. After that, they left me alone until the return of my official interrogator, Lebedev, from his vacation.

When I signed the concluding protocol, Taraskin was moved out of our cell, which again reinforced my suspicion that he was a snitch. Yet one should be extremely cautious when accusing somebody of being an informer. In the prison camps, incidents of prisoners collaborating with the camp authorities were quite common, but some cases turned out to be false.

Several days later, I was transferred to another cell. In the new cell, I met Stepanov, a geologist from Moscow, who was accused of sabotage, article 58-7 of the Soviet penal code. Several years back, he had served as the head of an exploration expedition, searching for Uranium in Siberia. He was accused of underestimating the prospects of a certain ore deposit.

He was about my age, unhealthy looking, fair-haired, with a lengthy mustache. He told me that many geologists all over the Soviet Union had been arrested this year, mostly in Moscow and Leningrad. Many of them were experienced and well-known scientists and professors.[6]

I do not remember Stepanov as well as Taraskin and Mustafa. One day, he returned from the interrogation and told me that he had signed his interrogation protocol. He did this without coercion and beating. He was sick and his willpower was weak. From my experience, only a few of the prisoners did not sign their protocols, and even though they did not admit any guilt, they were still sentenced to long prison terms. I met some of them during my time in the forced labor camp. As my interrogator, Lebedev used to say, "Every person arrested by the MGB will get his prison term," and the signature did not play any role at all.

Meanwhile, the months of August and September passed. My investigation was progressing. Lebedev returned from vacation, and I was brought again to his room. He was really angry that I had signed the closing protocol in his absence. He then fabricated one more protocol, in which he again mentioned the letter to Ben-Gurion and the name of the informer, Sasha Gordon. I had signed it. Many months had passed since my arrest, and I was sick and tired of this game.

The Encounter with Baazov

At the end of my investigation, Lebedev arranged a face-to-face meeting between Meir Baazov and me. Neither of us requested this meeting, it was all his idea. Before the encounter, he ordered me to behave like a "good boy," meaning that I should reaffirm all his lies and not dare to utter even a single word of truth. When Baazov was brought to the interrogation room, he looked much older. Before the arrest, he'd been a good-looking man, thirty-five years old. Now, his hair was gray and his features sagged. There was another investigator present at the meeting, at the rank of captain, who recorded the questions and answers.

The questions were addressed to both of us, but we were not allowed to talk to each other. Apparently, Meir had already signed his confession.

---

6   Later, in 1954, all the accusations against geologists were proved to be fabricated. Those who remained alive were rehabilitated and their rights restored.

His handlers had used a different interrogation method. They did not beat him; instead, he was put in a solitary cell for a long time, where he was exposed to frightening sounds until he began hallucinating. During the meeting, led by the questions of the interrogator, he testified against me. He confirmed that we both were members of a nationalistic Jewish organization and had committed all of the fabricated accusations.

"How can you say that?" I asked, but was immediately stopped by the interrogator.

Several days later, I was asked to sign a typewritten protocol of this encounter. Besides signing every page, I had to sign under each answer. Like all the other protocols, this protocol was also all fabrication and lies. The goal was to prove that the MGB had exposed a gang of dangerous criminals, who must be arrested, punished, and sent to remote places for forced labor work. This goal was not that easy to achieve. The main task of the investigators was to prove that behind the cover of the law obedient citizens and family members, loyal to the Communist Party, who for many years had diligently performed their civil duties and achieved outstanding results in their workplaces, were serial criminals The investigators were trying to accomplish this goal by putting together irrelevant bits and pieces of fabricated facts, conversations, and meetings. The most important part was the voluntary admission of their crimes by all the accused. We had to wholeheartedly confess to being Zionists and, therefore, the enemies of the state.

The protocol dealt again with the letter to Ben-Gurion. The question and my answer to it were as follows:

INTERROGATOR'S QUESTION. "Did Baazov know about the letter to Ben-Gurion?"

MY WRITTEN ANSWER. "Yes, the letter was devised, written, and sent to Israel by us."

Actually, this issue had not even been raised during my encounter with Baazov. If I had been given the chance, my real answer would have been as follows: "Neither Meir nor I was aware of the letter. I am not sure if the letter to Ben-Gurion exists at all. You have not shown it to me. I received negative answers to all my requests to see it. And even if Plotkin had actually written the letter, it was because you tricked him into doing it. It was you who provided him with the special ink and paper, and it was you who dictated it to him. This is a terrible and unfair provocation, intended to ruin people."

When I think about Lebedev, I feel repulsion and horror, like a fly would feel about a spider, or a mouse would feel about a cat. Not only had he beaten me, but he had also viciously vilified and insulted my very soul and my beloved family. He regularly shouted at me, intimidated me, and called me "brother Moshke." He referred to Israel as "a bunch of shopkeepers that got together and made themselves a state." He was merciless, I cannot forget that dreadful night, when I felt particularly weak and insane, and he kept beating me. Once, he tried to talk mildly to me and even told me a coarse anecdote, but he was not able to keep up a civilized conversation. He was incapable of any human relationship. He was an executioner, a cannibal without a human soul. He was a bloodthirsty animal at the rank of lieutenant colonel, with every means of oppression at his disposal.

Form 206

The stack of malicious protocols that did not contain even one grain of truth kept growing. At the end of 1949, nine months after my arrest, the investigators decided to wrap up the case. Perhaps they were under pressure to open new cases due to a large number of newly arrested prisoners, who required experienced interrogators—executioners. The tragicomedy of my investigation was coming to an end. The meeting with the prosecutor was ridiculous and sad. One night, I was woken up at three o'clock. By this time, my interrogation was already over and I was able to sleep during the night. Before entering Lebedev's office, I was ushered into another room, where my interrogator warned me in harsh words that he is going to "show me to the prosecutor," as if he was going to show me to a famous medical professor or, more accurately, show a horse to a buyer. I had to remember that the prosecutor was not my attorney. That he always conducts the case against a defendant, and strictly follows the rule of law. He reminded me that I should behave well and confirm everything that I had signed, otherwise he would "rip out my intestines."

After such a gentle introduction, he brought me to his office, where I saw a prosecutor, an overweight Jewish man, whose name was Doron. He was dressed in the uniform of a high-ranking officer; I felt as though a general was sitting in front of me. It seemed to me that his fat belly was jammed with the blood of innocent people, and there I was, in front of this devourer of human souls. He ordered me to sign form 206, confirming the conclusion of my investigation. The document had already been signed by him and by my interrogator. It declared that all three of us confirmed that the investigation of the criminal Zvi Preigerzon, accused according to articles 58-10 and 58-11 of the Soviet penal code, was complete. I was also supposed to fill the empty space in the form intended for my requests and complaints. However, this whole space had been crossed out, and at the bottom it already said that I approved all the protocols of my investigation.

I told them that I was not going to sign this form. That I had both complaints and requests.

"What are you complaining about?" asked the prosecutor.

In a nervous and trembling voice, as I was aware that this was my last chance to defend myself, I started listing all the lies and fabrications in the protocols. The most significant lie was about writing the letter to Ben-Gurion. I told him that I had never seen this letter, that the interrogator was the one who had told me about it.

Besides the prosecutor and my investigator, the captain who took part in my meeting with Baazov was also present in the room. When I stated all my complaints, the prosecutor asked the interrogator to bring a new form in order to write the document again. It was between three and four at night. All their dark deeds were conducted at nighttime; it appeared that these people were afraid of daylight.

The captain left the room for a few seconds and then came back and told us that it was late at night; all the office workers had gone, so he could not find a new form. Then the prosecutor asked me to come close. He showed me my notebook containing a part of my novel *When the Menorah Fades.* It was the notebook that I gave to Sasha for the doctor, who was supposed to bring it to Israel.

"Did you write that?" asked Doron.

"Yes."

"Was it your intention to send it to Israel?"

"Yes."

He handed me the notebook, opened the blank page at the end, and gave me a pen.

"Write!"

"What am I supposed to write?"

He dictated and I wrote.

"I wanted to send this notebook to Israel for publication."

The investigator corrected the words of the prosecutor:

"He did not *want* to send it; he *did* send it."

I wrote the following: "I sent this notebook to Israel for publication." Then I signed it and went back to my desk, next to the door. Form 206 was still there.

"Now you will sign," said Doron.

"I will not sign it. After all, I have presented you with my complaints."

"I have heard your complaints and will consider them."

"But it is written here that I do not have complaints. How can I sign that?"

"Sign it. Haven't you seen that we do not have the forms now," said the investigator.

"Sign, or we will arrest your daughter," he added.

My daughter, Nina, together with her friends, Leopold Vydrin and Anatoly Niankovsky, had gone to see the well-known Jewish writer Ilya Ehrenburg[7] to ask for his support for the State of Israel. After hearing this threat from the interrogator, I decided to sign the form.

On the same day, after signing the form, I again requested a pen and a paper from the guard on duty to write a letter of complaint. I wanted my interrogation file to hold at least a symbolic sign of resistance to all this nonsense. They did not give me the pen and paper, not on that day, and not on the following days. My interrogator told me that I would have an opportunity to express my complaints and requests to the judges during the trial. That was also a lie. There was no trial. All the protocols, together with form 206, were submitted to the "Special Council,"[8] which had issued a judgment in my absence. Among all the documents in my file, there was no trace of my resistance or objection to the accusations. Everything was perfectly legal.

---

7   Ilya Ehrenburg—Soviet writer and journalist, member of the Jewish Anti-Fascist Committee.

8   Special Council—also known by the name "Troika," a body consisting of three judges, who were granted the right to apply punishment "by administrative means," i.e., without trial.

At the beginning of November, I was called again to the interrogator and shown the documents in my file. The volume of documents was huge, more than two hundred pages. The file contained all the protocols, including the concluding protocol and other documents. There were also concluding protocols of the investigations of Plotkin, Baazov, Kahanov, and the statement of Brakker, an employee of the Lenin Library Hebrew Department. Apparently, Brakker had signed his statement under extreme pressure. It contained devious lies, a mixture of evidence and accusations that had never occurred and never happened. He had signed this statement five months before my arrest. Brakker was the last one of us to be arrested, besides Kricheli, who I had not yet met. In his statement, Brakker claimed that, during our frequent meetings, I spoke contemptuously about the heads of the Soviet state and the Communist Party and, if I remember it correctly, that I tried to convince him to get involved in the activity of our nationalistic group. I was not very close to Laser Brakker and had not seen him since the beginning of 1949. He knew the Hebrew language very well, and his wife belonged to the Luboshitz family, whose members included several famous musicians and violinists. Brakker's daughter was also a gifted violinist. I also remember that he borrowed a book from me, containing a selection of works by Bialik, and did not return it until the day of my arrest.

In my heart, I have no hard feelings about Brakker and the rest of my friends who testified against me in their protocols. I know very well, in my marrow, that it was impossible to resist and refuse to sign the fabrications of the interrogators. In addition to the accusation of writing the letter to Ben-Gurion, Plotkin also admitted to the accusation of being a spy. His interrogator used a corresponding article of the law in his indictment.

So, I was shown the documents in my file, and even though I was not given enough time to read the whole voluminous stack of papers, I signed the form confirming my review of it. And again, I was not allowed to submit any objections and complaints.

Part 3

Butyrka Prison

On November 12, 1949, I was transferred to Butyrka prison. At Butyrka, I had to go through the familiar customary reception, Again, I was locked in a box, was subjected to medical inspection, etc. Then, I was brought into a cell on the third floor, which was occupied by about thirty prisoners. There, I met several Jews, but I remember only a few of them.

I spent about a month in this cell. In Butyrka, my experiences were quite different from those in the Lefortovo prison. The wooden-plank beds were stacked very densely, so the bodies of the prisoners were pushed close to each other. We were allowed to sleep during the day. The food allotment was similar to the Lefortovo prison. There was also a prison shop. Those who had money in their accounts were able to buy premium food. The prisoners who did not have money used a shared account. Every prisoner with money had to contribute ten percent to the shared account. The money in the shared account was used to purchase bread and tobacco for prisoners that were hungry or were addicted to smoking.

It was already winter and snow was covering the ground; the sky was gray and bleak, and the white world unfolded outside of the window of the prison cell. Every morning, we were taken outside to the prison yard for a walk. The prison yard was subdivided into cells. We silently strolled under the falling snow, one after the other. During these twenty minutes of our walks, the women prisoners would clean our cell, wash the floor, and open the window for ventilation. I vividly remember the first moments after our return from a walk: the floor would still be wet and clean, and the air cool and fresh.

The matter of ventilation caused numerous quarrels among the prisoners. We were allowed to open the window at any time, and many liked the fresh air, but some prisoners were afraid of getting cold. This issue contributed to alliances and animosities between the prisoners.

A few days after my arrival at Butyrka, I was officially informed that my case was submitted to the Special Council. I had to sign an acknowledgement of receiving this information. It became clear to me that my fate would be decided in my absence. I asked again for a pen and paper, but was refused.

The month spent in Butyrka stays in my memory like a gray spot. I recall meeting Nahmanzon, who was an old Bolshevik[1] and had worked in one of the construction organizations. He wore a long, yellow, leather coat and often strolled back and forth along the narrow prison cell. Although he had been a party member for more than twenty-five years, he was arrested like an ordinary person. How could it be possible? He felt dismayed and often complained about the government. However, I think that he was not dismayed as much about the fate of the other prisoners.

I did not meet many noteworthy people in the cell; I remember when a common criminal, a jailbird, appeared in the cell. It is important to emphasize the difference, and the animosity, between the political prisoners and the common criminals, who were typically thieves, burglars, and bandits—in short, members of a shadow world. This common criminal was serving a twenty-five-year term and made several attempts to escape from the forced labor camp. He had a very sharp tongue, and anybody who tried to argue with him was immediately put down. Once, he replied to a young Ukrainian guy, who had been convicted by article 58 of the Soviet penal code for belonging to a religious sect:

"I am quite sure that you have never given even a ten kopek coin to a cleaning woman in a public toilet."

---

1   Bolshevik—a veteran member of the Communist Party.

The Sentencing

On December 10, after numerous requests, I was finally given a pen and a piece of paper. I wrote my petition in small letters because I intended it to be brief but comprehensive. I addressed it to the State General Prosecutor. In this petition, I wrote about the letter to Ben-Gurion that I had never seen, about the nationalistic group that I had never heard about, and about other false accusations.

At the time of my submitting the petition, I did not know that a week earlier, on December 3, I had already been sentenced by the Special Council. It appeared that they had given me permission to use a pen and a paper only when it was already too late and my petition was pointless.

On December 12, I was taken out of my cell to be officially sentenced. The procedure was conducted on the first floor, where about twenty prisoners from different cells were gathered in one room. One after another, we were called by name and were given the length of our imprisonment. To my delight, one of the prisoners in the room was Meir Baazov. Aharon Kricheli, a Jewish prisoner from Georgia, who was somehow attached to our "criminal group," was also there. Since Butyrka prison, the three of us, Baazov, Kricheli, and I had been together for more than a year.

The prison official who read the verdicts was a Jewish man of my age, dressed in an ordinary suit and wearing thick glasses. He was sitting and I was standing. We had the following conversation:

THE OFFICIAL. "So, what is your crime?"

I. "I am not a criminal."

THE OFFICIAL. "There are no innocent people among prisoners."

I. "It's you who says so."

THE OFFICIAL. "Are you a Jew?"

I. "Yes, I am a Jew."

THE OFFICIAL. "Do you speak Hebrew?"

I. "Yes."

THE OFFICIAL. "It's written in the Bible that one has to respect the authorities."

I. "I do respect the authorities, but the authorities do not respect me."

THE OFFICIAL. "By your resistance, you are harming all Jewish people."

I. "I have never committed a crime, not against the authorities, and not against the Jewish people."

THE OFFICIAL. "And now, you are standing here and continue to argue."

He was testing my nerves, but I remained silent.

"Sign this," said the man and handed me the verdict of the Special Council.

It was written there that on December 3, 1949, it was decided that Hirsh[2] Ben Israel Preigerzon was convicted to ten years in the forced labor camp for "participation in a nationalistic anti-Soviet organization and the distribution of illegal literature."

"Sign it" commanded the official. "Look what you have done to yourself."

"It's you who had done it to me. I am innocent."

He looked at me over his glasses. I signed my verdict and left the room; more precisely, I was escorted out of the room. Since my arrest, I had not been allowed to go anywhere without a guard. Soon, it became known that all political prisoners were given a ten-year term.

One of the other prisoners got a five-year term. He was accused of the sexual harassment of a twelve-year-old girl. According to him, he was working as a sport education teacher, and approached the girl and touched her legs to correct her posture during an exercise. The girl's parents submitted an official complaint to the school, claiming that he was touching her private places. This complaint was forwarded to the MGB office, and he was arrested. He was Russian, but had a Jewish wife who loved him very much. She sent him clothes, food, and other things before transfer to a forced labor camp.

After signing the receipt of my verdict, I was allowed to prepare a few documents, mainly powers of attorney. I wrote about five of such documents, which allowed my wife to receive money for the work that I had completed before my arrest. My wife confirmed receiving the documents.

---

2   Zvi Preigerzon's first name in Yiddish was Hirsh and it was written in his passport; his equivalent Russian first name was Gregory. Zvi was his first name in Hebrew. His father's name was Israel.

Church Cell

Before departure to Karaganda prison camp, I was transferred to the Church[3] building of Butyrka prison. Our cell on the second floor was quite large, the plank beds were stacked at two levels, and there were many more people than in the previous cell. Baazov and Kricheli were also there, along with a relatively large number of other Jewish prisoners. All the prisoners already knew their terms and had nothing to lose anymore. The rules were quite relaxed; we were allowed to lay in bed during the day, to talk, to sing, and to play chess. My wife sent me a large package with high boots, felt boots, warm clothes, shirts, etc. I gave the felt boots to Kricheli, but what was I supposed to do with the rest? During our transfer to the forced labor camp, I would have to carry everything by myself, so I had to put all my stuff into one large bag.

In the Church cell, I met Greenberg, a senior lecturer from one of the Moscow universities. He was around sixty, cleanly shaved with a plump belly, and had a habit of talking a lot. He was a veteran member of the Communist Party, and somehow was connected to the party faction that had been later denounced for treason. He had been arrested and convicted to ten or fifteen years. In prison, he became close to his fellow Jewish tribesmen. If I remember correctly, he was born in Shklov, Belorussia, and liked Jewish songs. As a boy, he met a Jewish peddler, whose trade was to go around the town and play records of Jewish songs, melodies, and prayers on a gramophone for a small fee. When the peddler came to his house, Greenberg, after a lot of begging, got three kopeks from his mother to pay him. The gramophone played a record of the "HaMavdil" psalm:[4]

He who makes a distinction between the sacred and profane,
Will pardon our transgressions.
He will multiply our seed and our means,
As the sand on the beach and as the stars at night.

---

3   Church—a building in the middle of the Butyrka prison yard, which was originally built to serve as a church.

4   HaMavdil—a Hebrew psalm that praises God as HaMavdil, the One who creates separation and division. Part of the ritual of Havdalah, which marks the end of Shabbat.

And now, fifty years later, he still remembered the psalm and performed it in the muddle of prisoners' clatter in the Church cell of Butyrka prison. I listened to this ancient song, and it warmed my heart. This psalm, like many other songs that I learned during these dark years, was helping and supporting me; it was a source of comfort and encouragement. After a few years, I learned about the death of Greenberg. He had suffered from cancer and committed suicide in the prison hospital. Together with him faded away the recollection of his story about the gramophone and the "HaMavdil" psalm

The Jewish Theater

In prison, we were not allowed to read newspapers or listen to the radio, so our only source of the news from the outside world was the stories of prisoners who had recently been arrested. That is how we learned about the victory of the Communists in China, and the closure of the Jewish Theater.[5] One of the recently arrested prisoners was a Jewish shoemaker, who had a small booth on Maroseika Street. According to him, he was arrested for cursing the Soviet government in a conversation with a tax inspector who had come to impose an additional tax on him. Most of the time, he lay on the top bench of the plank bed. I asked him about the fate of the Jewish Theater on Malaya Bronnaya Street. He replied that the theater remained open until the end of the season due to contributions from the Jewish audience, who had purchased seasonal subscriptions.

I had been familiar with this theater since the beginning of the 1920s when Solomon Mikhoels[6] and Benjamin Zuskin[7] were still young. Many of my memories are connected to this theater. I vividly remember the plays of Sholom Aleichem: *Three Raisins*, with beautiful Hassidic music, and *Two Hundred Thousand*; "The Travels of Benjamin III" by Mendele Mocher Sforim; *A Night in the Old Marketplace* by Isaac Leibush Peretz;

---

5 Moscow State Jewish Theatre—a Yiddish theatre company established in 1919 and shut down in 1949 by the Soviet authorities.

6 Solomon Mikhoels—Jewish actor and artistic director of the Moscow State Jewish Theater. Served as the chairman of the Jewish Anti-Fascist Committee during World War II. Stalin ordered his assassination in 1948.

7 Benjamin Zuskin—Jewish actor and director of the Moscow State Jewish Theater. As a member of the Jewish Anti-Fascist Committee, he was arrested and executed on Stalin's orders in 1952.

and *The Sorceress* by Abraham Goldfaden. All the plays were directed by Alexis Granovsky and the actors were Mikhoels, Zuskin, Minkin, Royzin, and others. Recently, I saw *Freylekhs* by Zalman Shneer-Okun and a new production of *The Sorceress.*

In the 1920s, as a poor student, I often went to the Jewish Theater by foot from the student's dormitory on Polyanka Street, where I lived. Even in the middle of the winter, I would go there without an overcoat, but with a tie around my neck. I did not have money for a ticket and waited in a convenient hiding place until the end of the first act. During the intermission, I blended in with the members of the audience who were smoking outside of the entrance door, and then entered the theater without a ticket. Many, many times I watched the last acts of *Three Raisins* and the rest of my favorite plays.

I also remember the Habima Theater in Moscow.[8] I saw performances of *Neshef Bereshit* [The Genesis Ball] and *Hahama, Hahama* [The Smart, the Smart] by Itzhak Katzenelson, *Pega Ra* [Devil] by Isaac Dov Berkowitz, with the actors Menahem Gnessin and David Vardi, S. Ansky's play *The Dybbuk*, *The Eternal Jew* by David Pinski, and *The Golem* by H. Leivick. *The Dybbuk* was a real event for me. Many Jewish folk songs became engraved on my heart.

---

8 Habima Theater—Moscow Jewish theater company that staged Hebrew-language plays until 1926, when it moved to Palestine.

Part 4

On the Way to Karaganda

One day, we got an order to collect our belongings and be ready for the transfer. We had no choice, but to comply with the order. I took my large bag with all my things and food and went outside with the other prisoners. We were ushered into a Voronok and packed very tightly. Being pressed against each other, we felt every bump on the road. I was desperately trying to look through a small window with metal bars to catch just a tiny glimpse of Moscow, where I had lived for more than thirty years. It was a winter morning in December. The Voronok passed through the streets of Moscow. Sometimes, I was able to see posters on the walls. Men, women, and children were strolling on the sidewalks, but nobody noticed the prisoners' car. The people's faces were indifferent and pale; it looked like the whole world was in mourning. The car stopped; we went outside. Somebody had been sitting on my bag, so all the food inside got squashed.

And there we were, standing at some dismal place next to train tracks that ran far away. A pack of prisoners with shaved heads, dressed in different types of clothes, and loaded with bags and boxes, some large and some small. My bag, as large as it seemed to be, was among the medium ones. Guards with automatic rifles surrounded us from all sides. We were lined up in a column, four to a row, and were warned that anyone who moved two steps to the left or the right of his position would be shot at once. We started walking along the rails until we reached an empty prisoners' railroad car, known as a "Stolypin carriage." One after another we entered the car.

The Stolypin Carriage

A few words about Stolypin carriages. I do not know why prisoners called it after Stolypin; maybe it was dated back to the time of the tsars when he served as prime minister. The carriage was subdivided into isolated cells with grilled metal doors locked from the outside. The keys from the locks were kept by the guard commander. The cell had two bottom and two top benches, and two baggage benches at the very top. The standard occupancy of each cell was ten people, but up to thirty prisoners, along with their baggage, were jammed into the cell. It was terrible. All the time during out travel, we were fed with bread and salty fish; sometimes we were given some sugar. There was no hot or cooked food available. In this car, and in these jam-packed conditions, we traveled many days. When we arrived at a large transit station, we were moved to a local prison for a few days, and then resumed our voyage.

During the journey in the Stolypin carriage, there was always a shortage of water. A water portion was given two or three times a day. A guard would open a small hatch in the door from the outside, fill a metal mug with water from a bucket, and pass it to the prisoners, one by one. With this water only, we had to relieve our thirst, even though our thirst was increased by the salty fish.

For me, the most terrible thing was going to the lavatory. It was located at the end of the corridor, where the armed guard watched the prisoners. Because of my ulcer, I suffered from constipation and the guard's presence caused me such stress that it was difficult for me to even urinate. If it took me more than one minute, the guard would start knocking on the door and shouting at me to finish up and get out. Sometimes, I was not able to do anything during this short time. And while I was returning to the cell, holding my trousers up, because I did not have enough time to fasten them, another prisoner was already running to the toilet.

Yes, it was terrible. There are two things that I recall with a shiver, the interrogator, and the Stolypin carriage. In addition, the atmosphere there was very close and stifling; most of the prisoners smoked cheap tobacco

(I had quit smoking in 1945), and this smoke filled the cell and got into my lungs.

And yet, I cannot say that I suffered all the time during transit. It is human nature to adapt to anything. A person's body and mind are able to adjust. A prisoner's mind is generally not predisposed to feelings of sadness, sorrow, and tears. And prisoners do not engage in constant complaining and weeping. On the contrary, a cheerful atmosphere of activity is quite common in prison, especially in the company of young men.

As we learned later, our destination was Karaganda. From Moscow, we were first transported to Sverdlovsk, where we climbed out of the carriage and were assembled in a column, four to a row. We were warned again about stepping out of line, that it would cost our lives; and there we were, a procession of tired and unshaven prisoners moving slowly towards the prison. When we arrived, there was a roll call, when the commanding officer of the transport handed us over to the prison management. They went through each one of us. When your family name was called, you had to step forward and loudly announce your first name, father's name, year of birth, the articles of your verdict, the length of imprisonment, and the date of your release. In my case, I had to shout: "Zvi, Israel, 1900, 58-10, 58-11, ten years, March 1, 1959." Then a new family name was announced, and the next prisoner would shout his details.

After the handover roll call, we were taken to a gloomy cell, which was already occupied by other prisoners. The prison in Sverdlovsk was much worse than Butyrka prison in Moscow. The cell was overcrowded, the food was awful, there was a permanent smell from the urinal bucket, the restroom was small and dirty, and the tap water drain was always clogged. With great difficulty, I found myself a place on the upper row of plank beds next to a prisoner from Germany who did not speak Russian at all, so I had a hard time understanding him. Even though he was a physician, he did not shave and did not wash himself. His clothes were worn and dirty, and he was always complaining about his health. Even now, I can hear him groaning on his upper plank bed in the neglected Sverdlovsk prison in the middle of December 1949.

Part 5

Karaganda

Sand Camp

From Sverdlovsk, we were transferred to Karaganda via Petropavlovsk. In Petropavlovsk, we had to wait several days for our Stolypin carriage to be attached to the train heading to Karaganda. The journey took at least seven days and it was extremely exhausting for me. For the whole time during transit I suffered from constipation and stomach pains. Finally, we arrived at Karaganda. We spent one day at the town's prison, where I was finally able to relieve myself and begin to feel much better. Then we were taken to the third division of Sand forced labor camp. Before our arrival, the camp had been occupied by Japanese prisoners of war, and their traces were visible everywhere—Japanese signs on the walls, pieces of Japanese newspapers, etc.

The prison camp was surrounded by a tall wooden fence. In front of it was an additional fence made of barbed wire, and the area between the fences was called the "Forbidden Zone." In the middle and at the corners of the wooden fence there were watchtowers with guards armed with automatic rifles. The fate of those who dared to enter the Forbidden Zone was to get a lead bullet.

The wooden fence was very thick, I could only see the sky above it, with sunlight during the day and stars during the night. In the mornings, I would often stare at the bright star, which winked at me, as if it was trying to calm and console me and inspire a desire in me to pray. It reminded me of my youth and my life outside of prison. And against the background of dark blue skies, burning with the sunrise, there was a watchtower and the silhouette of a guard holding an automatic rifle.

In the Karaganda region there were several prison camps belonging to the Sand group of camps, and the Prairie group of camps. These were high-security regime prison camps, intended for political prisoners sentenced by Article 58 of the Soviet penal code. Numerous forced labor camps were scattered across the vast territory of the Soviet Union, such as the Lake group of camps in Siberia, the River group of camps in Vorkuta, the Mineral group of camps in Inta, etc.

Camp Rules

The Sand and Prairie groups of camps had particularly strict administrative rules, much more rigorous than those in Karaganda camp, or "Karlag," which was intended for common criminals, e.g., thieves, robbers, murderers, etc. The regime in the Karlag was less tight and we, political prisoners, envied them. For instance, we were forbidden to communicate with the free people, who worked in the camp. This crime was severely punished. A prisoner was allowed to write only two letters per year; these letters were heavily censored and sometimes entirely banned, so communication with a prisoner's family was very irregular (in some cases, relatives did not receive letters from an imprisoned family member for many years). Prisoners who received packages or money transfers were allowed to confirm receipt by a brief postcard message, whose wording was defined beforehand (I wrote this message many times and still remember it: "My dear, I have received the package. Thank you. I am well and healthy. Yours Zvi"). If relatives wanted to get information about the health of the prisoner more often, they had to send money in small amounts—for instance, instead of a single amount of three hundred rubles, they had to send six times fifty rubles, and each time would receive a postcard confirming the transfer. The following are some of the rules, which illustrate the harshness of the regime in Sand camp:

—A prisoner's head always had to be shaved. All types of haircuts were forbidden.

—A prisoner always had to wear the camp's clothes.

—Every prisoner, except disabled ones, had to work. Those who avoided work were sent to carcer.

—Prisoners had to line up for roll call two times a day.

—Prisoners' belongings were regularly searched. All metal items were confiscated. Watches and alarm clocks were forbidden. Books in foreign languages that were published outside of the Soviet Union were forbidden. Searches were extremely rigorous, in particular before national holidays, such as May 1 and the anniversary of the October Revolution.

—Prisoners had to be in bed by a certain time. Until 1953, the doors of the prisoners' barracks were locked up from the outside. During the night, prisoners used awful-smelling urinal buckets.

—Prisoners had to stay in the barracks from a certain time in the evening until a certain time in the morning. It was like night arrest.

—Prisoners had to greet every guard and official in the camp. They had to remove their hat and say, "How do you do, Citizen Officer."

—Prisoners had to stand up in the presence of a guard or an official, especially if he addressed them.

—Prisoners were not allowed to have cash. Each prisoner was issued a card that showed his account balance and all his purchases. The card was stored in the financial office of the camp. Each time the camp store was open, especially when a new shipment of goods arrived, the financial officer was present at the store with all the prisoners' cards. Each purchase was accompanied by cumbersome calculations and numerous signatures.

—Alcoholic drinks and card games were forbidden.

—Communication between men and women was forbidden. Women's camps were entirely separated from the men's camps. For all my years in the camp, I felt as if I were in a men's monastery. In Sand camp, because of the tall fence, we could not even look at women from afar. Prisoners, particularly younger ones, suffered from this and conversations and stories about sex were very popular among them.

—Pens and ink were forbidden. Prisoners could use only pencils.

—It was forbidden to criticize or speak out against the camp management. There were numerous informers, whose task was to notify the operational officer,[1] or "Oper," about every violation of the rules and

---

1 Operation officer—a representative of the MGB in a camp, whose task was to spy on prisoners.

every word or action against the Soviet government, Communist Party, or camp management.

There were many other rules and limitations. To regular people, these limitations may seem insignificant and dull, but for us prisoners they were very real and caused us enormous mental and physical suffering.

The essence of life in the prison camp was always the fight against physical weakness and hunger. Hunger was the foremost issue, especially for those who did not receive food parcels from home. Prisoners doing hard labor had to supplement the regular camp food. Fat and sugar were particularly rare. Without them, prisoners had to eat more bread, but even the regular portion of bread was not sufficient. Other sources of food included getting additional helpings of soup and porridge in the camp's canteen, purchasing food in the camp store, and receiving personal food parcels.

Prisoners belonging to the "High Society" of the camp, among them the heads of the working teams, were able to get larger portions of meals in the camp's canteen. This was done unofficially. Prisoners who worked in the camp's canteen had higher status, and also belonged to "High Society." They gave their friends or other important prisoners larger or better servings of food, whereas the rest of the prisoners got regular, tasteless helpings of soup and porridge. All members of a working team went to the canteen together. The head of the team, or his deputy, would observe the distribution of meals among his team members. The teams typically received several additional food servings, and they were distributed among the most efficient workers and those who had close relations to the team head. Obviously, the heads of the working teams got the largest and best meals. Unlike the warm meals, the daily portions of bread and sugar were given to prisoners separately.

The prisoner camp menu lacked variety: a daily portion of rye bread (six hundred grams), gruel soup, porridge, and salted sprats in the morning; sour cabbage soup, porridge, and again salted sprats in the afternoon. Sometimes, we were given sour cabbage soup in the morning and the gruel soup in the afternoon. In the gruel soup, there often were pieces of unpeeled and unwashed potatoes. At the bottom of the bowl, there would be dark sediment of dirt. In the northern camps, particularly in Vorkuta, the food was better, but in Karaganda, we were always hungry. Young prisoners doing hard manual labor suffered from hunger much more. After the meal, many prisoners stayed in the canteen, hoping to get an extra helping of the gruel soup or leftover porridge. However, they were rarely successful, and very often hungry prisoners searched for food in the garbage bins. Sometimes, they were lucky and found a frozen potato. There were many hungry and feeble people in Karaganda forced labor camps.

The camp store was just a small booth that was closed most of the time. The food products were delivered to the camp very rarely. On such days, all of the camp's public life happened in front of the small store window. The prisoners formed a very long line; they pushed each other, the noise was very loud, often there were arguments, and even fights. Prisoners who received money transfers had their own accounts, recorded in the logbook. The procedure of buying food involved cumbersome calculations, corrections, and signatures in the logbook. Each purchase took a very long time, so all the prisoners waiting for their turn in the line were very stressed. By and large, prisoners tried to buy butter and sugar. Obviously, the heads of the working teams and the rest of the members of "High Society" made their purchases without waiting in line. Some of them used the money of their team members. "Give and take" relationships were common. There were wolves and there were lambs.

As I have mentioned already, due to my refusal to sign the interrogation protocols I was forbidden by my interrogator to make store purchases. This ban began in the Lefortovo prison in Moscow, but it remained active for some time after that in Karaganda camp. All this time, my devoted wife deposited two hundred rubles, the maximum allowed amount, in my account each month. So, in Karaganda, my account accumulated more than one thousand rubles, and for some time I was the wealthiest man among the prisoners. However, due to the long waiting lines, I was rarely able to use the camp store. Later, when I was transferred to Vorkuta camp, there were more than nine hundred rubles left in my account. As it happens, this money was lost during the transfer.

There were also some positive elements and rules in the prison camp that worked reasonably well. Although food was scarce and of poor quality, each prisoner was entitled to his portion of bread and sugar. During the food shortage years, until 1954, this was especially important. After that, bread was put on the tables, so prisoners could eat as much as they wanted.

The medical service was organized quite efficiently. The sanitary department was responsible for hygiene in the barracks and restrooms. There was a medical office that was open in the morning and the evening. The doctors were chosen among the prisoners, and often they were quite experienced. Medical experts included general physicians, surgeons, dentists, opticians, otolaryngologists, etc. In the large camps, there also were X-ray laboratories, and optometric and cardiological facilities.

If a camp was lacking certain medical resources, the sick prisoner could be sent to another camp with better medical facilities. While in Sand camp, I was sent to Maykaduk camp for a stomach X-ray examination. In the camps, there also were hospitals for seriously ill prisoners. The hospital medical staff was also composed of prisoners with medical education.

Often, the doctors tried to help the prisoners and kept them in hospital for some time, even after they had regained their health. Much depended on personal relations. Most of the prisoners tried to prolong their stay in hospital, where they did not have to work and the food was much better.

Cultural activity was centered in a prisoner's club. In the camp, there was a relatively large concert hall for 250-300 people, with a library, rooms for drawing, and an orchestra. The club was managed by an MGB officer and involved actors who played in the prisoners' theater, directors, painters, musicians, etc. In prison performances, the women characters were played by men. Sometimes we were shown movies.

In Sand camp, we were housed in barracks that were partly dug into the ground. The two-level plank beds ran along the walls, and prisoners densely lay on them so that their bodies were touching one another. The barracks were about thirty meters long and about ten meters wide. There were no dividing walls, only columns in the center of the corridor. At the entrance, there were public amenities, a washbasin, a urinal bucket, and a place to dry clothes.

The veteran prisoners typically took the bottom rows of the plank beds. However, one of the inconveniences of the bottom rows was that some prisoners from the top rows sat there during the day. I got a place in the upper row at the beginning.

Every prisoner sought to be in the company of decent neighbors, such as his friends, trustworthy people, prisoners with a similar background, education, interests, age, nationality, etc. There were prisoners of all ages, from eighteen to eighty, and even older, and of all nationalities: Russians, Ukrainians, Lithuanians, Latvians, Jews, Moldavians, Georgians, Armenians, Tatars, Belarussians, Germans from the Volga region, et al. There were also prisoners from foreign countries, mostly from Germany, Austria, Poland, etc. The foreigners were mainly held in the northern camps.

Injustice and disrespect did not always rule in the camp; there was also friendship, respect, brotherhood, and devotion between the prisoners. In most cases, such relationships occurred among members of ethnic groups. Many prisoners organized in groups and ran a common economy by sharing their belongings and food packages. They shared their meals equally, sometimes eating from the same bowl. Sometimes the prisoners formed larger groups, conversing, singing, and praying together.

Prison terms varied from five to twenty-five years. However, a prisoner's mentality was such that everyone considered himself innocent. Many prisoners complained that their prison terms were way too high, relative to the crime that had been committed. Most political prisoners, sentenced by articles 58-10 and 58-11 of the Soviet penal code, were, in fact, innocent. However, there were also dangerous common criminals, jailbirds, murderers, and bandits, among them those who collaborated with the Germans during the war (some of them were devotees of Stepan Bandera), and those who were involved in the persecution of Jews.

There were several cases of prisoner escapes from Karaganda camps, but only a few of them were successful. One prisoner hid under the seat of the car belonging to the camp management. Two officers, one of them a camp commander, were literary sitting on the man when the car left the camp. When the car stopped and the officers got out, the prisoner climbed out of the car and was immediately captured. Another time, two common criminals ran away from their workplace. This time, their escape was more successful; they had prepared civil clothes in advance and managed to avoid capture for several days. At these moments, the camp bustled with activity; a successful escape awoke hopes and dreams in the other prisoners and excited them. That is why the prison management always made every effort to catch fugitives and the punishment for escape was very harsh. In the end, both runaway prisoners were returned to the camp. We were told that they had been able to run as far as Petropavlovsk, where they were caught in a restaurant while drunk in a company of prostitutes. Both runaways were immediately sent to carcer and then to another camp with extremely strong discipline. That was a relatively mild punishment; the veteran prisoners told us that only a few years earlier runaway prisoners were beaten to death and their bodies were left outside to serve as an example to others.

When prisoners were transferred from a prison to a camp or from one camp to another, they had to stay in quarantine for a period of twenty-one days. During quarantine, prisoners did not have to work, and this was quite pleasant. After arrival at Sand camp, we spent the quarantine period in the barracks, lying on the plank beds and talking to each other. It was winter, and because of the cold it was difficult to go outside for long walks. The barracks hummed with the noise of prisoners' conversations, except at night, when other noises were heard.

During quarantine we had a medical examination. At that time, I was weak and was suffering from acute stomach pains, so I was rated as a disabled person, which turned out to be incredibly lucky for me. During my first year in the prison camp, I did not have to work. The status of a disabled person was coveted by every prisoner, but the actual number of disabled prisoners in the camp was small, about five or six people; we comprised a separate working team, and I was chosen to be a foreman.

There were four categories of prisoner health in the camp. The first category included prisoners who were fit for hard work; the second involved prisoners doing less difficult work; the prisoners in the third category did easy work inside the camp; and the fourth category was for the disabled, who did not have to work at all.

After quarantine, prisoners were divided into work teams. They mostly worked outside of the camp, mainly in construction. They built residential houses, the club building, office buildings, and a plant for the repair of the coal mining machines.

There were many informers among camp prisoners. The operational department of the camp, staffed by the MGB officers, recruited informers by various means, such as: exempting them from hard work, giving them a better food allowance, granting them permission to write letters home more often, giving them better clothes, etc. Maybe I am overestimating, but it looked like that there was a wide network of informers. Often, prisoners belonging to "High Society," who held supervising positions in the barracks, working teams, store, canteen, etc. were suspected of being snitches. The other prisoners hated their guts, and sometimes traitors were severely punished by beating, stabbing, and even murder.

My Morning Prayer

It is night; a dim light of an electric lamp is gleaming at the far end of the barracks. Everybody is fast asleep. One can hear the noises of heavy breathing, snoring, stammering, screams, nervous and fearful voices; it feels as if a miniature brass band is at work. The air is thick and suffocating. I am lying on my plank bed with my eyes closed and trying to fall asleep.

The winter nights are long. Morning arrives, but the small windows of the half-basement are still dark. At last, the door is unlocked and a cold and refreshing white mist fills the barrack. The prisoner on duty is taking the urinal bucket outside. Then, one hears the sound of the buckets knocking against one another; the prisoner on duty is bringing buckets with fresh water for washing and drinking. Most of the prisoners are still asleep. I get dressed and go outside for a morning walk. I am wearing quilted cotton wool-padded trousers, an old cotton wool-padded jacket, a fur hat with ear flaps, and old felt boots. I gave Kricheli the new felt boots that my wife sent me when I was in Butyrka prison. So, dressed like this, I start my morning walk and my morning prayer.

It snowed during the night, a minor snowstorm, and I have to make my own path between piles of snow. It is still dark; I make my way between the low barracks with flat roofs and keep praying. There is a light breeze; my nose and lips are getting cold. I go back and forth, faster when the wind is blowing at my back, and slower against the wind.

What was my morning prayer? I sang Hebrew songs, Yiddish songs, and Jewish melodies without words. Throughout my time in the prison camp, I collected Hebrew songs. Besides the songs that I knew from my childhood, I learned many other beautiful Hebrew songs from my fellow Jewish prisoners. I learned many songs from Yechezkel Pulerevitch, Israel Avrovich, Shmuel Halkin, Shaul Weissman, Mordechai Grubian, Yosef Kerler, and especially from Leonid Kantargi, my young friend, who I cherished very much. I learned several songs from Mustafa Adali, Abraham Shtukarevich, and Strongin. I wrote some of the songs myself.

In Karaganda, my collection of songs was still small, and every morning I recited the same songs. Over the years, I assembled more than a hundred songs, so I divided them between the days of the week. Every day, I sang different songs, including the Shabbat songs. In Vorkuta in 1954, Mordechai Shenkar managed to obtain the siddur,[2] and I learned the Song of Songs by heart.[3] Shenkar also helped me to learn several psalms, especially the Song of Ascents,[4] and I also used them in my prayers.

Refreshed, I come back to the barracks and wash my face and hands. We are waiting for breakfast. It is the usual morning routine in the barracks. Prisoners are climbing up and down the plank beds, the entrance door is opening and closing. The prisoner in charge is adding coal to the furnace. One can hear voices, yawns, and morning jokes. Some prisoners are still sleeping; they are really fortunate people. I typically sleep only five to six hours during the night and had trouble sleeping even before my arrest. But eventually those who sleep have to wake up, it is time to go to the canteen. During quarantine, the prisoners of each barracks eat separately. At normal times, every working team eats together.

Meir Baazov

From the day of my transfer to the Church cell in Butyrka prison, I became friendly with Meir Baazov and Aharon Kricheli. We were together all the time during the transfer to Karaganda and were placed in the same barracks in the prison camp. I got especially close to Meir, who knew Hebrew very well. He was born in 1913 in Georgia. His father, David Baazov, was a well-known rabbi and his brother, Herzl, was a Georgian Hebrew writer, whose books were published in Russian too. Herzl was arrested in 1938, accused of Zionism, and immediately executed. At the beginning of the 1940s, his father was also arrested and spent five years in prison. He was released in 1947, returned to Tbilisi, and died a year later. Meir's other brother, Haim, was a lawyer and was also arrested for Zionist activity.

---

2   Siddur—a Jewish prayer book containing a set order of daily prayers.
3   Song of Songs is a collection of ancient Israelite love poems that celebrate the beauty and power of God's gift of love and sexual desire.
4   The Song of Ascents is a special collection of psalms sung by Hebrew pilgrims on their way to Jerusalem.

Meir and I, both loved the Hebrew language with all our heart, we were devoted Hebraists and conversed with each other only in Hebrew. In Moscow, we used to read Hebrew literature together in Lenin Library. In the prison camp, we shared everything, like being a part of a commune. We shared food, clothes, and parcels from our families. We often told stories to each other. Meir was an experienced storyteller and his Hebrew was exquisite. No one was able to understand us in the barracks. Meir was a good person and I liked him very much, though he was extremely passionate, as many people from the Caucasus are.

To our disappointment, he did not get the status of a disabled person. He was given only the third category of health and had to work. His profession had been construction engineer, and he had to teach other prisoners how to build houses. Before the arrest, he had taught college students, and this work was familiar to him. As I had mentioned before, most of the prisoners in our camp worked in construction. So, several professional courses were organized to train carpenters, plasterers, painters, plumbers, etc. Almost everyone in the prison camp had to take these courses, so in the beginning Meir was quite busy. Soon, another prisoner with experience in construction joined him in teaching.

When the initial period of courses was over, Meir went through a tough time. As an engineer, he was ordered to oversee the construction work at one of the locations. But in camp conditions, it was not easy. He was responsible not only for the technical aspects of construction, but also had to report the amount of work accomplished by the working teams every day. The reporting documents were typically overblown. The members of the working teams tended to report higher results to get larger food portions. And the camp management wanted to receive their bonuses, and therefore, supported the practice of exaggerating the progress of construction. Meir was not ready to sign the overblown reports, and because of his fiery temperament his relations with the other team members and with his bosses went sour. So, very soon he was demoted to a regular worker and was ordered to work at a job that involved hard physical labor. The work was very difficult for him, and he suffered a lot. He started having rheumatism outbreaks, and Doctor Lemenev, the head physician at our hospital, exempted him from work several times. Meir even spent some time in hospital. Eventually, he had to continue working.

The Invention

As a professional engineer and as a professor at Moscow Mining University, I studied and taught the theory and practice of coal processing and enrichment. In the prison camp, I was not able to be idle all the time, so I started to work on the design of an improved coal processing machine, and later I was even awarded a patent for this work.

The work on this invention was done together with Andrey Usov, an experienced mechanical engineer. Before his arrest in 1947, Andrey had been a doctoral student at Leningrad Polytechnical University. Andrey was a very pleasant and educated man, and I became very friendly with him. During the war, Andrey served as an officer in the army. He was captured by the Germans and sent to a POW camp in Finland. After returning home, he was arrested by the MGB and sentenced to a ten-year prison term for being captured during the war. Initially, he was sent to a forced labor camp in the Ural Mountains, where he worked in a lumber factory. There, he invented an improved mechanical saw. In a work accident, he lost several fingers on his left hand. But he did not consider himself as a disabled person. He was able to write with his right hand, draw, make sketches, etc. He was very handy and inventive and could do many things. In Karaganda forced labor camp, Andrey worked as the head of a work team. He was highly respected both by his teammates and by the camp management.

It seemed that the camp management had instructions to support our work on the technical invention. Initially, through the MGB operation department, we submitted a short description and drawings of our invention to Moscow Coal Mining Agency. The agency replied that our invention was of interest and that we should be allowed to develop it further. So, the camp management provided us with a small room in the club building, where I had spent most of my time. We were also given an electrical lamp, drawing paper, rulers, pencils, and other items. Andrey Usov and Meir Baazov were also there when free of work. Another prisoner, Yakov Beilinson, also often visited us in this room. Unfortunately, after a short period of time, the room was taken back from us, and we continued working on the invention in our barracks. Under the light of the electric lamp, we were able to work in the evenings too.

Yakov Beilinson was an experienced transportation engineer, a highly educated man, about forty to forty-five years old, well built, with blond hair. He liked music and played passionately on the mandolin. Before his arrest, Beilinson had been a party member and worked as a manager at the Leningrad seaport. He had published major technical papers in scientific journals. During the war, his work involved interaction with representatives of the foreign countries who were supplying Russia with emergency help. He was accused of espionage and sentenced to twenty-five years in prison. Yakov Beilinson was respected by all the prisoners. He joined me and Usov in our invention activity and worked on a project aimed at improving the process of loading and unloading railroad carriages.

Beilinson did not receive packages from home and lived only on the prison camp food ration, which was not sufficient for him; so he was often hungry. On one occasion, his friends shared with him some butter, honey, and other food that they'd just got from home. He ate and immediately felt strong stomach pains. He was transferred to the hospital in another camp, where he was diagnosed with an intestinal obstruction and operated on. The operation was not successful, and he died three days later.

Baazov was a gifted mathematician. With his help, I was able to improve my math skills, which I had hardly used since my university days. I also read books on electronics, since I already had some ideas for a second invention—a coal enrichment machine that used X-ray radiography. I implemented this second invention later, in Vorkuta prison camp. I also read fiction, had my morning and evening walks, spoke Hebrew with Baazov, and sang Hebrew songs with Yechezkel Pulerevitch. I also spent time with other friends I had acquired in the camp.

When we arrived at the camp, we were allowed to send a postcard home with a return address. A month later, I received the first two parcels from home. My wife was worried about my stomach and sent me some special food. But by that time I was feeling much better. What we needed most were sugar and fatty food. Meir also received parcels from home, and we shared our food between us. All our belongings and food were kept in the storage room.

Life in the prison camp was very monotonous, but unexpected events sometimes happened, as in the case of the photographs. Family photographs enclosed in parcels and letters from home were forbidden and were confiscated by camp security. So, many family pictures accumulated in the camp's files. One day, this regulation was revoked, and we were allowed to receive family pictures on the condition that there were no images of people in military uniform. It was announced that the pictures would be distributed to prisoners in the storage room at a certain time. This was in winter; it was already dark, and heavy snow was falling. It just so happened that I was walking next to the storage room and saw people leaving it with photographs in their hands. They looked happy and had smiles on their faces. Almost everyone stopped next to the lamppost, under the falling, swirling, and dancing snowflakes, to look at the images of their relatives. One man was so excited and happy that he embraced the post with his hands and kissed the photograph. I also received a picture of my wife with my son, and it was a very moving moment for me.

Thieves and Bitches

Most of the prisoners in our camp were political, sentenced according to article 58 of the Soviet penal code. The common criminals were a minority. They were mostly jailbirds, who spent most of their lives in prison. Since there were few of them, they could not terrorize the political prisoners. They were mostly only pretending to work, so that other prisoners had to perform their jobs. This caused some protests, but many of the political prisoners were also not very enthusiastic about work either.

The common criminals had their own laws and customs. They were subdivided into two categories, "thieves" and "bitches." The thieves branded themselves as the criminal elite. They did not work and did not collaborate with the camp authorities. The bitches cooperated with the authorities and often worked as heads of the working teams. Thus, they defied the thieves' laws and were marked as traitors. According to the thieves' code of conduct, this was a capital offense, and bitches were often murdered by their own folks.

In the spring of 1950, the thieves seized the storage room at night. It was a huge event. They broke the locks, opened many cases and bags belonging to other prisoners, and started to eat their food. The camp guards arrived when the thieves were still in the storage room. They were ordered to come out, but they had closed the door and refused to leave the storage room until their stomachs were full. My bag got into their hands and I lost a large part of my food supplies.

One of the common criminals was stationed in our barracks. His name was Leonya. He was a young man with blond hair. He was quite pleasant and somehow became close to Yakov Beilinson, a friend of mine. Their plank beds were next to each other, so they talked a lot and Leonya respected Yakov Beilinson as a father. One day, Leonya was stabbed deeply by the other criminals. It seemed that they defined him as a bitch and had sentenced him to death. Leonya was taken to the hospital in another prison camp and we never heard about him after that.

Part 6

The Eynikeyt Group

Despite the harsh life in the prison camp, the thoughts of many prisoners focused on events that took place before their arrest, and even the most reserved of them were often disposed to share their stories with fellow prisoners. So, time and again, I heard the life stories of other people about their origins, experiences, achievements, and downfalls. I will try to write down some of the stories that I heard during my time in the camp.

I will start with the young guys from Zhmerynka, a small town in Western Ukraine, who belonged to a Zionist Jewish group called Eynikeyt, which means "unity" in Yiddish. The Eynikeyt group consisted of ten boys and one girl, Tanya Kerzman. Three of them were serving time in Karaganda prison camp: Alik Hodorkovsky, Eliyahu Mishpatman, and Sasha Sukher. Later, in Vorkuta forced labor camp, I met Misha Spivak, Meir Gelfond, and Volodya Kerzman, who also belonged to the group. After my release from the prison camp, back at home in Moscow, I also met Tanya, who at that time was a student at Saratov University.

Alik Hodorkovsky

I became very close to Alik Hodorkovsky, a young guy of medium height with a pleasant face, a trace of a black mustache, and dark dreamy eyes that turned fiery when he was excited. He was very generous and good-natured, and many of the prisoners liked him. Alik was also extremely sensitive to unfairness and was punished several times for his reaction to injustice. Once, in his presence, a guard abused a prisoner who was smoking on the way to work. For this offense, the guard made the prisoner lie down in the dirt, so Alik interfered, called the guard a "fascist," and was punished by being sent to carcer for several days. His father was a literature teacher and the headmaster of a local school in Zhmerynka and his mother was a librarian. They regularly sent him letters and parcels with food and books. Alik showed me their pictures.

The prisoners used to joke that there were two libraries in the camp, one in the club and the other was Alik's. He received many good books from home and let other prisoners read them. Even the camp administration borrowed books from him.

Alik possessed a kind of moral compass and was always striving for truth. The head physician of the hospital, Doctor Leon Lemenev, a man of around fifty, was one of the readers of his books. Dr. Lemenev was a veteran of the Communist Party and, before his arrest, had held a high-level position at the Ministry of Health. He was very fond of Alik and tried to help him. Even though Alik was quite healthy, Dr. Lemenev released him from work whenever he asked. He once put Alik in the hospital to rest and then prescribed him special food, which was much better than the regular camp food. Lemenev was a practical man with a kind heart; I also became quite friendly with him.

Alik had the first category of health and worked in construction outside of the prison camp. He did not have a profession and did hard physical work, carrying bags with sand, cement, slag, and gravel at the construction site. After graduation from a high school in Zhmerynka, Alik had continued his studies at the Odessa University Law Department. His goal was to become a lawyer and to defend unlawfully accused people. He was like Don Quixote, a fighter for justice; and, like Don Quixote, he was suffering greatly for his ideals. Many times, tired after a long day at work, he used to tell us about cases of dishonestly, misconduct, and corruption that he had encountered during the day. At one time, he was promoted to the much easier position of examiner and had to record the amount of work performed during the day. This sort of work involved cheating, and he often fought with other team members. In the end, our Don Quixote was sent back to do the hard and dirty work. He was very disappointed and Dr. Lemenev and I had to comfort and encourage him.

I spent long hours with Alik in the prison camp. He was very interested in the history of Jewish people and asked me to educate him. About a year before my arrest, I had read a book on Jewish history by Meir Balaban, and I did my best to narrate this book to him. I also told him Bible stories and the fundamentals and customs of the Jewish religion that I remembered from my youth. Most of these conversations were during our walks on the pathways of the camp. I told him stories from the distant past about faraway lands, and he listened attentively.

Before arrest, Alik had a girlfriend, whose name was Tzila. She was not a member of the Eynikeyt group but knew about its existence. She was not detained. When arrests began, she moved to her aunt's in one of the Middle Asian republics. Later in the camp, Alik learned from a letter from his parents that Tzila had continued her studies at Vinnitsa University as if nothing had happened. He showed me the letter. There was a hint that she was suspected of being an informer. Alik was terribly upset when he received the news. Even now, I vividly remember his sad eyes. "How is it possible that Tzila, such a lovely girl, could become a traitor?" The idealistic spark of his Don Quixote's nature flared into a fire. Every prisoner has yearnings and dreams, and life is unbearable without them; and at the age of twenty-one, the power of ideas is overwhelming. And now, all his dreams were crushed. How could I help such a sensitive young man?

In the summer of 1950, several new and more comfortable barracks were built in the camp. Baazov and I moved into one of them. Alik was also transferred to the same barracks. We occupied the lower plank-beds and Alik got an upper one. During his free time, Alik mostly read books that he received from home and from the library. He learned a lot, but the most important university was the prison camp itself.

Eliyahu Mishpatman

Eliyahu Mishpatman was Alik's cousin. He was a good-looking young man with broad shoulders, dark hair, and a very logical way of think-ing. He was born in 1929, like most of the members of the Eynikeyt group who were born between 1929 and 1932; only one of them was born in 1934. Eliyahu was not emotional like Alik—quite the contrary. He was very cautious with his words, and I loved him for his common sense and logical approach to life. Eliyahu had graduated from a high school in Vinnitsa and started studying at Kiev University while residing in his aunt's home. His mother still lived in Vinnitsa and his father had been killed during the war. Eliyahu had been arrested in Kiev several months after the detention of the other members of the Eynikeyt group. According to him, his connection to the group had only been casual. During interrogation, somebody had mentioned that Alik had a cousin who knew about the group. In the camp, Eliyahu did hard labor, even though, as I remember, his lungs were in bad shape. One day, there was a fire in the factory where he worked. There was a panic, part of the outside fence was destroyed, and there was a real possibility to escape the prison camp. Eliyahu told me later that the temptation to run away was very strong, but eventually he had decided against it.

Sasha Sukher

Another member of the Eynikeyt group in our camp was Sasha Sukher. During the war, as a young boy, he had spent more than two years in the Zhmerynka ghetto. Sasha wore glasses; he was an intelligent young man and liked to read and play chess. Sasha was not doing hard labor; from the very beginning he was appointed to be an examiner and had to record the amount of work done during the day. For a long time, all three friends belonged to the same working team, headed by Konoplev. They had good relations with Konoplev and ran their economy together. Konoplev was originally from Siberia. His prison term was only five years, and he regularly received parcels from his young wife, who lived in Novosibirsk. He was a pleasant, straightforward, and educated man. Both of us were imprisoned in Lefortovo at the same time. His cell was next to mine, and it was him who I had communicated with by knocking on the wall.

Sukher was a quiet and silent young man, deeply immersed in his thoughts. He did not like to talk much about himself and gave the impression of being in another world. However, when one of the prisoner who was much stronger insulted him as a Jew, this quiet guy immediately began fighting. I do not remember the outcome of this fight, but the very fact that he chose to fight says a lot about Sasha. Alik Hodorkovsky would behave similarly, but his decision would come from the heart, whereas Sasha's action would be based on his principles as well as his heart. Unlike Alik and Eliyahu, Sasha had seen a lot during his life. In the ghetto, as a punishment, he had once been buried alive up to his chin in a hole. His profound inner concentration hindered his relations with friends. Alik and Eliyahu were much closer to each other and shared everything—maybe because they were cousins.

Even though I am trying to arrange my memoirs in chronological order, perhaps it is appropriate now to describe the other members of the Eynikeyt group. I met them later in the Vorkuta forced labor camp, where I spent the last three years of my imprisonment. There, I encountered Misha Spivak, whose prison term was twenty-five years, Volodya Kerzman, and Meir Gelfond.

Misha Spivak

Misha was a pleasant young man with broad shoulders and a baby face. He had a strong Jewish provincial accent and drew his words out, so his speech often sounded like a song, which was very enjoyable to my ears. He was very talkative. His friends, Meir Gelfond and Volodya Kerzman, could not bear his chatting, and their relations were often quite tense. Misha had been arrested in Lvov, where was studying at the university. Like Sasha Sukher, he had gone through the hell of a ghetto, where he had suffered a lot. His mother loved him passionately. Her letters were full of love, concern, and sadness. She worked as a shopkeeper and his father was an accountant. Her income was much larger and she was the dominant figure in his family.

Misha was a pragmatic young man and cared a lot about the material aspects of life, a trait that his friends did not particularly appreciate. Despite his shortcomings, I liked Misha. He was working in the coal mine and had good relations with his team members. He was the only one among his friends who was motivated to advance in the prison camp. He took a training course for heads of the working teams and successfully passed the tests. I helped him in some of his studies. Even though he was just a young Jew from a small provincial town, he was appointed as head of the working team maintaining ventilation of the coal mine.

I did not interact with Misha very often, as I preferred talking with people who spoke Hebrew and knew Hebrew songs, but I vividly remember him on one of the warm summer days. The sun was high in the sky and green spikes of tall grass were growing in the open spaces of the camp. I was strolling with Misha Spivak along the path inside the camp and enjoying his wonderful Jewish accent. He was talking about revenge, but we both knew that these were just words.

Misha became friendly with Leonid Aronov, a former professor from Moscow Steel University. Professor Aronov was a tall, strong man, fifty-eight years old, and had a fifteen-year prison term. I will write more about him later. At the time, I was not able to grasp a rationale for their friendship, Aronov was a grown-up man who had experienced a lot in his life and Misha Spivak was just a green youngster. Strange relationships flourished often in the camp for instance, the friendship between Doctor Lemenev and Alik Hodorkovsky, or between Volodya Kerzman and Menahem Levy.

Volodya Kerzman

Volodya Kerzman was the most handsome guy among the members of the Eynikeyt group. He was of medium height with a pleasant face. His eyes radiated warmth, and he was not shy of his gold tooth. Before the arrest, Volodya was studying at Leningrad Medical University. He was very cordial and kind and was always ready to share everything he had with other prisoners, which was very unusual, as many people in the camp were sick with the greediness disease. I spent many hours with Volodya; he wanted to learn Hebrew, but lacked persistence and commitment. He told me that girls were always very fond of him. One of the girls in the Eynikeyt group, Tanya, was his girlfriend. He told me about the Zhmerynka ghetto, where he was during the war. There, at only thirteen or fourteen years of age, he had sex with girls.

In the camp, Volodya became very close to Menahem Levy, who was like a father to him. Volodya's mother had died when he was young, and his father had married for a second time. His relations with his father's family in Zhmerynka were not very good. Volodya was supported by his elder brother, who loved him very much. Even though his brother was married and had children, he regularly wrote Volodya warm letters and sent him food parcels. After his release from the camp, Volodya got a job at a factory in Vladimir where his brother worked as an engineer.

Volodya told me a lot about his life in Leningrad. There were also stories about his victories with girls, even with middle-aged ladies. I remember the comic verses that somebody composed about Volodya in Yiddish:

> Here is Kerzman Wolf,[1]
> He likes to play a duet.
> With a girl in bed.
> Who wants to work in a coal mine?
> Run to the forest, enjoy the sunshine.

Kerzman was quite healthy; he was in the first category of health and had to work in the coal mine. But he did not get along with the head of his work team. Once somebody called him a "kike" and he got in a fight with him. Other prisoners joined his foe and Volodya was badly beaten. The marks of this fight remained on his face for a long time, but he carried them with pride. Eventually, after many pleas supported by bribes, his health status was changed to the second category, and he was supposed to be released from work in the mine. However, the head of mining operations refused to let him go. The official reason was that Volodya was neglecting his work duties, but we all knew that the head of mining operations was an antisemite. He insulted Volodya and called him dirty names. Volodya replied to him in kind. This was in 1954; prisoners at that time had more freedom. Eventually, Volodya refused to go to work in the mine and was put in a carcer.

Towards the end of his stay in the carcer, he was visited by Colonel Bogaenko, a commanding officer at Vorkuta prison camp. Volodya requested a transfer so that he could work aboveground, in accordance with his new health category. Bogaenko promised to transfer him, but Volodya had to continue working in the mine for a certain period of time. The mine was always short of workers and there was a surplus of laborers aboveground. Volodya returned to the mine, but Bogaenko did not deliver on his promise, so Volodya refused to continue working as a miner and was sent to the carcer again. This fight continued for a long time, and we supported Volodya during this difficult period. Eventually, he was transferred to the mechanical repair factory and worked as a

---

1   The name of Volodya (diminutive of Vladimir) corresponds to the Hebrew name Zeev, or wolf.

carpenter, making wooden molds for metal forging. He was hired with the help of David Kogan. I will write more about him later. Volodya did not have any experience as a carpenter and initially worked as an apprentice. The head of the forge operation in the plant was a young woman engineer, who noticed the good-looking young man. I do not know all the details, but according to Volodya he enjoyed working with her. One day, he was suddenly transferred to a different work team that was doing hard labor. He had no choice but to accept this change; it was still much better than underground mining, where numerous accidents happened.

Meir Gelfond

Now, I will turn to Meir Gelfond, the most talented and remarkable member of the Eynikeyt group. He was a good-looking and good-natured young man, with a sharp mind, pleasant manly voice, dark eyes, and a piercing gaze. The sharp mind in combination with diligence promised a lot, and Meir had what it takes. I should also note how motivated he was. He was the only one who decided to learn Hebrew in the prison camp and, in fact, accomplished a lot: he started talking Hebrew after several months of training. I taught him by heart every day. In Vorkuta prison camp, writing in Hebrew was forbidden and searches of prisoners' belongings were conducted frequently. Before his arrest, Meir had been studying medicine; and in the prison camp he worked as a medical assistant. He chose to specialize in ophthalmology and was quite successful in this goal. He assisted Dr. Petrov, an experienced ophthalmologist, who was very fond of Meir.

Meir was less affectionate than Kerzman; he was more rigorous and pedantic, and was relentless and very efficient in his work. He would scorn hapless people who lacked purpose in life. But everyone has his shortcomings and for Meir this was a minor issue. He always treated people fairly and was respected by many. I heard a lot about his intelligence from his friends in Karaganda camp, and when I met Meir in Vorkuta he proved to be worthy of their praise. He was a true Jew and as a member of the camp's medical department helped many Jewish prisoners get released from work or have their workload lightened. As I write, Meir is graduating from Karaganda Medical University, and I am sure that he will become a knowledgeable and outstanding physician.[2]

After my release from the camp, I met another member of the Eynikeyt group, Tanya, Volodya Kerzman's girlfriend. Both of them spent a night in my apartment in Moscow. Due to the brevity of our meeting, we were not able to have a meaningful conversation, but all her friends spoke very warmly about her. She'd also been arrested and had behaved bravely during interrogation. Tanya did not betray her friends and was sentenced to eight years in the prison camp. Now she is studying at the university in Saratov, where her sister lives.

Zhmerynka

I have done my best to describe the seven members of the Eynikeyt group. Now it is time to talk about the group itself. Zhmerynka was a small provincial town in the southeastern part of Ukraine. Before the war, it had a significant Jewish population. The Jewish kids went to the Soviet schools together with the children of other nationalities and did not receive any special Jewish education. They were all young citizens of the Soviet Union. At school, they were taught the history of the USSR and Russian literature: Pushkin, Lermontov, Gogol, Turgenev, Tolstoy, Chekhov, Gorky, and Mayakovsky. They never even heard about Moses, King David, King Solomon, the prophet Yeshayahu, the prophet Jeremiah, Shabtai Zvi, Baal Shem Tov, or Binyamin Zeev Herzl. Jewish culture was foreign to the young pioneers. They were aware that their parents belonged to the Jewish nation, but besides occasional antisemitic incidents, their Jewishness was meaningless to them. Inspiring slogans floated in the air: "Love and Friendship between Nations," "Brotherhood," "Soviet Motherland." And the young chicks absorbed these slogans and believed in them. Soviet propaganda became part of their life. It was a golden period in their serene childhood; their world was full of happiness and flowers. And suddenly the war broke out.

---

2   Meir Gelfond (1930-1985) was released from the prison camp in 1954 and became an expert cardiologist. He worked in one of the Moscow hospitals and remained close to Zvi Preigerzon until Zvi's death in 1969. He was active in the Soviet Zionist movement and emigrated to Israel in 1971, where he continued working as a cardiologist.

The war destroyed the peaceful life of Zhmerynka. Instead of summer vacation—blood and ruins. During the first few days of the war, Hitler's divisions occupied vast territories of Ukraine and Belorussia. The young Jewish kids started to realize that they were somehow different from their Ukrainian and Russian friends. Terrible rumors about the Nazi persecution of the Jews filled the air. The Germans were slaughtering all Jews, irrespective of their age—the old and the young. It was the first time that they had faced the fact of their Jewish origins. The problem was crucial: it was a question of life and death.

The Ghetto

Some Jewish families were able to evacuate to the eastern parts of Russia, to distant, unfamiliar, and cold lands. But the advance of the German tanks was extremely fast; they passed through Zhmerynka and continued further and further to the east. The Zhmerynka region fell under the rule of the Romanian government. The Romanian attitude towards the Jews was not as brutal as the German's. They did not murder; they just plundered them and put them in ghettoes. All the Jews from the region were gathered into a small part of Zhmerynka, the size of a few streets. There were also Jews from Romania, Serbia, and other countries. It is not clear why Hitler, whose power was absolute, allowed Antonescu to avoid imposing the "final solution" policy on the Jews. Maybe it was due to the fact that Romania, as a junior ally of Nazi Germany, was able to preserve a degree of political autonomy.

Sasha Sukher, Volodya Kerzman, Misha Spivak, and many other young boys and girls found themselves in the Zhmerynka ghetto. They spent about three years there, from the ages of twelve to fifteen. Adolescence is a critical age for youngsters. During the teenage years, people's eyes open and the surrounding world shapes their minds, casting its stamp on their whole life.

I learned a lot from these three young men about the life in the ghetto, but this is not the right place to go into detail about this important subject. Perhaps someone who experienced life in the Zhmerynka ghetto should describe and document all the facts about it. I can only point out the deep scars that the ghetto left in the minds of these young people.

In my opinion, the ghetto, in some respects, was very similar to the prison camp; on the other hand, they were quite different. The following things were similar. They both imprisoned people, restricted their freedom of movement, crowded them into a small place, and put them under total control of the authorities. In the forced labor camp, a few selected prisoners had power over the rest of the inmates so the prison authorities did not have to deal with all the prisoners, just with the few appointed ones. The ghetto had the same set up: a Jewish administration, which included a police force, took care of all the needs of the ghetto's inhabitants. The head of the administration in the Zhmerynka ghetto was a Jew from Romania, whose name was Greenstein or Greenberg. He exercised his power quite assertively, including punishing of the fellow Jews. Misha Spivak told me that his mother was once beaten for being absent during work time.

I cannot judge the head of the Jewish administration of the Zhmerynka ghetto. I have heard a lot about his efforts to help the Jewish prisoners, about his hard work to feed them, protect them, save them from extermination. In the ghetto, there were several factories, and their produce was used to feed the ghetto population. There were sanitation, medical, and cultural units, which played a significant role in the life of the ghetto. There were arrangements with the Romanian authorities regarding prisoners working outside the ghetto. All of this was the responsibility of the ghetto administration, which he headed. That said, I have heard that he behaved improperly towards some of the residents and that some of the money collected for common needs found its way into his private stash.

In the prison camp, men and women were separated from each other, whereas in the ghetto families were able to stay together. In the camp, everyone had to bear his own burden, but the prison term provided some certainty; in the ghetto, however, the length of imprisonment was indefinite and everyone was under the threat of sudden death. The Germans frequently entered the ghetto, conducted searches, and murdered people. A common aspect of both the prison camp and the ghetto was that everyone nurtured hopes and dreams of a better future. Survival was impossible without hope.

The life of those teenagers who were lucky enough to escape the Germans and reach distant parts of Russia and Middle Asia was not easy either. They had to adjust to a new environment and often faced hunger, cold, and hard work. They worried about their relatives and friends who remained in the occupied territories or were fighting the fascists, as well as about their lost homes and property. They often faced acts of unbridled antisemitism from the local population. Being a displaced Jew brought an additional weight. The flames of the furnaces that burned the bodies of Jewish men, women, and children in Majdanek and Treblinka cast dreadful shadows in the minds of all Jews, wherever they were.

.After the turn in the war and the retreat of the Germans, Zhmerynka was liberated by the Soviet army and the gates of the ghetto were flung open. People started to come back from their places of escape and life in Zhmerynka slowly returned to normal. The teenagers started going to school again and, as before, continued to study Turgenev, Gorky, and Mayakovsky. But the events that they experienced, the rivers of blood that covered the country, left bitter scars in their fragile minds. Young people are not capable of total hypocrisy. Their Jewishness troubled them. The German occupants put this issue in front of them as a crucial one, or, more accurately, as an issue of life and death. Hitler proved that the assimilation of Jews was not the answer: Jewish "half-breeds"[3] or even "quarter-breeds" were also slaughtered in the concentration camps.

The Zionist Group

Another answer to this question was the creation of the State of Israel. To be like all other nations. National pride touched the entire Jewish population of the Soviet Union. In addition, antisemitism raised its head in the country and contributed to the resurgence of national feelings.

The time spent in the ghetto also contributed to the revival of national feelings among the youth. In the Zhmerynka ghetto, they got to know Zionists from Romania and Moldavia, who managed to continue their activities and propaganda even there.

It happened that Misha Spivak, a young guy of sixteen, a member of the Komsomol,[4] who went through the seven circles of hell in the ghetto, started writing short stories and even a novel, the contents of which did not quite comply with the official policy of the Soviet Union. He showed

---

3   "Jewish half-breeds" was the legal term used in Nazi Germany to denote persons deemed to have both Aryan and Jewish ancestry.

4   Komsomol—the youth division of the Communist Party.

his works to his friends and they started to discuss and even argue about them. I do not know who initiated the group, or suggested its name Eynikeyt—Unity. At about the same time, the novel *The Young Guard* by the famous Soviet writer Alexander Fadeyev was published and widely discussed in the Soviet press. It was about a group of young partisans who were fighting the German occupiers in the Ukrainian city of Krasnodon. It is quite possible that the book also influenced the youngsters. In any case, the name Eynikeyt was chosen and the group was formed.

The common link between the Young Guard and Eynikeyt was that they both had a traitor. The MGB knew about everything that was happening in the group. Unlike the Young Guard, the members of Eynikeyt were not involved in any real actions. The members of the Young Guard had a goal—to fight the despised German enemies by brutal means. The members of the Eynikeyt group did not hate the Soviet authorities and did not fight against it. Their activity was limited to distributing leaflets in the local synagogue and calling on Jews to emigrate to the State of Israel. They claimed that emigration was the real answer to the Jewish problem.

After graduation from high school, the members of Eynikeyt went to universities in Vinnitsa, Kiev, Lvov, and Leningrad. Misha Spivak moved to Lvov and was in contact with the local Zionist group. When he returned home for the summer vacation, he tried to organize a "Spivak group," but tensions were starting to grow between the friends. The traitor continued his disgusting mission and the amount of information collected by the MGB was increasing. In 1947, the group ceased its activity. The young guys grew up and everyone went on their own way. The burning wounds of the war started to heal and they became interested in other matters. But the material collected about them by the MGB still existed.

At the end of 1948, with the beginning of the campaign against Zionism, the members of the Eynikeyt group were the first to be arrested. These young Jewish boys and girls faced brutal interrogators, like innocent lambs chased by wolves. During the search of Misha Spivak's home, they found his novel. The MGB had a considerable amount of evidence against him. He was sentenced to twenty-five years in prison and the rest of the group to ten years. Their mothers, fathers, brothers, and sisters became the families of "Enemies of the State." The years that they spent in prison camps, until the end of Stalin's atrocities, left deep scars in their souls—scars that could never be erased.

Part 7

The People in Karaganda Camp

In Karaganda camp, I also encountered members of Zionist organizations from the republics that were occupied by the Soviet Union in 1939-1940, such as Western Ukraine, Moldavia, and the Baltic states. Most notable were the members of Beitar. I had never heard about this organization before.

Beitar was a Zionist Youth organization founded by Zeev Jabotinsky,[1] who was greatly admired by its members. Jabotinsky was a very gifted and strong-willed person, a fearless fighter, prominent orator, publicist, poet, writer, and translator. He created and led the far right wing of the Jewish Zionist movement; he was sometimes even called the leader of the Jewish fascists. During World War I, he had served as a commander of the British Army's Jewish Legion. I learned a lot about Beitar from a Jewish prisoner from Kovno,[2] Yechezkel Pulerevitch,[3] who I got to know in Karaganda forced labor camp.

---

1 Zeev Jabotinsky (1880-1940)—Jewish Zionist leader, who cofounded the Jewish Legion of the British Army during World War I and established several Jewish organizations, including Beitar and Irgun.
2 Kovno or Kaunas is the second largest city in Lithuania after Vilnius and an important center of Lithuanian economic, academic, and cultural life.
3 Yechezkel Pulerevitch (1914-1995)—one of the leaders of Lithuania's Beitar organization before the annexation of Lithuania by the USSR in 1940. He was a Gulag prisoner from 1941-1954. In 1965, he emigrated to Israel, where he founded the Prisoners of Zion Association.

Yechezkel Pulerevitch

As I mentioned earlier, I arrived at Karaganda Sand camp at the beginning of 1950. At that time, the camp was almost empty. The Japanese prisoners of World War, that were stationed there were moved out shortly before our arrival. During the first ten days, the camp was filled with newly arrived and veteran prisoners, some of whom came from the Ural Mountains. One of the prisoners in this group was Yechezkel Ben-Moshe Pulerevitch. He was stationed in the neighboring barracks, and one day he approached Baazov and me while we were sitting on our plank beds and speaking Hebrew. He was very surprised to hear Hebrew in the prison camp and immediately started talking to us in the language. We were very glad to meet him. His Hebrew was rich and fluent, and when we got to know him better we learned to enjoy his cordial spirit.

When we first met, Yechezkel was thirty-six years old. He was of less than average height, solidly built, bald, and with gray eyes and a slightly sharp chin. Yechezkel was born in Lithuania. During World War I, his family moved to Southern Ukraine, where they experienced the dreadful events of those years. In 1920, following the agreement reached between capitalist Lithuania and Communist Russia, they moved back to Lithuania. His family was very poor, and his mother died when he has quite young. In 1928, as a schoolboy, he joined Beitar, which was very popular among the Jewish youth, especially in Kovno (Kaunas). He was a devoted member of Beitar and named his son Shaby after the Beitar hero Shlomo Ben Yosef, who was hanged by British soldiers in Palestine. Eventually, he became one of the local Beitar leaders. When the Soviet army occupied Lithuania in 1940, he was arrested and sentenced to ten years in the Gulag. In Karaganda camp, Yechezkel's work was not very hard and he was quite healthy. Before his transfer to Karaganda, he was held in another camp in the Ural Mountains and worked there as a logger. Yechezkel regularly received letters and food parcels from his wife, who was working as a seamstress and raising their son in exile in the Altai region.

We became close friends and I loved Yechezkel with all my heart. Those ten months that we spent together in Karaganda prison camp left me with very pleasant memories. As a disabled person, I was released from work and often waited for him at the end of his working day. I vividly remember a day when we walked back and forth along the prison camp's barbed wire fence speaking Hebrew. It was quite warm, the sun was setting in the west, the skies were bright and blue. Yechezkel told me about Beitar in Kovno, about the objectives and aspirations of this organization. Besides Beitar stories, Yechezkel told me a lot about his childhood and his life in Kovno, about his songs and dreams. Many of the Hebrew songs that I learned from Yechezkel, were written by him.

Beitar was an international organization with its center in London. At that time, the Beitar section in Kovno numbered hundreds of young men and women. They sported special brown uniforms and had their own clubs and training camps. Beitar members were sang their own songs and regularly took part in street rallies. When Zeev Jabotinsky, the commander of Beitar, visited Kovno they met him with songs, flags, and flowers, and Jabotinsky recited his rousing speeches.

Several years before his death in 1940, Zeev Jabotinsky left Histadrut[4] and founded a separate Jewish Revisionist Zionist Union which had its own congress. It was based on capitalist values and had an extremely anti-Arab ideology. He declared that Jews had to conquer the whole Land of Israel by all means. One of the poems that he wrote served as Beitar's guideline. It contained the verses: "Two banks has the Jordan—/ This is ours and the other is as well." I was raised on the idea of friendship between all nations, and this ideology was rather new and foreign to me. I argued a lot with Yechezkel on the issue.

The Lithuanian authorities were not very friendly to the Zionist organizations; nevertheless, Jewish schools, unions, meetings, and rallies were permitted. Most Beitar activities were conducted at the club where the Zionist youth met in the evenings. The young men and women took part in these meetings together. They conducted discussions, debates, learned Hebrew, and sang. Every Beitar member had to learn the Hebrew language. On certain days, Beitar held official meetings with music and songs, which were even broadcast on the radio. Yechezkel composed the song "We Forged Desire from Iron," which was based on Beitar ideology:

---

4   Histadrut—the General Federation of Jewish Labor in Palestine, founded in 1920 by David Ben Gurion.

We forged desire from iron,
And we learned the skills of defense.
We swore to give our lives
For the sake of building the state.

And if an Arab stands up as an obstacle
On the way to the resurrection of the nation,
We, Beitar's members, have all sworn
That we will not be afraid of blood.

I learned many Hebrew songs from Yechezkel. These songs were like prayers for me; they gave me immense emotional support in prison. Even now, I remember more than twenty-five of these songs. One of them, "If I Die on My Watch," goes like this:

If I die on my watch, slashed by a dagger,
I will sing the songs of Beitar 'til the last moments.
If my destiny is to give my life for freedom,
I will find the strength to break my chains and die in high spirits.
If I freeze to death in prison,
The sun will rise again and the eternal light will shine.

Another song was "The Unknown Soldiers," which made a deep impression on me. Yechezkel sang it in a deep, raspy voice in the slow rhythm of a parade march. The verses of this song were gloomy and despairing; they matched the music very well. The song "In the Fields of Galilee" consoled Yechezkel during his time in prison. It reminded him of Israel, and he sang it with passionate excitement:

The hills of Galilee, I swear on the blood of your heroes
To keep fighting a war of labor, a war or revenge—
Revenge for the heroes of Tel Hai[5]

---

5   Tel Hai—a Jewish settlement in northern Galilee. In 1920, a military engagement in Tel Hai between Zionists and Arabs resulted in the deaths of eight Jews, among them Joseph Trumpeldor, who together with Zeev Jabotinsky cofounded the Jewish Legion.

I will never forget Yechezkel. He was my friend and I loved him like a younger brother. He sweetened my life and supported me during my first year in the prison camp. Almost every evening, we walked the same trail along the barbed wire fence speaking Hebrew and singing Hebrew songs. And at sunset, bright colors appeared on the horizon and a pleasant mild breeze arose from the prairie behind the fence. Then the skies turned dark, and the first stars appeared, one after another. Miserable scenery surrounded us—overcrowded barracks, dust, dirt, the hard work of prisoners, their hopes, dreams, and songs. But the heavens above us were vast and clear with bright, blinking stars. And the guard towers of the prison camp loomed over the fading colors of sunset.

At the beginning of November 1950, Yechezkel's prison term came to an end. A month before his release, he wrote a petition to the authorities in which he asked to join his wife and son, who lived in exile in the town of Slavgorod in the Altai region. However, his petition was left without a reply, and he was sent to the Krasnoyarsk region in Siberia to work as a logger. His wife and son Shaby joined him there.

We spent the day before his release together. Fall in Karaganda was quite nice. It was relatively warm, the bright sun cast golden light on the prairie, white clouds sailed across the sky. We sat on a bench next to the wooden board displaying prison camp posters. He told me about the last days of Beitar in Kovno, after the Soviet army occupation of Lithuania in 1940. The Beitar organization was banned and its members dispersed. Some of them were arrested and some started new lives. But the Hebrew songs did not fade away: they live their own lives. And here and there, on different occasions, their voices and melodies will sound again and again, songs of humor and sadness, songs of young people who lived long ago in the country of Lithuania. Their songs will spread throughout the whole world; they will disappear and come to live again.

In other prison camps, I met more Beitar members from Lithuania (Avrovich, Shtukarevich, etc.), but no one became so close to me as Yechezkel. He was respected and loved not only by the Jewish prisoners, but also by the Lithuanians, whose language he knew very well.

Aharon Kricheli

One of the challenging tasks in the prison camp was deciding how to spend one's free time. Prisoners were separated from their families, women, sport, entertainment (movie nights were very rare, and not all prisoners were allowed to attend them). The prison camp routine was very rigid, so everyone had to find his own way to spend their free time as pleasantly as possible. Many prisoners made themselves busy by talking to each other, telling stories, singing songs, playing chess, checkers, dominoes, and reading books. Some handcrafted small figurines and toys from wood or clay or drew sketches. Some people, like Aharon Kricheli, were rather desolate and were not able to find the mental strength to adjust to life in the prison camp.

Aharon Kricheli, a Georgian Jew from Tbilisi, was a member of the Communist Party and, before his arrest, served as the head of the Jewish Department of the Georgian National Museum. He was of medium height, with trimmed mustache, as was Georgian custom, and had a short beard that was turning gray. He was very thin and looked unhealthy, not only as a result of the insufficient prison food ration but also because of his lack of appetite. His face and body were covered with boils and bandages.

Somehow, Kricheli had been attached to our "Zionist group" by the MGB investigators and sentenced to ten years in the Gulag. The only possible reason for his arrest was his acquaintance with Meir Baazov, who occasionally visited the Tbilisi museum during the war. Now I understand that the real reason for his arrest was the desire of the Soviet authorities to destroy all signs and artifacts of Jewish culture—religion, books, theaters, museums, and even Jewish tradition itself. Every Jewish person, devoted to his nation, who dared to speak up, was arrested. By working at the museum, Kricheli was involved with the preservation of Jewish culture, and this "offense" was good enough to banish him from his normal life for ten years. The formal cause for his arrest had been easy to fabricate.

Life in the prison camp was especially challenging for Kricheli. He did not want, and was not able, to adapt to it. Like myself, he was given the status of a disabled person and was exempt from work. But, unlike me, he had not found any area of interest. He often sat outside his barracks, sometimes squatting against the wall and looking indifferently at the world. His knowledge of Hebrew was weak; we mostly spoke Russian. He spoke Georgian with the other Georgian prisoners and with Baazov. His relations with Baazov were rather tense. He held Baazov responsible for his arrest. Baazov was arrested in October of 1948, and during his interrogation had mentioned Kricheli in one of the protocols. But it is reasonable to assume that Kricheli would have been arrested anyway, even without his connection to Baazov.

Since I was close to Baazov in the camp, Kricheli directed some of this animosity to me as well. Nevertheless, I respected Kricheli, and we often talked about his life in Georgia before his arrest. Once, he opened his heart and told me about his love for a woman that had lasted throughout his life. She sent letters to him at the prison camp. Kricheli also had a young daughter, who was very close to him, and her letters were full of admiration, respect, grief, and empathy. She was still a high school student and wrote about her studies, grades, etc. I read her letters with respect; my children did not write to me often. It was a period of terror and fear, and my wife did not allow them to communicate with me.

Dr. Leon Lemenev

Doctor Leon Lemenev was an intelligent and energetic man of less than average height and around fifty. He was a kind person and, even though he was not at all religious, he had a warm Jewish heart. He was very good at his job, his clinic was well organized, and he had good relations with his superior officer, who oversaw the medical work in the camp. Lemenev was a veteran of the Communist Party, and before his arrest had held a high-level position in the Ministry of Health. He had been arrested in 1950 and accused of collaborating with two former coworkers, who had been arrested and executed in 1937. It was written in the protocols of their interrogation that he had been aware of and supported their anti-Soviet activity. I remember his case because he asked me to prepare a petition to the Central Committee of the Communist Party.

In his previous work, Lemenev had never worked as a physician; his experience was mainly in coordinating and managing medical organizations. But he quickly adapted to his new camp position. He asked his wife to send him various medical books, mostly on internal and family medicine, and even received the latest medical journals.

We became good friends. In the evenings, after his clinic hours, he would come to my barracks, tap on the window next to my plank bed, and I would come out for a walk with him. Sometimes, he would invite me to his office in the clinic and we would play chess using a set that had been made by the prison craftsmen. As I remember, he was not shy about receiving presents from prisoners who asked him to be released from work. His responsibilities were quite wide, and exempting people from work was one of them.

Lemenev regularly helped prisoners, especially during the medical commission period, the examination that determined a prisoner's ability to work. As I mentioned earlier, I was given the status of a disabled person until the end of 1950 because of my duodenal ulcer. The medical commission held in December upgraded my status to the third category—"Fit for easy work." At that time, I felt much better; my stomach pains had ceased and I had gained some weight.

The medical commission was comprised of several physicians. Its chairman was a medical officer, a Jew with the rank of major. The other members were a woman doctor and another major, who was in charge of our prison camp's medical service. Dr. Lemenev, who reported to him, loudly read prisoner medical files. Many of the prisoners in the camp were young and healthy. In most cases, the procedure was very quick and simple and lasted less than a minute per person. The disabled prisoners were examined at the end of the line. During my examination, Dr. Lemenev tried to help me keep my disabled status. He mentioned my age (fifty), my heart condition, my ulcer, and the problem with my spinal cord. But nothing worked. The commission chairman kept declaring: "Fit for easy work." Dr. Lemenev even took me to the hospital at another camp for an X-ray examination and attempted to persuade the medical officer in charge of the X-ray laboratory to confirm my disabled status. However, the X-ray examination showed that my ulcer had healed. It turned out that the inferior prison food was somehow beneficial to my stomach and gave me an unexpected benefit; after a year in the prison camp my ulcer was gone.

So my status was changed and I was assigned to the working team headed by Koniuch, who treated me quite fairly. I mainly did indoor office work that took me only a few hours a day.

Itzhak Kahanov (Kogan)

During my brief stay in the hospital at the camp where I was sent for the X-ray examination, I met Itzhak Kahanov (Kogan), who was also a member of our "Zionist group." He was working there in the club. Before his arrest, Kahanov had led a philharmonic orchestra in a provincial town in Central Russia. In the prison camp, he was able to get a job in his own profession. He was responsible for the local orchestra, cultural events, and the distribution of books and newspapers. We were both very glad to see each other. He was a tall man with broad shoulders and had lost some weight since our last meeting in Moscow. Many prisoners from different places were brought to his prison camp for medical examination, so Yitzhak was well informed about what was happening in the other Karaganda prison camps. He told me that Zvi Plotkin's health had seriously deteriorated. During his first year of imprisonment, Zvi had done hard labor, and only later had received disabled status. We also talked about our life in the prison camp. He was quite optimistic and tried to reassure me. Even now, I remember his encouraging words, that despite all the hardship we will reach a "safe harbor." While he spoke to me, his blue eyes shined brightly.

Motl Grubian

Many Jewish writers and poets were arrested in 1948-1949 after the Soviet authorities launched an antisemitic campaign. The authorities shut down the Jewish Antifascist Committee, closed the Jewish Theater, the Yiddish publishing house Emes, the magazine *Eynikeyt*, and all other Jewish cultural institutes. Among those arrested were well-known Jewish poets and writers: David Bergelson, Itzik Feffer, and Leib Kvitko—all of them were later executed. Yechezkel Dobrushin died in 1953 in Abez camp. Also arrested, were Shmuel Halkin, David Hopshtein, Itzik Kipnis, Heft, Yosef Kerler, Yakov Shternberg, and many, many others. Motl Grubian was one of them.

Motl (Motele, Matvey) Grubian[6] was served as a medical assistant under Dr. Lemenev. He was a well-known Jewish poet, who had published his poems in Yiddish magazines, such as *Eynikeyt* and *Heymland*, as well as abroad. He often liked to brag that his poems were published even in Montevideo. He limped on one leg due to a wound from the war. He was a heavy smoker and his fingers were yellow from tobacco. I got to know him fairly well. He liked to talk about his wife Dina, who was Russian and did not appreciate his Yiddish literary work. When he was appointed as a medical assistant, he asked her to send him medical textbooks. In one of the books, she had written: "To my butterfly, in hopes that you will let go of your fantasies and start learning a real trade."

Grubian had good relations with the camp censor. He was an excellent chess player and they often played together. It helped him to get permission to keep his book of Yiddish poems *Gezang vegn Mut* (Song of Courage), which was sent to him by his wife. I read it several times and enjoyed the lyrics. Some of the poems touched my heart, such as "Das Mamas Zeygerl" (A Small Clock), the Minsk songs, folk songs, etc.

Motele once told me that inspiration (he called it "the Holy Spirit") usually came to him in the morning hours. He used to write in bed and kept a sheaf of paper next to it. He was possessed by his writing, starting immediately after waking up and working until two or three in the afternoon. He wrote and corrected, wrote and corrected, and after each correction he stared a new page, rewriting all of the text from the very beginning.

Grubian's prison term was ten years. In the first protocol that he had to sign, it stated that he was an American spy (after all, his poems were published in Montevideo). He signed it and declared: "Even if I sign a hundred such protocols, you will never turn me into an anti-Soviet person."

I enjoyed talking to Motele. He told me what was going on behind the curtain in the Yiddish literary world in Moscow and Minsk and about his performances in cities with large Jewish populations. His poems were very popular, and he enjoyed the admiration of the Jewish public. I believed him—his poems were really marvelous. He continued writing

---

6   Motl (Matvey) Grubian (1909-1972)—Yiddish poet, who fought in World War II. He participated in the battle of Stalingrad and was wounded three times. In 1949, he was arrested and sentenced to ten years in the Gulag. He was released in 1956.

poetry in the camp. The name of one of the poems was "De Yiddishe Shurelech" (The Yiddish Lines). In other poems, he wrote about an executioner standing behind him and about a hole filled with worms and him inside.

Grubian loved to sing sweet Yiddish songs. Some of the songs belonged to his "Golden Fund." I learned several songs from him. One of the songs, by a young Jewish girl, can be translated as follows:

> I am completely surrounded by troubles, Mother;
> The troubles turn me round and round like a barrel.
> I would not trust our youngsters:
> They are like the dogs in the marketplace.

Another romantic song was also about an unfortunate love:

> The ink is black, and the sheet is white;
> So why is my heart disturbed, what is bothering me?
> No food or drink will be tasty to me
> Unless you hold my head in your arms
>
> When I see your pretty face, your slender body.
> An invisible fire is burning in my heart;
> There is no medicine to heal my wounds.
> The only remedy is to see you, my love.

Grubian's folk songs were notable not only because of the beautiful words; they also had very lovely melodies. I used one of his melodies to compose a song about the prison camp: "I Was Convicted to Ten Years."

> I was convicted to ten years,
> Without any fault on my side;
> But even on my death row
> I will never abandon you, Zion.

As a medical assistant, Grubian was not particularly liked by the prisoners. He sensed their attitude and attributed it to antisemitism. He was not well organized and felt a bit miserable. We were all miserable, but most of us tried to hide this feeling deep inside. Motele was not able to deal with his misery. Before his arrest, he had been living a full life, enjoying wine, women, and intense emotions. And here in the prison camp, he was a hated medical assistant. He had to carry his large medical bag with a red cross on it in all seasons—spring, summer, fall, and winter.

Kreinman

Among the other Jewish prisoners in Sand camp, I remember Kreinman. He was about thirty-five years old, from Bucharest. His father was quite wealthy. His family owned a shoe factory, a chain of shoe stores, and several bus lines in Romania. When the Soviets took over Bessarabia, their assets were confiscated, and his family, along with other wealthy families, was detained. Eventually, his father died, Kreinman himself was sentenced to ten years in the Gulag, and his mother was exiled to Siberia. She sent him very weird and sentimental letters, written in a highly refined and eloquent Yiddish. It seemed that she was frustrated and suffered a lot from the change in her lifestyle. Once a prosperous lady, engaged in charity and philanthropy, she had now been thrown into the harsh, impoverished, and starving reality of exile.

Kreinman behaved strangely. His speech was distorted by secrecy, odd hints, and murky claims. His way of speaking Yiddish was very similar in style to his mother's letters. His words were somewhat veiled and exalted; sometimes, he spoke in a whisper with his eyes wide open. Perhaps that way of speaking was quite common in Romania. He told me about his life in Romania before the arrest, about his family, about times long gone.

Once, Kreinman showed me a recent letter from his mother. She had written about her misery in her highly eloquent style, as though arguing with somebody. Yet there was no self-pity; instead of complaining, she was just pouring out her soul. It was in the evening; we were sitting in the densely packed barracks. Some prisoners were chatting loudly, some were playing dominoes, banging the domino pieces against the wooden desk. It was very noisy, the smell was awful, and the air in the barracks was yellow from the smoke. Outside, there was a snowstorm, and the strong wind was hauling, and spinning the snowflakes into huge banks of snow.

Kreinman's black hair was combed; he was always neatly dressed, proving that even the prison uniform could be tidy and worn with elegance. His shoes were always clean, and the number patch was accurately fastened to the back of his coat. Even though he was a veteran prisoner, his behavior and speech showed him to be a free man, a man who could ignore the present and live in the past. Like every other prisoner, he strived to evade hard labor. It turned out that he was good at wood carving, mostly in making racing horses. The camp authorities liked to receive free presents from prisoners, and it helped him to obtain a release from hard labor. He always managed to take care of himself.

Once, I went to see him in his barracks. He was sitting on his plank bed and carving a small galloping horse. Its legs were very powerful and its head was raised high. I was quite sure that with this figure he was expressing his craving for freedom. Yet, this expression of his aspiration was intended for a particularly cruel and ruthless camp officer who aroused fear in the prisoners. This horse was destined to sit on the officer's desk, while Kreinman was destined to wear a crisp camp number on the back of his prison coat.

There were several craftsmen in the prison camp. They used the machines in the carpentry shop to make magnificent chess figures, marvelous boxes, wooden travel cases, etc. One of the prisoners from Lithuania made amazing painted boxes from straw. In Karaganda forced labor camps, prisoners were allowed to send home few things that they did not need. Dr. Lemenev sent several parcels containing such artworks to his wife. A chess set and several straw boxes made by prisoners were among them.

Leib Pashtandiker

Besides the people described above, there were many other Jewish characters in the camp. For instance, Leib Pashtandiker, a food engineer, who before his arrest had worked, and probably continues to work now, at the Mikoyan food factory in Moscow. We arrived at Sand camp together and he occupied an upper plank bed in our barracks. He was a member of the Communist Party and was sentenced to ten years for some political blunder that he had made in his youth. He had a wife and two children in Moscow and received food parcels from them. He told me that he had not always been devoted to his wife. Many women were employed at the factory—some of them were quite pretty—and serving as a chief technologist, Leib was not going to miss any opportunities. However, I did not get to know him very well and he did not make a deep impression on me.

It is quite possible that the love adventures recounted by prisoners were, in fact, not that spectacular in reality. These stories were probably told in compensation for the total absence of women in the prison camp. It is only natural that, under such conditions, prisoners were very focused on sex and exaggerated their experiences. I had never heard such stories before the prison camp. Even serious, grown-up men, who in normal life would never have taken part in such exchanges, were very keen to participate in conversations about sex. The demand led to supply. Some prisoners were very skilled storytellers on such matters.

Jabotinsky

At the end of 1950, another Jewish prisoner, Jabotinsky, arrived at our prison camp. He was about my age, from Moscow, where he had worked at the Stalin Automobile Factory. He told me that more than a hundred Jews, employed in the administration and technical departments of the factory, had been arrested. The director of the factory was Lihachev, a decent man, who was not afraid of hiring talented Jewish employees. By the way, after Stalin's denunciation, the factory was renamed after Lihachev. Among those arrested were Lihachev's deputy, the principal mechanical engineer, the managers of the production departments, and leading engineers. Even the Jewish female physician who headed the factory's medical services and the Jewish manager of the cafeteria, whose name was Solomon Fayman, had been arrested, as well. I had met Fayman in Vorkuta camp and will write more about him later. The officially announced, fabricated allegations for the arrests were sabotage and membership in an illegal Jewish organization whose goals were to establish control over the factory and divide all the high-paying jobs among Jews. The physician was accused of giving preferential treatment to Jews and Fayman was accused of providing the Jews with the best nutrition. All those arrested received twenty-five-year prison terms, and unlike other prisoners, they had to do hard labor, irrespective of age or health.

Before his arrest, Jabotinsky had been a member of the Communist Party and had headed one of the production departments at the factory. He suffered from heart disease and because of his health condition was supposed to be exempt from work. Dr. Lemenev tried to help him, but in vain. His personal file had the official inscription: "Only hard labor"; and the head of the camp administration had no choice but to assign him to a team doing hard work. As a result, Jabotinsky suffered a stroke. Dr. Lemenev, on his own responsibility, transferred him to the hospital in another camp, but I do not know what happened to him afterwards.

I remember another Jewish prisoner from Telenesti, Bessarabia, who had been arrested at the age of seventeen, in 1942. When we met he had already spent more than eight years in the prison camp. At the beginning of the war, he had left his home and wandered in the vast Russian countryside. He did not have a passport and eventually, after many risky adventures, had been arrested and accused of spying. At that time, every unfamiliar person was suspected of being a spy. Conditions in the prison during wartime were very harsh and he was very weak from hunger. So when the interrogator had told him that if he admitted being a Romanian spy he would be immediately released, he had agreed. As a result, he had received a sentence of fifteen years in the prison camp.

When I met him, he was already a veteran prisoner with seven more years to serve. Despite all the suffering, he had a naive and innocent smile on his childish face. He was assigned to a team doing hard labor and was always hungry. We often helped him with food. He told me a lot about his life in Telenesti. Those were the golden days of his youth. A young man's life had been quite easy then: family, friends, school, holidays, sunny bright days, a marketplace full of fruits and grapes from the vineyards. He remembered having a girlfriend with dark braids and laughing eyes. I enjoyed listening to the Yiddish songs of his youth.

Michail Yankovsky

I also remember many non-Jewish prisoners I encountered in Sand camp in Karaganda. One of them was Michail Yankovsky, a strongly built pleasant man of about forty, with straw-colored hair. Before the war, he had been a stage director at one of the Leningrad theaters and had also directed several movies. During the war, he had served as a military officer and had continued to serve in occupied Germany, where he'd been arrested. In the camp, Yankovsky worked as a chief economist. I was not familiar with the scope of his work, but his position was quite prominent. He received food packages from his sister in Leningrad and was not shy of taking bribes from prisoners in exchange for granting them relief from their workloads.

Yankovsky's living conditions in the prison camp were quite convenient. He shared his food with Melnikov, a young man, who was working in the camp as an electrician and often received food packages. Melnikov's father, an important party official, had been arrested and executed in 1937, while Melnikov himself got a twenty-five-year prison term and was scheduled for release only in 1962. Both Yankovsky and Melnikov belonged to the camp's "intelligentsia," a select company of educated prisoners who often spent time discussing and arguing between themselves. They also read a lot, getting books not only from the camp library but also from other prisoners, mainly from Khodorkovsky. Yankovsky was a good speaker and liked to tell stories and debate. He was stationed in the "High Society" barracks, and every time I visited, I heard his loud voice arguing with Melnikov, Dobrzinsky, and other prisoners.

Yankovsky was often present at the camp's club, where he directed a group of prison camp actors and staged several performances. The club was headed by a prisoner named Smirnov, a tall, pale man, who, before his arrest, had had something to do with the artistic community. Smirnov was also responsible for the orchestra, library, and newspapers. He was a pleasant man, but many suspected him of being an informer, which was quite possible considering his challenging position, in which he often had to interact with the camp authorities. Later, I heard that he had died in the camp from the flu. After my release, I met Yankovsky on the train on my way from Vorkuta to Moscow. It was at the beginning of 1956, and at that time he was working in the theater in the Komi Republic.

Bokov

There were many talented men in the camp. One of them, Bokov, was an artist. He graduated from the famous Academy of Art in Leningrad. He was about forty years old, a bit plump, and had dark hair and a sizable Russian mustache. According to him, he had been sentenced to ten years in the Gulag because, while a student in the Academy, he had voted for an opposition proposal at a Komsomol meeting.

Bokov was a very gifted artist and worked at the club barracks. His first drawing was a copy of a well-known Ilya Repin masterpiece: "The Cossacks Writing a Letter to the Turkish Sultan." He made it with oil paints using a colored reproduction of the original. This picture was hanging on the wall of the cafeteria. It made a deep impression on the prisoners and the prison camp authorities, not only because of its likeness to the original, but also due to its vivid depiction of the free spirit of the Cossacks. Bokov told me that he had copied this picture before, during his studies at the Academy, from the original that was exhibited in the Museum of Russian Art in Leningrad. Later in the camp, he made copies of several other pictures, among them "The Unequal Marriage" by Vasily Pukirev.

Bokov mostly painted pictures for the camp authorities, but he also drew sketches of prisoners. He made their portraits in exchange for tobacco. He was a habitual smoker and always had papirosa in the corner of his mouth. I happened to be one of his clients. He drew a picture of me for a few wraps of tobacco.

Ermakov

Ermakov was a typical of working team leader. He was a Russian of thirty plus, who had been transferred to our camp from the Far East, together with Dobrzinsky. They arrived at the beginning of January of 1950, and we were stationed in the same barracks. Ermakov was originally from Bryansk, a town in the west of Russia, close to the border with Belorussia. He had been sentenced to ten years in the Gulag for the "betrayal of the Motherland." He had used to be a member of the Communist Party and was captured by the Germans during the war. Upon return from captivity, he had been in the police.

There was something cruel about him; his face was very smooth, without any sign of a stubble. He had a sharp nose and chin; his eyes were gray. He was well built and was usually dressed quite neatly. However, there was something repulsive in his voice, in his smile, and in his way of speech, which was very dirty and crude, full of swearing and cursing. He was frequently involved in fiery arguments, which led to real fights.

In such confrontations, Ermakov often had the upper hand, for which he was respected by other prisoners. The men of his type could be categorized as the "wolves" of the prison camp. Everything he did was for his own sake. He chose the members of his working team based on the amount of food parcels that they received from home and their willingness to share them with him. He regularly cheated in the daily reports of his working team, which was quite common in the camp, and did not push prisoners too much. When needed, he was even capable of doing the daily work by himself. He comported himself in a straightforward and self-respectful way with the camp authorities.

Ermakov was obsessed with women. He often talked about his womanizing skills and past endeavors. He always kept a photograph of one of his lovers in his pocket and before going to sleep he would loud announce that he was going to "sleep with her." He kept a photo album containing pictures of his lovers and relatives and frequently wrote letters to them in a somewhat illiterate but elated style.

Our relationship was a bit strange. Baazov and I were not among his friends, but we did not avoid him. Baazov was more sensitive than me and sometimes got into arguments with him. I never clashed with Ermakov, not only because of my attitude—"Let the dog bark"—but because he had never confronted me directly, verbally or physically. However, his presence was felt very strongly in the barracks. After telling somebody one of his exceptionally crude and dirty jokes, he often glanced at me, as if assessing my reaction. Even now, I remember those piercing glances. I have an unsubstantiated feeling that he was somehow involved in the persecution of Jews during the war. If I need to create a "villain" character one day, I will use him as a model.

Other Characters in Karaganda Camp

Dobrzinsky was also among the camp "intelligentsia"; he was a Polish man and was responsible for the camp's work schedule. He was about thirty, a former officer in the Polish army led by Anders. He had been caught in some petty felony and convicted to ten years in prison. He also liked to talk a lot and received bribes from prisoners. He had a wife and a son who had been exiled to the Russian Far East. His wife was working as a schoolteacher and often sent him warm letters.

The head foreman, Vania, did not belong to the camp "intelligentsia." He was a plain, coarse, and powerful Russian man, responsible for sending prisoners out to work, either voluntarily or by force. Those who refused to work had to deal with the foremen and were often severely beaten. The camp administration turned a blind eye to such cases. In general, the foremen were the guard dogs of the administration. Vania was an adept bribe-taker, and he expected that Baazov, like other prisoners, would share his food packages with him. But Baazov was reluctant to do this. His relations with Vania went sour and he was assigned to a working team engaged in digging, which was very unfortunate.

Many of the heads of the work teams were also very rude to the prisoners; but some, like Konoplev, behaved reasonably well. The head of my working team, Koniuch, was also a decent man. He was about twenty-five years old, from West Belorussia. He was quite educated and liked to read books and talk about general matters. His working team was employed inside the camp and consisted of old, sick, and disabled prisoners. The daily tasks of our working team were not hard. We were mainly assigned to repairing and cleaning jobs inside the camp grounds. I was not close to him, but I acted respectfully. In general, I always treated members of the camp administration with respect, even the less important ones.

Among other prison personalities, I remember an Armenian hairdresser, thirty-plus years old. He was a veteran prisoner who had known better days and even spent some time abroad. To me, he looked like an skilled criminal: his language was very crude (typical prison camp slang) and, needless to say, he belonged to the camp's "High Society." His occupation was very popular. Many prisoners, and even the camp authorities, guards, and officers came to him for a shave and a haircut. Obviously, they were served without waiting in line. The compulsory short haircut for all prisoners was done using a mechanical shaver. Once, He offered to let me skip the line if I bought him a new shaving blade and perfume from the camp store. He knew that I had money in my account, and I had to comply with his request.

Many of the religious prisoners were Catholic Lithuanians. In Sand camp, I met two Catholic priests, both of whom were employed as regular workers. The name of one of them was Akavichus. He was a very devout man and regularly walked back and forth on the path outside the barracks while whispering prayers. He was a little above thirty and was highly respected by the Lithuanian prisoners. The second priest was even younger. He had a very pleasant face—one might say the face of an angel—a very nice smile, bright white teeth, and a lovely voice that touched people's hearts. He was admired by all the prisoners.

Most of the Lithuanians were committed believers and wore crucifixes. During Catholic holidays, the Lithuanians used to gather in our barracks, where both of the priests were stationed. They collectively prayed and sang Lithuanian songs. Sometimes, the young priest sang psalms solo, such as "Ave Maria," "By the Rivers of Babylon," etc. His voice was so magnificent and touching that all the prisoners listened to him in absolute silence.

One day, the young priest was sent back to Lithuania. When he left, there was a general feeling that something had faded away in our lives, but we were very happy for him; we thought that he was going to be released. However, I met him a year later in Vorkuta camp. He told me that due to some additional evidence his case was reopened in Vilnius and, as a result, his ten-year prison term was increased to twenty-five years. After the departure of his young friend, Akavichus kept praying during his walks outside of the barracks.

Many Ukrainian prisoners were from Western Ukraine, Galicia, and Bukovina, occupied by the USSR in 1939. Most of them belonged to the Ukrainian Greek Catholic Church which, contrary to the Russian Orthodox Church, considered the Roman Catholic pope as their principal authority. During holidays, they sang melancholy Ukrainian songs. At Easter, prisoners gathered in groups outside the barracks, and prayed and sang beautiful folk songs. Alcohol was forbidden in the camp and, instead of being joyful, holidays in the prison camp were a rather sad time. Spring arrived and the snow melted, but the earth was still wet. Benches were placed outside the barracks, and on Sundays prisoners enjoyed the bright sun; they rested on the sloped roofs of the barracks, talking to each other, and singing. In spring, when the warm winds began to blow, every prisoner dreamed about escape, about freedom, home, and women. At such times, the camp administration took extra measures to prevent prisoners' escaping. To relieve the tension, they spread false rumors about possible government decrees to commute prison terms and release prisoners.

In Karaganda camp, I wrote a petition to Stalin appealing for my release and submitted it to the camp administration. After some time, I received a negative reply. During the years of 1950-1953, it was impossible to get your case properly reassessed. The release of political prisoners only started in 1954.

At the end of 1950, Usov and I received a negative decision from Moscow regarding our invention. We appealed the rejection and continued to work on the more advanced version. At the beginning of March 1951, I was visited by Major Abramov, the head of operations at the camp. It was during the morning, when most prisoners were at work, and I was doing my daily assignment. He inquired about my family and the invention, and reminded me of its rejection. Overall, I sensed his negative attitude towards me.

A few days after his visit, my name appeared on a list of about twenty prisoners that were to be transferred from the camp. I received this news in the evening and was told to gather my belongings and to be ready for the move the next morning. For me, this was like thunder on a bright day. Generally, prisoners hate being transferred to another camp; they even do not like to be moved to another barracks. A human being, like a cat, can adapt to his surroundings. Even though my situation was far from being comfortable, the new place could be much worse. During these fifteen months in Karaganda prison camp, I had gotten used to the camp routine, to my work, and the people surrounding me.

The order for my transfer did not mention the destination. This added to my nervousness. I thought of different possibilities and assessed the speculations of the camp's "experts." Among their suggestions, was the unlikely possibility of my release, transfer to a special engineering design group in a different camp, or transfer to another camp, located further away from Karaganda to distance me from my relatives living there. The last possibility was the most probable. The camp administration disapproved of prisoners whose families lived close to the camp. A few months before that, a group of prisoners with relatives in Karaganda was transferred out of the camp.

Indeed, my wife's family lived in Karaganda. My mother-in-law, my wife's sister, and my wife's aunt lived there with their families. Karaganda was well known for its coal mines. During the war, I worked there as an engineer in one of the coal mines, and my family was also evacuated there from Moscow. My wife's family, originally from Kharkov, Ukraine, were lucky to escape the German occupation and joined us in Karaganda. After our return to Moscow in 1943, they chose to stay there. In one of her letters, my wife mentioned that she was planning to visit her mother and sister, and maybe even me, in Karaganda. It was quite possible that the censor, who was examining prisoner's mail, informed the camp administration about that.

Another possible reason for my transfer was my expertise in coal enrichment. The engineers in this field were in high demand in the northern area of the USSR, especially in Inta and Vorkuta.

I have spent a year and three months in the 3rd division of Karaganda Sand camp. It was a difficult time. The rules in the camp were very harsh. I had almost no connection with my family. But there were also several bright spots related to my friendship with Yechezkel Pulerevitch, Andrey Usov, Meir Baazov, fellows of the Eynikeyt group, Hebrew songs, and my "morning prayers." There were clear skies and a bright morning star that winked at me and comforted me during the hard times. There also were golden evenings, with sunsets turning into dark and starry nights. However, all this splendor took place behind the barbed wire fence and watchtowers of the prison camp with guards armed with automatic rifles.

Part 8

In Karaganda Transfer Camp

With deep feelings, I bid farewell to my friends and fellow inmates. Together with a group of prisoners and our personal belongings, I was put in the back of a truck reinforced with high wooden side shields to prevent the possibility of our escape. Two guards, armed with automatic rifles, were also there. It was the middle of March. The snow was still at the sides of the road and in the fields. We drove towards Karaganda. With inquisitive eyes, I looked through the slit in the side shield of the truck at the world outside. We passed the street where I used to live in 1941-1943. Karaganda had expanded a lot during the seven years since I'd left it; new construction sites were everywhere. I was especially impressed by the Maykaduk, a brand-new suburb of Karaganda.

After about half an hour, the track stopped at the entrance gate of the 5th division of Sand prison camp. It was a transit camp used for prisoners who were going to be released or transferred to other camps.

I stayed at the 5th division prison camp for about a month, until April 20. On arrival, our belongings were put in storage, and I was given a place on a bottom plank bed in one of the barracks. It was a large and packed place. Together with me, there were about twenty other prisoners from my previous camp, who had relatives in Karaganda. It was the beginning of spring, the snow had almost gone, and the bright sun was bringing the land back to life. But the high wooden fence divided us from free life outside. And inside the fenced area, there were prisoners with number patches sewn to their backs, sleeves, and hats. Soon, we were required to do some maintenance and cleaning work inside the camp. It was an easy job, and I remember the month spent in the 5th transit camp mostly as leisure time.

Abraham Shtukarevich

In the transit camp, I became acquainted with three Beitar members from Kovno who were very familiar with Yechezkel Pulerevitch. The first was Abraham Shtukarevich, who I met soon after my arrival. He was one of the leaders of the Kovno Beitar organization. Abraham had been accused of spying for Israel and convicted to fifteen years in prison. It was his second prison term. He had served his first five-year term during the war and had worked as a logger in the Ural Mountains. During that time, his wife, Masha was evacuated to Siberia and later returned to Lithuania. He told me about the feelings of excitement and passion when he suddenly and unannounced came back to her after his release. In 1946, they settled in Vilnius, where he was employed at a publishing house. During that time, their daughter was born. He described his second arrest, as follows. During one of his business trips to Moscow in 1948, he had gone to see opera at the Bolshoi Theater. Next to him was a couple, a man and a woman, who were speaking Hebrew between them. Shtukarevich, who was fluent in Hebrew, could not hold back and joined their conversation. They happened to be employees to the Israeli Embassy. The man, whose name, as I recall, was Oren, gave him his phone number. Shtukarevich later called him and even met with him. After that, he was arrested, accused of being an Israeli spy, and was held under investigation for the next two and a half years in the MGB prison in Moscow. Then, he was sentenced and transferred to Vorkuta.

Shtukarevich was roughly forty years old, of medium height, with a broad face, and had few stainless teeth in his mouth. He had black hair, and even though he shaved his beard, his chin was always covered with black stubble. We became very close and often conversed in Hebrew. There was a large open square with several benches in the middle of the camp. I remember sitting with him on one of the benches and listening to his stories and songs.

Israel Avrovich

Israel Avrovich, another former member of Beitar, arrived a few days later. He was an old friend of Shtukarevich from Kovno and they spent many hours together. They preferred to speak Yiddish, the language of their youth. Shtukarevich, who had lived in Vilnius before his arrest, had a lot to tell him about their common friends. Avrovich was a bit plump, but had a very delicate soul; he was around thirty, knew Hebrew, and sang Hebrew songs with a very pleasant voice. He used to be a soloist of the Kovno Beitar choir. Israel Avrovich was also a poet, with many his own songs and verses. I liked Israel Avrovich very much, but to my disappointment he was not fond of sharing with me the treasure of his Hebrew songs; it is more accurate to say that he did not like repeating them to me several times so that I could learn them by heart. Nevertheless, I managed to pick up nine songs from his repertoire.

Later, another Beitar member from Kovno, Binyamin Robinson, was also transferred to the 5th camp. He was not as active in Beitar as Shtukarevich and Avrovich, but also spoke Hebrew. He was a war veteran, decorated with numerous medals for his war service. He had been convicted in 1950 to eight or ten years without any plausible cause.

Zinovy Shulman and Lublin Gymnasia in Odessa

Zinovy Shulman was a well-known singer of Yiddish songs. I knew him from my childhood when his nickname was "Zuzia." In 1916-1918 we studied together at Odessa Seventh Gymnasia, which had been transferred from Lublin, Poland during World War I, and thus, was informally called Lublin Gymnasia. It shared a building on StaroPortoFrankovsky Street with Second Odessa Gymnasia. We studied during the second shift. The school headmaster's name was Yarema. He had developed a method for teaching Latin and had also written several books on this subject. My favorite teacher was the Russian language instructor Kozlov. He was rather old, with a red face, white mustache, and a slightly hoarse voice. I was one of his favorite students and he always gave me the highest marks for my essays. Back in my youth, I loved to dream and to put my dreams into writing. I still remember many of my teachers from that time, more than thirty-five years ago. The math instructor was Alexander

Ivanovich, a tall young man with a pale face. He had a deep pleasant voice and often coughed. Once, I wrote a sentimental essay in French about falling autumn leaves, which was appreciated by my French lady teacher. I remember the old baron, who taught German, and had a lot of trouble with the students.

Most of the students at Lublin Gymnasia were Jews. War refugees were given special permission to learn in high school; they were exempted from the "Jewish percentage rule" that was in effect in the large cities of the Russian Empire. I was also a war refugee. During the war, my family moved from the village of Shepetovka in Western Ukraine to Krolevets in the Chernigov region.

Among the students at Lublin Gymnasia, I remember Zuzia Shulman, Ziniuk, Polishuk, and Medvedev, all of them also Jews. Zuzia was a bit plump, with a pleasant face, black hair, and slightly protruding eyes. He was the son of the famous cantor Boris Shulman from the Odessa's Great Synagogue. However, I preferred attending Brodsky Synagogue, where Pinhas Minkowski performed with a boys and girls choir. They sang Jewish prayers and hymns, accompanied by magnificent pipe organ music.

Almost every Saturday and on Jewish holidays, especially during Selichot prayers on Yom Kippur, I went to Brodsky Synagogue to listen to Minkowski. In those years, Jewish cultural life in Odessa was thriving. Haim Nachman Bialik, Yosef Klausner, and Avraham Usishkin were still active there, and the publishing house Moriah was working at full strength. Klausner, who at that time was around forty, was my Hebrew instructor. I went to his house to borrow Hebrew reading books. I remember that at the first meeting he gave me an entire book of poetry by Judah Leib Gordon, with a black cover. Yosef Klausner and Boris Shulman are still alive. But all my recollections are from a different era. To understand these people, one must leap across an unfathomably wide gap of time. And here, at the beginning of spring of 1951 in the 5th division of Sand camp in Karaganda, I met the prisoner Zinovy Shulman, my former school friend Zuzia, son of Boris Shulman.

Before his arrest, Zinovy Shulman had resided in Lvov, Eastern Ukraine, and had been known as a performer of Yiddish songs. He had a Russian wife, who had also somehow been involved with the art. In 1947, he'd been wrongly accused of an attempt to escape from the Soviet

Union and sentenced to ten years in the Gulag. He told me that some-body offered to help him escape; at that time it was possible to travel from Lvov to Poland. But he had refused and immediately reported the inci-dent to Soviet authorities. Zinovy was rather short, with a pleasant small face and piercing eyes. He was dressed in an oversized pea coat.

After the war, several Yiddish singers were popular in the Soviet Union, among them Appelbaum, Lubimov, Sarah Fibich, Zinovy Shulman, etc. I liked Sara Fibich and had even met her in 1945 at the home of the poet Shmuel Halkin. Shulman was very popular among the Jewish public and was also making money on the side by performing at synagogues during holidays. In Sand prison camp, he agreed to sing for me only after a good deal of persuasion. One of the songs that was new to me was called "Baranovichi"; it was named after a small Ukrainian Jewish town. Shulman had a hard time in the camp. Somehow, he was not capable of doing even an easy task. Eventually, he was assigned to do hard labor, and complained about it all the time. His goal was to have a full-time job as a singer at the prison camp club. He was an excellent performer of romantic Russian songs and arias from operas. However, at the time of my departure from Karaganda, he was still far from reaching this goal. Shulman was preoccupied with self-respect, and most of the time complained about his bad luck in life. A year later, I met his brother, Arkady, in Vorkuta camp. I will write more about him later.

Gitterman

Another Jewish prisoner at the transfer camp was Gitterman, a man from Bessarabia, who was set for release from the camp. He had a pleasant face with raven-black hair, red cheeks, and fiery eyes. His Russian was heavy accented with a burr. He had been arrested in 1941, before the war, and had completed a ten-year prison term, "from ding to ding." In the camp, he was in charge of the canteen, which was a very important position in those years, especially when food was scarce during the war. His large trunks in the storage room were filled with stuff that he had amassed. I did not get along with him very well; there was something rotten about his mindset. He bargained about everything for his personal gain. He told me that during a food shortage, when prisoners were ready to give anything for a piece of bread, he used his position to receive sexual favors from a female nurse who was working in the camp medical department. The price of making love was a portion of bread, about three-quarters of a pound.

Spring was coming; it was hovering in the air. One could feel the crisp breeze of its brand-new wings. The camp's ground dried up and fresh patches of green grass appeared here and there. Everyone has expectations and hopes; this is especially true for prisoners in transitional camps. Our barracks were like a railway station; some prisoners were entering and some were leaving. Those to be released were awaiting the last day of their term. In this case, the regulations were very precise. Prisoners who had finished serving their time were released promptly from the camp, without delay.

One day, there was a surge of anxiety in the barracks. One of the prisoners had had a heart attack and was going to die. It happened during the night hours when the barracks doors were already locked from the outside. The prisoners started pounding at the door and shouting. It took a long time to open the door and get the physician inside. When the physician arrived, the prisoner was already dead. He had finally become a free man. Evidently, it was not easy for a person with heart disease, who had spent long years in the prison camp, to survive the stress of the transition to freedom.

Memories of the various prisoners I met in the transfer camp come before me like distant silhouettes. I recall myself strolling with several Jewish prisoners inside the camp, under the bright spring sun, and listening to a story about the German occupation of Polonne, a small Jewish town in Eastern Ukraine, where one of the prisoners had lived before his arrest. Everyone was recounting his own misfortunes. Shepetovka, Sudilkov, Khrolyn, Polonne—these were the places of my youth. Jewish life there did not escape its fate.

I also remember meeting an engineer with a Caucasian name, an expert in shipbuilding. After his arrest, he had spent several years in a special mechanical design prison camp near Moscow. The conditions there were much better than in the regular camps. The food ration included white bread, butter, and sugar; they were able to use the library, and even received a salary. It was truly a paradise. At the time of our conversation, most of the prisoners from such technical prison camps had been transferred to regular forced labor camps with high-security regimes.

The daily routine of the prison camp went on and on. The unsavory food in the canteen was based on millet. Each day we were given millet porridge, millet soup, rye bread, and a piece of broiled fish. I had lost my spoon and was forced to sup my soup and porridge straight from the aluminum bowl. A prisoner could not maintain his refined manners, even if he was an aristocrat or a lord. In prison camps, degradation occurs rather fast. In the canteen, there were long dirty tables and shaky benches. On the walls, there were reproductions of work by well-known Russian painters: "The Hunters at Rest" by Perov, "Bears in the Forest" by Shishkin, "Alenushka" by Vasnetsov, and a still-life of meat and fruits, items that none of us had tasted for a very long time. And with these art masterpieces as a backdrop, a middle-aged Jew would be sitting on a long and shaky bench together with his fellow prisoners, slurping millet porridge straight from the bowl. And outside, one could feel the presence of the spring, the fresh wind caressing, whispering, and hinting at new hopes and dreams.

Part 9

On the Way to Inta

Finally, our group of prisoners from the third division of Sand prison camp set out for transfer. There was a rumor that a few of us, including me, would be sent north to Inta. We were told to prepare for the move. I was able to buy a wooden suitcase from one of the prisoners and packed my belongings. In preparation for the move, I took the suitcase out of the storage room and put it under my plank bed. Soon after, we had to go outside as the names of the prisoners to be transferred had been announced at the camp office building. That day, my name was not mentioned. Our group was divided into two parts, and I was in the second one. When we returned to our barracks, the first part of our group had already left with their belongings. Later, I found that somebody had opened my suitcase and stole all the food, the leftovers from the last package from home. Everything else was intact. The prisoners told me that my food was stolen by a seasoned thief, who I met later in Inta.

Our group left the next day. We were transferred to the train station and put into the Stolypin carriage. Farewell, Karaganda, we are heading north through Petropavlovsk, Sverdlovsk, Kirov to Inta. And here it was again, my beloved Stolypin carriage with overcrowded sections, more than thirty prisoners with their belongings in each one. I managed to get a place on the bottom bench and put my suitcase under it. My place was next to the metal lattice door with the opening for food distribution. The food ration was the same as before—bread and salty fish, which brought on thirst, and water twice a day. It was difficult, very difficult, especially during restroom time. Again, everything was done in a rush; the guards shouted and pushed prisoners. Those with delicate souls suffered the most.

The voyage from Karaganda to Inta lasted twenty-two days, including stops in the transit prisons of Sverdlovsk and Kirov. By that time, I was an experienced, veteran prisoner and had seen a lot. During transit, I encountered more Gulag prisoners.

Michael Ibambletov

Michael Ibambletov was originally from Bessarabia, which had been occupied by the Soviet army in 1940. He was about fifty, well built, with a pleasant appearance, gray hair, and large black eyes. Before the occupation, he had been a wealthy man, served as a town mayor, and had been one of the leaders of a local conservative party. Even though he had already completed his first ten-year term in the prison camp and was now serving a second one, his spirit was not broken. He told me a lot about his life back in Bessarabia. Michael was very familiar with human nature and was good at analyzing the factors that influenced human behavior. He was able to find an optimal course of action under any given circumstance. Michael was a smart and humble man, and I learned to respect him. When we arrived at Inta, Michael managed to dodge hard labor in the coal mine and was assigned to the canteen as a cook. In 1951, when prisoners were not paid for their work, everyone tried to get an easy and convenient job.

Kononenko

Another prisoner, who I knew from the Sand camp, was Kononenko. He used to serve there as a medical aid, which had been his profession before arrest. He was originally from Pyatigorsk, in the North Caucasus, where his wife and parents were still living. According to Kononenko, he had been arrested for dodging military service. Moreover, he was suspected of collaborating with the Germans during the occupation. Kononenko was about thirty-five, of medium height, broad-shouldered, with blond hair and blue eyes. He often wrote letters to his wife and used to read them to me. He even read me some of his poetry, which was written in a quite analphabetic manner and sounded awful to me.

There was something repulsive about him, even though he was neatly dressed and proudly carried his medical bag with a red cross. However, Doctor Lemenev and the major responsible for the medical service in the camp did not trust him; and eventually he was assigned to regular hard labor. It is quite possible that he tried to get close to me because of my friendship with Doctor Lemenev. Later, his wife arrived at Karaganda and he managed to meet with her. They came up with a clever ploy. Before the start of the workday, she would hide at a place outside of the camp where his team was working. When prisoners arrived, Kononenko could sneak away and spend time with her in private. Eventually, their ruse was discovered and, as a punishment, Kononenko was transferred to Inta.

During transfer, Kononenko joined a company of common criminals and thieves. His behavior underwent a drastic change. His cultural veneer peeled off and he started to act like a veteran criminal; and, according to the criminal way of conduct, he began to intimidate and exploit other prisoners. Even his style of speech changed into the usual, coarse camp jargon. He became very aggressive and got into physical fights with other prisoners.

Yes, something was disgusting about Kononenko; there was not even a trace of kindness or compassion in him. He always put his interests above everything else. But despite being a crude and egotistical man, he could also pretend to be a decent person. In different situations, he was able to alter his way of talking—from vulgar and abusive language to tender speech. But maybe I am mistaken in my judgment of my fellow prisoners. I tend to describe them in black-or-white terms. But human nature is never black and white; it can take on all kinds of shades, depending on circumstances. Thus, it is possible that Kononenko, in some ways, was not such a bad man.

Alexey Ivanovich

I met Alexey Ivanovich in the transit camp and we became quite close on our way to Inta. He was originally from Dnepropetrovsk, Ukraine, and had been a member of the Komsomol at the local university. At one of the meetings, long before the war, he had unintentionally voted against the party line and was exiled to Siberia. Later, he'd been arrested and given a ten-year prison term, which he had spent in Karaganda camp.

After his release in 1948, he remained in Karaganda and found work as an accountant in one of the government offices. His wife, who he met in Karaganda, was employed as a nurse in a local hospital.

Soon after his release, he was arrested again, without any fault on his side. From what he said, during 1949-1950 there was a directive from the MGB Moscow office to arrest those who had already served time for anti-party activity. At the office where he worked, there was an informer, who reported on him and, even though he was very careful and did his best not to utter even a word against the party or the government, he was sentenced to an additional ten-year prison term. His wife was also arrested.

Alexey Ivanovich was about forty years old. He was quite chubby, with a bald head and pleasant round face. Despite his large belly and baldness, his face was somewhat youthful, and the wrinkles at the corners of his mouth revealed an innocent, and rather sensible, childish smile. We became close and stayed together during transfer. We were in the same section of the Stolypin carriage, or next to each other on the plank beds in the transfer prison cells. He was extremely talkative and I spent long hours listening to him.

What did we talk about? He had seen a lot during his life and his memory was quite vivid. He told me about his youth in the Southern Ukrainian city of Dnepropetrovsk in the 1930s, about the Komsomol, about his exile to Novosibirsk. He also told me about his first arrest, interrogation, and life in the prison camp during the war. He was not a stranger to women and told me about several of his escapades in this area. Here is one of the stories from his first prison camp period. Alexey Ivanovich was a diligent worker and the camp authorities treated him fairly. Once, he was appointed as a coachman in the stables, even though he had no previous experience with horses. He hauled building materials, such as stones, lumber, sand, and clay, and was allowed to stay outside of the camp. There, he came across a widow who lived not far from the camp. Her husband had been killed in the war and they both needed consolation and solace. At first, Alexey Ivanovich only "comforted" her during the daytime, but soon he managed to spend time with her at night too. The story was quite unusual and very romantic. After our arrival at Inta, he was initially assigned to hard labor, but he was soon able to get a job as an accountant.

Ostrovsky

And there was another prisoner, Ostrovsky, a Russian man, forty-six years old, who I had met during the transfer to Inta. Like Alexey Ivanovich, he was also serving his second prison term. His head was skinny and bald with a sharp chin and faded blue eyes. Both had a common character trait: they liked to talk. But Ostrovsky also liked to gossip. Each prisoner, especially those who had spent a long time in prison, had their own way of looking at the world. Some saw the world as a total mess, some became frightened, some dived into religion and prayer. And each prisoner nourished hope. Ostrovsky was no exception; his worldview was very dark. He saw the world as a dreadful place, the "Kingdom of the Devil." People, in his view, were hostile to each other; and even though they suffered under the Devil's rule, they took every opportunity to hurt each other. The strong took advantage of the weak, and the weak did the same to those weaker than them. There was no limit to the degree of weakness, as there was no limit to the degree of strength. It was the philosophy of a hapless lamb that had been left at the bottom of the ladder while others ruled at the top. Ostrovsky talked and talked, gave examples, and expanded on his theory of an unjust world where the righteous suffered or were exploited by criminals who enjoyed life.

After many long and tedious days of travel, we arrived at Sverdlovsk. Again, we went through the grueling routine of transfer to a local prison, with roll calls and guards armed with automatic rifles. We arrived at the prison in the evening and were ushered into a long, narrow, and over-crowded cell with a double-decker row of plank beds on each side. The cell looked like a coffin. We were among the last to arrive. There were no unoccupied plank beds left, so I, together with other prisoners, had to sleep on the floor under the lower row of plank beds. The overstuffed place evoked the feeling of a mass grave. Nevertheless, everyone did his best to adjust to these conditions. I lay in the darkness with my eyes open. Next to me were my fellow prisoners, and until this day I remember this feeling of brotherhood that comforted me in the darkness. The next day, we were moved to a larger cell, where I was able to get a plank bed.

We spent about a week in this cell at the end of April 1951. It was a large square cell, crammed with double-decker plank beds. The cell had two small windows, fortified with iron grills and shields, to make it impossible to see what was going on below on the ground. As in many other prisons, the outside world was reduced to a small patch of heaven behind the window grills.

When I think of those days in the Sverdlovsk prison, I recall the loud and dirty voice of the jailbird Fedia; he swore all day long, except in his sleep, and he liked to sleep long hours and snored loudly in his sleep. The only time he behaved relatively quietly was during meals and when listening to the storytellers.

Storytellers were frequently found characters in prison camp. They were greatly admired by the common criminals, who enjoyed listening to their narratives, which frequently lasted hours, and sometimes even weeks. Those gifted with the talent to tell stories enjoyed special status in the camp hierarchy. Nobody would dare to harm them. Even seasoned thieves, who usually ruled prisoner camps, respected them. Most of the stories belonged to romantic fiction, derived from literature. But since well-read professional storytellers were rare, there were also talented impostors who made up their own stories. Large groups of prisoners gathered around such skillful storytellers, who unfolded intricate details about love and jealousy, loyalty and betrayal, courageous noblemen, lovely duchesses, ugly old sinners, brave military officers, beautiful princesses kidnapped from their castles and suffering at the hands of an evil sorcerer, and, again, love and jealousy, princes, and princesses. The plots of such stories were always very romantic and sentimental; they went back and forth, taking unexpected turns and twists.

We were lucky to have one of these storytellers in our cell; and Fedia, who was the chief bully in the cell, was also the chief listener. Prisoners listened to these naive stories with great attention. Those were the quiet hours of noisy, daily cell life.

Ordinary people, like children, mostly enjoy stories with plots based on "Cinderella." They start with a beautiful but clever poor girl, who works very hard, or a young man, who suffers at the hands of evil people or dark forces. Eventually, they manage to overcome all obstacles and live happily ever after. Many popular books or movies, such as: *The Prince and the Pauper, Robinson Crusoe, Treasure Island*, many novels by Charles Dickens, Mark Twain all fall into this category. The plots of prison camp stories were often composed by using such patterns.

My memory and imaginative abilities were somewhat impaired while in the camp, so I was not among the experienced storytellers, who assembled large crowds around them. Nevertheless, sometimes I also told some of my favorite stories to a close circle of listeners, who attended to them with sincere interest. One of my favorite stories was "The Million Pound Bank Note" by Mark Twain.

Every day, we were taken outside for a twenty-minute walk. Spring had arrived in Sverdlovsk and the sunny weather was warming hearts. Forty or fifty of us were strolling in line, one after another, round the small prison yard, fenced in by tall wooden walls. We had to keep silent, and some of us were absorbed in thoughts and dreams. Most of the time, I strolled with my hands folded behind my back, daydreaming. The back of the prisoner walking in front of me served as a guide because my sight was aimed high above the fence to the skies, which we were allowed to see only during the short twenty minutes.

In those twenty minutes, our cell was cleaned, the window was opened, and the floor was washed by the women prisoners. So, when we returned from our daily walk, the cell looked refreshed and the air inside was less thick. The mood of the inmates was improving and the sun's rays were piercing through the window. However, the shadow from the bars, crossing the bright square of sun on cell floor, reminded us of prison.

One day, we were given the command: "Get outside with your belongings." And again, roll calls, a line of four prisoners, four in a row, train station, guards with automatic rifles in front and behind us, a familiar command: "Those who make two steps to the right or left will be shot." And again, loaded with our possessions, we made our way into the Stolypin carriage.

The next stop was the prison in Kirov. It was not as gloomy as the prisons in Moscow and Sverdlovsk; it looked more like a prison camp, with wooden barracks and fences. In the barracks, there was a central corridor with cells on each side. The doors had spyholes. Before we were allowed to enter the cells, our belongings were meticulously searched. The guard who was searching my case found my book *Coal Enrichment* and started to turn the pages. When I told him that I was the author, he was quite impressed, ceased the search, and asked me to collect my stuff and proceed. The plank beds in our cell were single level, which was much more comfortable. It was the spring, the season of nature's revival, the season of hopeful feelings and dreams. Fedia continued to swear during the day and snore during the night. Our small group consisted of Michael Ibambletov, Ostrovsky, Alexey Ivanovich, and me. We all stuck together. Those were the people that were close to me.

Part 10

Inta Mineral Prison Camp

On May 12, 1951, we arrived at Inta, a small town in the Russian's Far North. From the small train station, we were transported by a local narrow-gage train to the 5th division of Mineral camp. It was already evening; wet snow was falling from the gloomy sky. We had to wait for a long time outside of the gate with our belongings. Then, after a roll call and a search, we were ushered into the barracks with double-decker plank beds. I put my stuff into a storage room and took a walk around the camp. The camp was surrounded by flat tundra with occasional small birch trees. The trees looked dwarfish, miserable, and sick. Even though it was the end of May, snow kept on falling. It was cold and the future in this new place with unfamiliar people looked gloomy.

The next day, there was a medical commission and again I was given the "Fit for easy work" status. I felt weak after the transfer, and the local physician sent me to the hospital. But before I was able to get there, I had to work for a few days in a coal quarry near the camp.

The 5th division of Mineral camp in Inta was larger than the third division of Sand camp in Karaganda. It numbered several thousand prisoners. There also were about seven hundred women prisoners, who were kept separately. We were able to see them from a distance. The women's barracks were surrounded by a barbed wire fence and at the entrance there were women guards. The women were dressed in worn-out peacoats with number patches and heavy camp boots. Most of them looked pale and neglected.

Many prisoners, especially those from Ukraine, belonged to various Christian religious groups, such as Baptists, Evangelicals, Seventh-day Adventist, Jehovah's Witnesses, etc. One of the prisoners working with me in the coal quarry was Maksimov, a passionate Evangelical Ukrainian young man from Rovno, about twenty-five years old. He had a pleasant and honest appearance, black eyes, and a lovely voice. He was an avid believer and possessed a very strong will and spirit, virtues inherent to leaders and prophets. He had been sentenced to twenty-five years for wandering between Ukrainian villages and teaching the Word of God. We talked a lot. He knew the Old Testament very well and it seemed like he was trying to convert me to his religion. I remember his lovely songs, especially one with its melody borrowed from a well-known revolutionary song. This song kept sounding in my ears a long time after I heard it. Most of his songs were about consolation and hope. They had simple words, simple rhymes, and simple, pleasant melodies, which easily captured people's hearts. All the Evangelical prisoners in our barracks gathered around Maksimov. To me, he remains a symbol of a pure soul.

Before my arrest, I had been working on the first part of my novel *When the Menorah Fades*,[1] in which I depicted some Evangelicals who saved a Jewish girl from being killed by the Nazis during the German occupation of Ukraine. In the camp, I learned that most German Lutherans also belong to the Evangelical church. It was impossible to reconcile a man like Maksimov, with his pure angelic soul, and the atrocities of the Nazis.

I also met Mustafa Adali, with whom I had shared a cell in Lefortovo prison in Moscow during my interrogation. He was working as a night watchman and tended a furnace in a vegetable greenhouse. He told me that all his hopes about freedom had been in vain. Instead of being released, he had been sent from Lefortovo prison directly to Inta. His face was pale and he looked shabby. Clearly, life in the north was not very agreeable to this man who had grown up in the south.

---

1   Published in Hebrew in Israel in 1966. English translation published by Academic Studies Press in 2020.

Michael Ibambletov managed to get a job as a cook in the camp's canteen and treated me to fried fish. He was a wise man and knew a lot about how to survive. Life had treated him cruelly, but he had been as able to withstand its severities; and now, dressed in a white apron and a white hat, far away from his dear Bessarabia, he was standing next to a burning stove and frying fishes for the inmates in a prison camp in the Far North of Russia.

In the canteen, I also met the thief who had stolen the food from my suitcase in Karaganda transfer camp. He was part of a team working on the renovation of the canteen. I had a chat with him, obviously not about the theft. There was no grudge left in my heart. Acts of theft were commonplace in the camp. Theft was even viewed as an art that required dexterity and quick hands.

After several days of work in the quarry, I was sent to hospital and stayed there for about two months. This period did not leave deep marks in my memory. In hospital, I did not become close with anyone and can only talk about people who stood out because of their appearance and behavior. One of them was Starostin, who served as a superintendent in the hospital barracks. He was one of the famed Starostin brothers, who were well-known soccer players. He was a quiet and relaxed man and performed his duties with ease. He and his brother had been convicted to ten years of forced labor, without cause. Another person in the hospital was a disabled elderly Catholic priest from Lvov. He had completed serving his term some time ago, but could not be released from the camp. According to regulations, he was not allowed to go back to his hometown. He did not have any relatives, so the camp authorities did not know what to do with him. The priest had a noble face and a big gray beard. Most of the time he played chess, checkers, and dominoes. He did not speak Russian, only Polish, so I could not talk to him and was not able to find out his personal story.

Another character, whose plank bed in the hospital was next to mine, was Lavrov, an army colonel from Leningrad. Even though he was serving a twenty-five-year prison term, he was treated quite well by the medical personnel and the camp authorities. He was very fat and, according to his diagnosis, had been wounded in the belly. However, during the two months that I spent next to him, I never heard him complaining about stomach pain. He often received parcels and letters from home, and even the daily newspaper *Pravda*, which was extremely unusual in the camp. Most of the time he lay in his bed, reading and playing chess. We even played chess together a few times. He was not a kind man. I once asked to borrow his newspaper, but he refused to give it to me. When our names were included on the list of the prisoners to be transferred to Abez, he went to the chief officer of the camp and was able to get his name removed from the list. It looked like Lavrov had bribed him with goods from his packages. I was not that lucky.

I also remember Misha, a young, nice-looking, and somewhat shy Ukrainian guy, about twenty-four, whose plank bed was under mine. He was working in the coal mine, but got sick with lung disease and stayed in hospital for a long time. He told me about his work in the mine and the coal excavation and enrichment. According to him, there were no safety practices in the coal mines the prisoners were not particularly interested in increasing coal production. They were intentionally sabotaging the coal mining equipment by mixing coal-rich pieces with bare rocks. Misha was a Catholic; he showed me his prayer book in Ukrainian that had been published in 1943 during the German occupation.

I only met a few Jews in the Inta hospital. One of them was a red-haired theater playwright from Leningrad. We only talked once about life in the hospital, and this conversation was not noteworthy. Another was a disabled Jewish professor, also from Leningrad, whose prison term had already elapsed. Because of the regulations, he was not allowed to return to his hometown. His daughter petitioned for his release to Luga, a small town in the Leningrad region, but her request was denied. The professor was mentally ill. I remember his head, which resembled that of a shorn lion, with sad and faded eyes, a look of shame, and a prison number attached to his sleeve.

Life in the Inta hospital was relatively easy, I mostly lay on my plank bed above Misha, reading books and thinking. Every day, we were visited by a young Georgian prisoner doctor. The patients respected him; it was his duty to decide about our release from hospital. Obviously, everyone was eager to continue their pleasant life in hospital. The hospital barracks were cleaner and less crowded, we did not have to go out to work, and we were given a larger food ration, including some sugar and butter and about three hundred grams of white bread. The rest of our life was like that of regular prisoners. Twice a day there was a roll call, though we were not required to get off our beds. The guard who performed the roll call was dressed in a white gown and did not shout our names very loudly. Every week, we were taken to the bathhouse. It was summer, so we wore hospital gowns and slippers. In Inta, they were conserving water, so we were given only a limited amount of water per prisoner in a small bucket.

As I mentioned earlier, part of the camp was occupied by women, and there was a separate hospital barracks for women next to ours. Several women had young children, some of whom had been born in the camp. I often saw our Georgian doctor playing with a three-year-old boy, holding him in his hands and stroking him. Even though the prison authorities did everything to separate between men and women, they could not completely prevent romantic encounters. Human nature bloomed even in the camp and prisoners experienced normal, or even stronger, feelings of love, affection, happiness, and jealousy. Many women tried to get pregnant intentionally. From time to time, some pregnant women and young mothers with children were released from the camp.

During my time in hospital, some prisoners were released or "expelled" from paradise and new ones took their places. These changes happened quite slowly. At the end of my hospitalization, the Georgian doctor was replaced by a woman doctor, a prisoner of about forty years old. She was of short stature, plain-looking, and very serious-minded. The hospital prisoners treated her with respect. They tried to show her their manly spirit and, instead of complaining in order to extend their stay in hospital, some of them answered questions about their improved health truthfully. I was no exception and told her that I was feeling much better. The result of my honesty was quite unexpected. I was included in the list of the prisoners to be transferred to Abez. My health status was also upgraded to the second category—"Fit for work."

The announcement about the transfer came like thunder on a bright day, without any warning. It was in the afternoon, and in the evening of the same day we had to leave the camp. I tried to submit a swift appeal, pointing out that my profession was useful in a place with coal mines; but my request was denied. The transfer numbered about three hundred prisoners. Those to be transferred became very agitated. Prisoners got used to their life in a camp, and now they had to move to the unknown. In the evening, one could see Zvi Preigerzon with his head lowered, a bag on his back and a suitcase in his arm, obediently standing in a line with hundreds of other prisoners waiting for transfer.

After a long and gruesome search, we walked along a dusty road, loaded with our belongings and escorted by armed guards. It was late in the evening in the middle of June, but the sky was still bright. It was the season of White Nights in the North. This time, we were ushered into a regular railway freight carriage. The carriage had rough, unhewn wooden plank beds and a urinal bucket, which was much more convenient than in the Stolypin carriage. I got an upper plank bed and put all my stuff there. The carriage was crowded with prisoners, and again one could hear the familiar noise of conversations, disputes, laughter, jokes, and coarse prison camp swearing.

Part 11

4th Abez Prison Camp

The journey from Inta to Abez took two or three days. Abez was a small village with a railway station, between Inta and Vorkuta, in the Komi Republic in the Far North of Russia. In Abez, there were six forced labor camps belonging to the Mineral camp group, administrated from Inta. Four of the camps were for men and two for women. We were put into the fourth prison camp. It was a large place confining several thousand prisoners. I stayed in this camp for five months, from the middle of July to the middle of December 1951. The camp was intended for elderly, sick, and disabled prisoners, who were not suitable for hard labor. The prisoners did not have to work outside of the camp: they were mostly busy maintaining the camp itself.

We arrived at Abez in the afternoon and were taken straight to the canteen. It was a bright and sunny summer day, with a pleasant warm wind, and prisoners sat at long tables outside of the canteen. Despite the nice weather, the food itself was far from being decent. When I think about my first meal on that day, I see in front of me small, salted capelin fishes—wretched and tasteless food. The piles of dusty capelin fishes that nobody wanted to eat were heaped on the dirty and dusty tables.

The 4th Abez prison camp was spread across a wide terrain with tens of barracks. In the middle of the camp stood a large brick building, a former auto repair garage. There were barracks for regular and disabled prisoners, a large medical office, a hospital, a long-term care facility, administration buildings, and restroom cabins.

Due to my upgraded health category, I was assigned to a team digging sand at the banks of the river Usa. The sand was for plastering the walls of the barracks. We had to load the sand into carts and take it to the camp. A cartload was about two to three hundred kilograms, and I was part of a team of five. The distance was quite large and the path sloped towards the river. We had to heave the loaded cart up the slope, yet on the way back we could take a rest; the empty cart rolled almost by itself. Needless to say, on our way back and forth we were escorted by armed guards. Those were bright and warm days of summer. The path through the marshland and tundra was quite dull, but at the riverbank the picture was quite different. The sight of flowing water, the bright skies reflected in the river, and the absence of the barbed wire fence were very pleasing to our hearts.

When all the required sand was brought in, our team was given another assignment—to dig a ditch carrying wastewater, including human excrement, outside of the camp. It was an innovative way to deal with the excrement, to let it flow naturally. However, the angle of the slope angle was not large enough, so it was necessary to dig a special ditch. The excavation work was performed by several teams under the supervision of the prisoners Kalinin and Kargin. Kargin had some experience in topography and carried a geodesical instrument that looked like an optical level-measuring tool. Thirty years before that, back in the mining university, I studied geodesy and gained some practical experience in using such measuring instruments. During the excavation, I got to know both Kalinin and Kargin, and even gave them some advice regarding the direction of the ditch, which was not a trivial issue at all. I do not remember if the project of the gravitational flow of excrement from the camp to the tundra was successful; it looked like the ditch could only be used for liquid waste. Solid waste had to be carried from the camp in barrels drawn by horses.

The Engineering Team

Kalinin had a small team of engineers working in a room in one of the administration barracks. They worked on the design, construction, and maintenance of the engineering facilities in the camp. I had a set of drafting tools with me that my wife had sent me at Karaganda camp. Such tools were in high demand among the engineers in Kalinin's team. I told Kalinin about the drafting set and showed him the textbooks on coal enrichment written by me. I am not sure what influenced him more, the drafting set, the books, or the fact that I was receiving food parcels from home, a potential source of additional nutrition to him. The result was that he agreed to transfer me to his team as a draftsman. I stayed on this job for the rest of my stay at Abez.

The prison camp had several engineering facilities. One of them was an electrical generator that provided power, not only for the camp, but also for the railway station. The facility included two ancient steam engines operating the electrical generator. The second facility was a pump station that supplied drinking water from an underground well. Initially, Kalinin assigned me as an assistant to Suchoruchko, who, besides other things, reviewed inventions proposed by prisoners.

Suchoruchko

Suchoruchko was from Prague, Czechoslovakia, and claimed to be Czech. However, I believe that he was either a Jew or a half-Jew. I came to this conclusion based on his Jewish appearance and because he openly despised and hated Jews. I did not like Suchoruchko, and not only for his antisemitism. Nobody liked him. I think that even his wife hated him. Suchoruchko was below medium height, with a wide face, piercing eyes, and hid his baldness by combing his hair from side to side. He was a chain smoker and had a mean-sounding voice. He was also quite illiterate and liked to gossip a lot about the people around him. In Prague, he had been involved in a shady business and, eventually, had become quite wealthy. When the Germans had occupied Czechoslovakia, he'd presumably joined the fascists and might even had got blood on his hands. Even though he despised people, and scoffed and mocked those who depended on him, he knew very well how to kowtow to those above him, the camp administration, who in turn despised him. He liked to eat well, was quite lazy, and did not miss an opportunity to avoid any kind of work; but this trait was typical of all prisoners.

As a reviewer of prisoners' inventions, Suchoruchko was expected to understand at least something about technology. However, he was quite illiterate, and not only concerning technical issues. His lack of education, however, did not prevent him from pretending that he was an expert in all kinds of technologies. I suffered a lot while working for him. As a draftsman, I was supposed to prepare drawings of prisoners' proposals in different technical areas. For instance, Suchoruchko wanted to design a washing machine to relieve the hard manual work of prisoners. In the camp, there were experts in different areas, and one of the prisoners had proposed such a machine. My task was to transform his ideas into technical charts and drawings. It took me two or three days to prepare high-quality three-view projection drawings of the proposed machine. When I showed my work to Suchoruchko, he looked at the drawings like an ignoramus and did not understand anything. He got very nervous, started shouting and swearing at me, and ordered me to make a draft that any layman could readily understand. I refused and advised him to show my drawings to a prisoner from Germany, who was an expert mechanical engineer. Eventually, the German engineer approved my drafts, and Suchoruchko had nothing to do but accept them and burden me with another assignment.

I do not recall the name of that German engineer. He reported to a chief mechanical engineer called Lihachev, who in turn reported to the head of our technical team Kalinin. He was about thirty-five years old, had a wife and kids in Germany, and was serving a twenty-five-year prison term. He was a very pleasant person and an expert in mechanical design. Unfortunately, soon after my arrival, he became sick and was taken to the hospital, where he died several days later.

Lihachev

Lihachev was a tall man, about forty-five years old, from Leningrad. He had graduated from a technical university and worked several years in different Leningrad factories. He was an experienced engineer, but for some reason his relations with Kalinin were rather tense. After the death of the German engineer, he was left without help and started giving me drafting assignments for steam engine parts. I did this work well. The parts based on my drawings were successfully used for steam engine repair. So Lihachev requested my transfer to his group as a draftsman. Lihachev was a decent man, and I was delighted to work with him. He had a small office in the steam engine building, where his technical team was stationed.

I started getting a lot of assignments from both Suchoruchko and Lihachev. The quality of my work was quite good, and Kalinin commended me and put my name on a list of distinguished workers. Kalinin also helped me to get a new peacoat, as mine was all worn out and had patches all over it. It was a really a big deal; new peacoats were only given to prisoners once every two years, no matter what condition the old one was in. My old peacoat was given to me just before my transfer to Inta and normally I would have had to wait for a long time before getting a new one.

Kalinin

Kalinin was a professional engineering manager and had considerable influence on the camp administration. He used to be a military officer at the rank of colonel and was serving a ten-year prison term. He was a very practical man and was able to communicate effectively with both the prisoners and the camp administration. Being a veteran prisoner, he knew well how to use the crude camp slang and liked to tell salty jokes. Kalinin and Kargin were close to each other and shared their food with each other. Kargin and a few of the other prisoners working under Kalinin often received food packages from home, and Kalinin was not shy in helping himself to their food. However, I could not claim that food packages played the main role in his choice of subordinates. The most important virtues were professionalism and the quality of work.

Kargin

Kargin was above fifty. He was a typical Russian intellectual, had a cordial way of speaking, wore glasses, and had a goatee. He was serving a twenty-five-year term. His family in Leningrad was quite wealthy and he often received letters and food packages from home. He was also a former military officer. During the war, he had been imprisoned in Finland. According to him, he'd been chosen as a headman in the officer's barracks and had to interact with the German administration, which was regarded as collaboration with Nazis. Kargin spent most of his time in his barracks. His closeness to Kalinin enabled him to be absent from the office. He liked to sleep a lot and enjoyed sincere conversations.

Boris Ivanovich

In terms of sleeping, Kargin was completely outdone by Boris Ivanovich, another prisoner who worked in our office; he slept more than twelve hours a day and also snored loudly in his sleep. Boris Ivanovich was a veteran political prisoner, he spent more than fifteen years in prison camps, since 1937. Boris Ivanovich was about fifty years old, a railroad engineer by profession. He was of short stature, had black hair, a loud baritone voice, and a thunderous laugh. Even now, I vividly remember his loud waves of laughter. Before Abez, he had worked as a manager in the construction project in the oilfields next to Ukhta prison camp. Despite spending a long time in forced labor camps and his advanced age, Boris Ivanovich looked quite healthy and was always in a good mood. Life was not treating him well. His wife divorced him, and he did not receive any letters or food parcels. Nevertheless, he had a good sense of humor and treated life in the prison camp with irony. I enjoyed his companionship; he was a very good man, and not only while sleeping. When the camp received a commission to build a new train station, he was appointed as the project manager. All the work teams heads respected him a lot.

Zeleny

The office workers often mentioned the name of Nikolay Ivanovich Zeleny, an engineer who used to work in the office for a long time and had been temporarily transferred to another prison camp to consult on a technical project. One day, he returned to our camp and was warmly greeted by everybody. Zeleny was a Czech from Prague, an experienced railway mechanical engineer. He was highly respected and regarded as the most experienced engineer in the office. He liked to make technical drawings and his drawings were perfect. One could say that drafting consoled him during his imprisonment. In his youth, he went to high school in Russia, and his Russian was very good. He was well educated and intelligent and never used dirty words. Zeleny was very tall, with a smooth elongated face and a pleasant smile, and liked smoking a pipe. He had seen and experienced a lot, understood human nature well, and was a fascinating conversation partner. He did everything in a very relaxed and simple manner, as he was smoking his pipe.

Although Zeleny and Suchoruchko were both from Prague, they were completely different from each other. Zeleny was respected and loved by all, but nobody felt affection for Suchoruchko. A short time before my transfer from Abez to Vorkuta, Zeleny was asked by Inta camp's management to help design a local coal factory.

The camp barracks had central heating, which used hot water supplied by the steam engines. In August and September, we were busy repairing and checking the insulated underground pipes. The repairs involved digging ditches and many prisoners were engaged in this work.

Later, Zeleny suggested that I should work on an exhaust system for the large cooking cauldrons in the kitchen. There were seven cauldrons used for soup and porridge. The steam from the cauldrons and the smoke from the coal-burning stoves filled the kitchen, so it was hard to breathe or see anything. The air circulation was insufficient and the only way to ventilate the kitchen was to open the doors and let fresh air in. In winter, this led to considerable temperature swings and many people got sick. I had no previous experience in ventilation and had to learn about it from textbooks that I found in the office. Eventually, with the help of Zeleny, I made several drawings. Even though he too was not an expert in this area, he was able to give me sound advice. Again, I was impressed by his logic and technical abilities. Yes, he was really a great engineer.

Later, we worked together on another project—to increase the output of the piston pumps that supplied water. The pumps were very old and all worn out. Zeleny asked me to do calculations and prepare drawings of spare parts.

The winter began in September. Both steam engines were heavily used, one for heating the barracks and the other one for electricity. Tension grew between Lihachev and Kalinin. Kalinin and Zeleny were mostly involved in construction. One of Kalinin's main projects was building a clubhouse. The work continued during summer and fall and was completed at the beginning of winter. Lihachev was more involved in the maintenance of the machinery—the steam engines, heating pipes, the power station, the electrical network, etc. Eventually, the camp management had to intervene and it was decided that Lihachev would no longer report to Kalinin. He was given independent authority. Afterwards, Lihachev asked me to work as a draftsman on his projects. Kalinin refused to let me go and this argument went on for some time.

Eventually, Lihachev succeeded in convincing the camp management that he needed his own draftsman, and I was informed that from now on I would work for him. I had to move to Lihachev's office, located in a small room in the building that contained the steam engines and the electrical generator. Besides me, there were two other people in the room: Lihachev and Hoffman. The room was rather dirty, and the steam engine operators, electrical technicians, and other workers were always entering and leaving. Kalinin's office was much cleaner and neater, in comparison.

Isaak Hoffman

I became close friends with Isaak Solomonovich Hoffman, who worked in Lihachev's office. He was one of the nicest people that I encountered during my time in the camp. Hoffman worked for Lihachev as an engineer, and was responsible for documentation. He was about fifty years old, of medium height, with gray hair, a thin elongated face, and a pleasant voice. Before his arrest, he had worked as a metallurgist in a government office and had been given a ten-year prison term for no reason. And here I was, working with this amazing man in Abez forced labor camp, in Lihachev's dirty office. But even inside an unremarkable ring bezel, the glitter of the diamond breaks through and brightens the dull world with its luminous rays. Hoffman was a very kind man, always ready to share the food that he received in packages from home with other prisoners. When people entered our room, Hoffman often treated them to sugar. In Abez, my ulcer got worse and I often experienced strong stomach pains. Sometimes, I even had to lie down on the floor and wait until the pain passed. When Hoffman learned about my illness, he started treating me to the small buns of white bread that we were given once a day. Initially, I refused his offers. In the camp, there was an unspoken rule not to take anything from other prisoners' food rations. But he strongly insisted, and, eventually, forced me to take the buns, so I accepted his kindness until I felt much better.

Hoffman was a very intelligent and clever man from Moscow. To this day, I remember his gentle voice. He told me a lot about his life experiences—events, meetings, and adventures. He understood human nature and could describe a person in only a few words. Like me, he detested Suchoruchko, although he had very good relations with other prisoners and was respected by them; and not only because of the sugar that he offered them. He liked to play chess and was one of the best players in the camp. When I played with him, he always won the games. As a young man, I used to play chess, but later I decided to stop playing. I concluded that it was a waste of my time and that I would rather use my free time for more meaningful things. In the camp, after a nine-hour workday, I devoted my free time to inventions, meetings, and conversations with other prisoners, especially those who spoke Hebrew. Although Hoffman did not speak Hebrew and was far from Jewish culture and traditions, I am sure that in his heart he was a real Jew. He was a very smart and creative man and was able to raise himself above our ordinary, dull life. He always strived to make proper choices and decisions.

Hoffman was not fond of Lihachev and believed that he was not treating me fairly. Lihachev was saddling me with a large amount of work. I had to draft numerous three-view projection drawings of steam engine parts to be ordered from distant factories. The steam engines were very old and required frequent repairs, so Lihachev often rushed me. Sometimes, he even tried to help me, but it was better if he didn't. One of the parts that was made from his drawings was not right and was found to be useless. Lihachev accused me of the mistake, even though Hoffman checked the issue and found that the draft had been done by him. I did not argue with Lihachev, but Hoffman was outraged at Lihachev's injustice towards me.

In Abez, I received a positive reply regarding my machine for coal enrichment, the invention that I had submitted together with Usov back in Karaganda. Our application was approved and a patent was issued for this invention later on. In addition, I started designing a new machine for crushing coal. Hoffman became interested in this project. I did the calculations and Hoffman helped me with the mechanical design. I very much enjoyed my interactions with Isaak Solomonovich Hoffman. We spent many days together in a small office. We used to talk a lot, work a lot, and then talk again.

Shmuel Halkin

The 4th Abez prison camp was blessed with Jewish prisoners. After work, I met my friends, many of them Jews. The most remarkable among them was the Yiddish poet Shmuel Ben Zalman Halkin. I came across him in the first days at the 4th Abez camp. I knew him from Moscow and had once visited him at home with Baazov. In the camp, he had a relatively easy job as an office worker in the firefighting team. Even though he suffered from heart disease, he was not given "disabled" status and had to work. Halkin was over fifty, heavyset, and carried the head of a lion on top of his wide shoulders. In the camp, his lion's hair was cut short, but a lion remains a lion even with a cropped mane. Halkin was extraordinarily gifted; he was one of the most talented Yiddish poets in the Soviet Union. He composed and published a lot, and everything he wrote was blessed by God. He was a fascinating conversation partner and often shared reminiscences, songs, and melodies with me.

Halkin knew Hebrew and even wrote poetry in Hebrew in his youth. He told me about his early life in a small Belorussian town, about his father, Rabbi Zalman, and his mother. One of the Hebrew psalms that he sang to me was called "Don't Be Afraid, My Servant Jacob." He had learned it from his father. His mother knew many Yiddish folk songs and Halkin loved to sing them. Halkin was a very warm and friendly man, not only in appearance, but in his very heart. He had good memory and recited his poems and songs to me, by heart. I learned many Yiddish poems, melodies, and songs from him. Every conversation with Halkin was enjoyable. He loved and respected his wife. After his arrest, she had declared: "If Jewish literature is now under arrest, Halkin's place is also in jail." Halkin was her entire life; she regularly wrote to him and sent food packages. Thanks to her, his food ration in the camp was adequate.

After two or three months, something happened and Halkin was moved from his easy office job in the firefighter team to hard physical work. It was already winter and his working team had to shovel snow for about four hours a day. I remember Halkin pulling a heavy sled loaded with snow, dressed in a worn-out peacoat, its fur collar upturned, and a shabby fur trapper hat with one earflap down and the other one up. There were other elderly prisoners with him, many of them over fifty. They had all been brought to this gloomy place in the Far North and had to do hard work under cold and clouded Northern skies.

Leib Strongin

Before arrest, Leib Izrailevich Strongin had been in charge of the Yiddish publishing house Emes [Truth] in Moscow. During Stalin's antisemitic campaign, when all of the Jewish cultural organizations were wiped out, Emes and its manager had also been terminated. Strongin had been sentenced to ten years in a forced labor camp, without any fault on his side. The closure of the publishing house happened suddenly. Only two weeks before, the government had approved the purchase of a second printing press. The publishing house had been thriving, and its publications were in high demand. And one day, it was abruptly closed and all the employees arrested.

Strongin was four years older than me, but quite healthy. In the camp, he had to do ordinary work, but did not complain. He'd been a laborer in his youth and remained one in his soul. He was an amicable and simple man and a veteran member of the Communist Party. Even under the harsh conditions of the labor camp, he had not lost his fortitude and took all the hardship in his stride. And here we were together with Leib Strongin, dressed in peacoats and walking outside the barracks. Strongin was murmuring some Yiddish folk song:

> I am sitting and playing the guitar
> And singing a song to myself.
> No one feels my suffering,
> Only God himself.

He had seen a lot in his life, and if he could still sing folk songs, it meant that there was still heart and soul left beneath his black peacoat with a number patch on its back.

Gregory Shitz

Gregory Shitz was a former editor of the Yiddish weekly magazine *Eynikeyt* (Unity), the official organ of the Jewish Anti-Fascist Committee.

He was around fifty, looked strong, and always walked with his head proudly raised. Even though he looked quite healthy on the outside, he was suffering from heart disease and was given disabled status. I was able to talk to him only a few times. For some reason, we did not become close; he was a very proud man and kept me at a distance. Maybe it was because of his illness. I was not particularly impressed by his knowledge of Jewish literature. But, obviously, as the editor of a Yiddish magazine, he must have had a sense for literature; he knew all the Jewish writers, poets, and journalists in the Soviet Union. The last time I saw him, we walked outside the barracks after the evening roll call. We walked slowly on the snow-covered path without talking much, almost in silence. It looked like he was deep in thought. I did not sense any internal strength or resiliency in him; it was as if his soul was broken. Later, he got very sick and died in the camp.

Yakov Shternberg

The Yiddish poet Yakov Moiseevich Shternberg was another Jewish dignitary in the camp. He was over sixty, looked rather old, had a bowed back, wrinkled face, and dressed in an oversized and shabby peacoat. He was originally from Romania and, besides writing poetry, had been a theater director and concert administrator. His shabby appearance, however, hid a highly intelligent and knowledgeable man, who had seen a lot and experienced a lot. I learned to respect him and enjoyed talking to him. Most of the time, Shternberg behaved himself with restraint, but during our conversations he revealed the depth of his mind and anyone listening to him would notice that he was really an extraordinary man. He knew some Hebrew, but all his writings were in Yiddish. When he recited his poems, I always felt refreshed, as though I was drinking fresh fruit juice. As a young kid, at the beginning of the century, he had corresponded with, and even met, Bialik, who had praised his poems. Sternberg was also well known in Romania and Serbia for the theater productions and concerts that he organized.

Sternberg told me a story about Khayele Grober, a former Habima actress, who toured Jewish towns and performed Jewish folk and Hassidic songs. She had once gone to Bucharest for a concert, where Sternberg was responsible for arranging her performance. But when he went to her hotel to greet her, he was not impressed by her at all. She seemed uncommunicative and not particularly attractive. He had tried unsuccessfully to get rid of the assignment, but it was too late. Khayele Grober was already quite famous by then and many people wanted to see her perform. When she appeared on the stage and started to sing a Hassidic song, the entire audience became very excited, Sternberg among them. Her voice was very touching, deep, and pure, and when looking at her gestures and movements one could vividly picture a Hassidic rabbi. Sternberg admitted that it was the first time in his life that he had witnessed a brilliant performance. The concert had been a huge success and Sternberg became one of her most passionate admirers. In his opinion, Khayele Grober was the best performer of Hassidic songs.

Sternberg was not very social and preferred to be alone, as if he was deeply immersed in his soul. Sometimes, during the day, he tried to avoid me and responded to me only with brief sentences, mostly about the daily camp routine. But in the evenings he opened his heart and turned out to be very talkative.

Weissman

I was able to talk to Halkin, Strongin, Sternberg, and Shitz only a few times during my time in Abez. Maybe it was because they did not speak Hebrew. However, I became very friendly with Weissman, who was a fluent Hebrew speaker. I spent almost every evening with him. Weissman was about sixty, ten years older than me, and had disabled status. He was from Kishinev,[2] where he had worked as a high school teacher and headmaster. He used to be a member of Bund[3] in his youth, and was given a ten-year prison term for previous political activity. Weissman was of short stature, with small red eyes and a hoarse voice. He was stationed in the barracks for disabled prisoners. In the evenings, after my work,

---

2   The capital of the Republic of Moldova. Until 1940, it belonged to Romania. In 1940, it was annexed by the Soviet Union. In 1941-1944, it was occupied by the German and Romanian armies. In 1944-1991, it was a part of the Soviet Union.

3   The socialist Jewish labor movement strongly opposing Zionism. It was active in Russia and Eastern Europe in 1897-1923. During Stalin's rule, it was dissolved and banned, and its members were persecuted.

we would meet outside his barracks, and walk together, while talking Hebrew, until evening roll call.

In his youth, Weissman had studied at a yeshiva[4] with a renowned tzadik,[5] who was also his distant relative. He told me a lot about Hassidic customs and sang me some Hassidic songs. He had spent a large part of his life as a Jewish educator and had also been involved in a campaign against Zionism in capitalist Romania. But in his old age he felt defeated. He felt depressed by the fact that he had to live in a dirty and filthy barracks and was forced to shovel snow during the Far North's cold winter. It seemed that he had started to reexamine his life and, particularly, his resistance to Zionism.

Such feelings were not unique to him; I heard similar thoughts from other Jewish prisoners. In the end, Zionism prevailed against all other varieties of Jewish politics and, after fifty years of struggle, led to the establishment of the State of Israel. Now, Bund and other non-Zionist organizations are long gone. One prisoner told me that it was a pity that they had neglected Zionism and allowed others, unintelligent people, to pursue it. He was convinced that all Zionists were uneducated simpletons and that all refined intellectuals were against it. Eventually, after the establishment of the Jewish state, many of its former adversaries among the diaspora Jews turned into Israel supporters. History does not judge the victors.

The Coachman

There were many other Jewish prisoners in the 4th Abez camp. One of them was a bearded man from Kiev, about fifty-five years old, a former coachman. He had been accused of terror and sentenced to twenty-five years. Here is his story. Before the war, his son had been engaged to marry, but something happened, and the wedding was canceled. The bride's parents were annoyed. In addition, during one of his trips outside town, they asked him to bring them a cow. He brought them a cow, but it turned out that the cow did not produce any milk. So they became even angrier and the father of the bride wrote a letter to the MGB accusing the coachman

---

4 A Jewish educational institution that focuses on the study of traditional religious texts.
5 A title in Judaism given to people considered righteous.

of insulting Stalin and claiming that Stalin should be murdered. In those years, such an accusation was enough not only for a twenty-five-year prison term, but also for execution. I vividly remember that old man with his sad eyes. He was an unsophisticated religious Jew. Once, he showed me a self-made hand-written prayer book containing several pages. One of the Jewish prisoners, risking punishment, helped him to write them. The prayers were incomplete and written in large letters. He treasured those pages and was hiding them deep among his belongings. He read these strange holy letters, which in the camp were twice as holy for him, and poured out his very heart. Later, this old coachman died in the camp. And if there is any justice in this world, his place is between the tzadiks.

The name of another veteran Jewish prisoner was Levin. He had spent more than twenty years in forced labor camps and was currently serving his third prison term. He was imprisoned for the first time in the 1920s and the second time in the 1930s. Apparently, in his youth, he had been a member of a political party that opposed Stalin, and because of this his entire life had been ruined. He looked like a nobleman and wore glasses. He liked to talk a lot and had a sharp tongue. As a veteran prisoner, he was respected by the other inmates. Levin read a lot and liked to talk about the books that he read. Troubles kept following him. His third prison term was coming to end, but according to regulations certain political prisoners were not allowed to be released. So the camp authorities searched for a reason to keep him in the camp. They found two stool pigeons, one of them from the camp library, who reported that Levin cursed the Soviet authorities. The camp administration conducted a brief field tribunal and extended his prison term.

The barracks for disabled prisoners was located next to the barbed wire camp fence, and across the fence there was a railway that was used by the freight trains that hauled coal from Vorkuta. Once a day, a passenger train from Vorkuta to Moscow passed by the camp. The windows of the train cars were brightly illuminated, and with yearning eyes we looked at the free men and women who had no idea what was happening just a few meters from their train.

Evening roll call was held in the camp's yard. All the prisoners lined up outside—a sea of black peacoats with number patches sewn on the back. When the guards were counting the inmates, one could hear bits and pieces of conversations between prisoners. I remember that sometime in August the camp administration issued an order commanding all prisoners to remain in their barracks after evening roll call. However, the order was not strictly observed and we continued walking outside after the roll call. One evening, Weissman, Sternberg, and I were standing outside the disabled prisoners' barracks after roll call. Suddenly, two guards appeared and ordered us to approach and explain why we were outside the barracks. We started to improvise. Weissman and Sternberg claimed that they were going to the restroom and I told them that I was returning from work at the power station. However, it did not work and they punished us with a night in the carcer.

On our way to the carcer, we met another prisoner, who was standing outside the barracks. In line with camp rules, he greeted the guards: "How do you do, comrade officers." One of the guards commanded him to join us. "We are not your comrades. You have to say: 'How do you do, citizen officers.'" All four of us were searched and ushered into a small dark cell with only one folding plank bed. When we sat down on the plank bed it immediately collapsed and overturned the bucket filled with urine and feces. We thus found ourselves on the cell floor in total darkness covered with the contents of the bucket. We started shouting and knocking at the door. After a long time, the door was opened, and eventually we were given some rags and a bucket of water to clean the cell.

What could we do? If there is no justice, even among the immortal gods, what can be said about our unhallowed reality? So I knelt down and started to wipe the spilled, stinky gold. The three others followed suit. As one can imagine, this work gave us a lot of pleasure. Eventually, we succeeded in cleaning the floor and even rinsed it with an additional bucket of water. We waited for some time and after the floor had dried out all four of us laid down on it and spend the whole night in this pleasant fashion. After this, our evening walks lasted only until roll call.

I was stationed on the top plank bed in the barracks designated for the camp's "High Society." Our barracks were much more comfortable and cleaner than the barracks for the disabled prisoners. Most of the camp dignitaries, including Kalinin, Kargin, Boris Ivanovich, and the kitchen, office, and medical employees were stationed there. The barracks had an orderly, a young prisoner from Azerbaijan, a diligent guy who was responsible for cleaning. The washbasin was located at the far end of the barracks, opposite the entrance. The barracks had central heating and all the plank beds on the bottom and top levels were arranged in the same neat fashion.

Winter had arrived in Abez already in September. For the first time in my life I observed the Northern Lights, which occurred quite often that year. When I looked up at night, the skies were illuminated with colorful bright snakes crawling and meandering between the bright stars. On the horizon on sunny days, it was possible to see the Northern Ural Mountains covered with snow, a drastic change from the flat tundra surrounding the camp. Occasionally, freight trains passed by. The noise of approaching train carriages loaded with coal got louder and louder and then faded.

In winter, several changes were made in the camp canteen and, as a result, the quality of the food improved. Among other things, they started to fry the salted capelin fishes, which made them more suitable for eating. Even Weissman, who mostly ate food that was sent to him from home, started coming to the canteen. I did not like the salted capelin fishes, but regularly ate the gruel soup and porridge, together with rye bread.

The storage room for prisoners' belongings was organized quite efficiently. A special kitchen was set up next to it to prepare warm food from prisoners' supplies. It was very convenient. In the packages from home I was getting porridge concentrates and some other products that required cooking. Halkin, Kalinin, Kargin, and other prisoners regularly used this kitchen. First, one had to withdraw the products from the storage room. The withdrawal amount was meticulously weighed and registered. Then, one had to submit the food to be cooked to the kitchen. The food was prepared by the prisoners who worked there. Next to the kitchen, there was a room with small tables and chairs, like in a real cafeteria.

Performances by prisoner-actors were held in the club. Among the actors was a former professional singer. Even though he was quite old, his voice was still strong. Unfortunately, after a while he was transferred to ordinary work and was not allowed to perform any longer. Maybe he was also a victim of those two stool pigeons.

One day, I was called for a meeting with an interrogator, who asked me questions about a Jewish engineer I used to know in Moscow. He asked if the engineer was involved in "nationalistic activity." I refuted the accusation and told him that the engineer was a devoted Communist and that I had never heard anything criminal from him. The interrogation was conducted without pressure. In the end, I signed the protocol, which was written exactly according to my testimony.

I was also invited to the office of the chief officer of the 4th Abez prison camp, who advised me to start working on compressing coal powder bricks. It looked like he had received some information from Inta about my professional experience. This was a hopeless task in the camp's conditions. I had no binding material and no hot press. Inta coal was very brittle and its small grains could not be formed into bricks without a proper binder. At first, I tried to use water, the only binding material that was available to me. I prepared several frozen balls of coal powder mixed with a small amount of water. In addition, with the help of Kalinin I built a small hand press to form coal bricks. However, the firing of the coal bricks in the furnace was unsuccessful. The ice melted very fast and the coal powder blew away before being ignited.

In the middle of December 1951, I was informed of a further transfer. Yet again, as in previous cases, it was very inconvenient. I had become accustomed to the place, people, and my work. But what could I do? The order was to "gather your belongings," so I gathered my belongings and managed to bid farewell to my close friends and coworkers. I went to Weissman's barracks. We sat together on his plank bed. I shook hands with him several times and exchanged a few words. How can one say goodbye to a disabled, elderly friend? We were very sad and both of us knew that we would most likely not see each other again. I also went to Halkin to hear his lion's voice again. I went to the office to say goodbye to Boris Ivanovich, Leykachev, and Hoffman. Hoffman was my devoted friend and parting with him was especially difficult. This time I was alone on my way to Inta. My belongings were searched and I was taken by a guard to the train station. Outside reigned an eternal polar night. We went to the station on foot and waited for the train in the small main hall. It was very strange to be outside of the barbed wire fence, to see ordinary people, men and women, who sat next to us and waited in line for the ticket office. Then the train came.

I arrived in Abez in July of 1951, when the skies were bright and the days long, and left in December, when darkness, extreme cold, and piles of snow covered the whole world. And if there is something left in my memory from Abez, it is the daunting gloominess of the tundra.

My transfer to Vorkuta was requested by special order. The management of Mineral camp was at Inta and my journey to Vorkuta went through Inta. Again, I was placed in the 5th transit camp, where I was treated in the hospital between May and June of that year. This time, I was there only two or three days, but I had time to see some of the people that I knew before. In Inta, I was given worn-out felt boots and sent to Vorkuta in the Stolypin carriage. This time, the carriage was almost empty. Besides me, there was only one prisoner—a thief. He gazed at my belongings, but the armed guard was sitting in the corridor and he did not dare to rob me. The train ride lasted only one night. The next morning, we arrived at Vorkuta.

Part 12

Vorkuta

The way from Vorkuta train station to the transfer camp was long and covered with snow. It was very cold. We had to walk and carry our belongings all the way, through the ascents and descents of the road. There were several books in my suitcase and it was quite heavy. Other prisoners in our column were younger and stronger, so I started to fall behind, but eventually was able to reach the destination.

Barracks Number 18

The transfer camp where we arrived was called 62nd Vorkuta camp, a part of the River camp group. It was the sixth camp that I had "visited" during my prison term. After being searched, we were taken to barracks number 18. But before that we were advised to leave our belongings in the storeroom. I heeded the advice and, as I found out later, it was not superfluous. The 62nd transfer camp was intended mostly for common criminals, thieves, robbers, and even murderers, and barracks 18 was jointly occupied by political prisoners and common criminals. A gang of thieves operated in the barracks and they stole from the political prisoners.

The two weeks that I spent in this barracks were awful. The door was always locked during the day and night. Prisoners were allowed to leave the barracks only for work or to go to the canteen. So we were stuck in this unpleasant and broken-down place, filled with the suffocating smell from the urinal bucket. I was not able to wash myself throughout this time. But the most dreadful experience was the robber of the political prisoners by the gang. The guards knew about it, but did not interfere. It was quite possible that some people in the camp administration were benefiting from this robbery. The guards regularly brought in groups of newly arrived political prisoners, along with their belongings, and some of them had valuable things in their possession.

Robberies usually happened like this: the lights suddenly went out and in total darkness the gang of thieves attacked the newly arrived political prisoners. One could hear noises and the sound of fighting, punching, and deep breathing, voices threating and persuading, cries for help, and cries of despair. All this lasted only a few minutes. And then it was all over, the lights went on again, and everything was as usual. The stolen items were smuggled out of the locked barracks through a broken window. Apparently, the gang's accomplices were waiting outside. By the way, this window remained broken all the time during my stay there, even though it was quite cold inside the barracks.

My place was on an upper plank bed not far from the entrance door. By chance, next to me was the plank bed of Volodya, the gang's leader, a good-looking young guy. He was a veteran thief; it was already his third term in prison. Volodya himself did not take part in the thieving. He only gave orders to his henchmen. Normally, he behaved in a civilized manner and was a pleasant partner in conversation. Some of the well-educated political prisoners even became friendly with him. Among them was Kostia Amarnetov, who often chatted with Volodya, and since my plank bed was next to Volodya's I was able to listen to their conversations.

Volodya's current prison term was seventeen years. He told his life story in a very calm manner. Together with a friend, he had brazenly burgled of a store in his hometown in the Moscow region. They took all the cash, more than fifty thousand rubles. Initially, he had been arrested for a petty crime; the store burglary was added to his case during interrogation. There were several large bags among his belongings. I never saw him opening those bags, but can imagine that they contained the most valuable items stolen from prisoners.

Some of the common thieves I encountered in the camps were quite smart, pleasant, and good-looking young people. Their common trait was that they loathed any kind of work and were after a luxurious life. They wanted to grab all of life's splendor, with all the bells and whistles. The typical attributes of this luxurious life included alcohol, girls, fine food, elegant clothes, card games, and entertainment. And because such a lifestyle required money, they needed a great deal of money in their pockets. A thief does not steal because he is greedy; there is nobody more generous than a thief. Money is not his ultimate objective; it is simply the means with which to attain life's pleasures. And here, in this wretched barracks 18, in the obscurity of Vorkuta prison camp, this pleasant, fine-looking, and healthy young man, who could have made humankind better, was stealing the last valuables of poor and unfortunate political prisoners.

Once, a group of about ten political prisoners from Lithuania was brought into our barracks with their belongings. Many of them were young and strong. They managed to occupy empty plank beds that were close to each other. After the door was locked, one of the prisoners was able to warn them about the gang operating in the barracks. After some time, the light went out and the gang attacked them. In the darkness, one could hear the sound of a serious fight, which lasted for a long time. I overheard one of the thieves creep over to Volodya's plank bed and ask him in a whisper if they should use knives. Volodya said no and, finally, the thieves retreated. When the light was back on, it appeared that the thieves had won the battle, despite the group's resistance. Only a few of them had signs of the fight on their faces, whereas the Lithuanian guys were severely beaten and robbed. They decided to call the guards and started shouting. After a long time, the door opened and the camp's officer on duty, accompanied by two guards, entered the barracks. The mugged Lithuanian prisoners complained about the robbery and threatened to complain to the camp management and the Moscow administration.

After that, several camp officials, including the chief officer and many additional guards, assembled in the barracks. They lined us up in the middle and started a search. Some of the robbed prisoners helped in the search. However, none of the stolen goods was retrieved. Everything had been thrown through the broken window and collected by the thieves' accomplices. One of the robbed Lithuanians was determined to get back his new high boots. He pointed at the thieves who had taken part in the robbery and several of them were taken out for interrogation. The Lithuanian guy was also moved out of the barracks because there was a danger that the thieves would take revenge on him. After a while, though, we heard a rumor that he had been knifed by the thieves and had died.

Luckily for me, the thieves did not touch me. All my stuff was in storage and my felt boots were so old and worn out that they were of no interest to anybody. Moreover, I had number patches sewn on the back and sleeves of my peacoat, as was the custom in Abez. However, in Vorkuta camp this was a sign that a prisoner had been sentenced to hard forced labor. Such prisoners were particularly revered, so the thieves treated me with some measure of respect. Despite all the political prisoners' requests to be separated from the criminals, the situation did not change during the time that I spent there. Separation only took place several months later.

The canteen in the 62nd camp was terrible and very dirty; everything there, the floor, the chairs, and the tables looked filthy. We were mostly served salted fishes in the mornings and evenings. Next to the canteen, there was a store where one could buy sweets and sausages. However, political prisoners had no money, and even if they did have some money it was immediately stolen by the thieves.

The prisoners in barracks 18 were not required to do regular work, but sometimes we had to carry out occasional assignments. I was once required to peel potatoes in the canteen. The potatoes were frozen; it was impossible to find any unfrozen vegetables in Vorkuta in the middle of December. The potato peeling machine broke, so we had to do the work manually. We had to sit in a very uncomfortable position and the work was very tedious. Yes, those two weeks in barracks 18 were a nightmare. Nevertheless, I met there several interesting people; some of them were Jews. In those years, there were quite a few members of my nation locked up in forced labor camps.

Kuznetsov

Even though he had a Russian family name, Kuznetsov was a Hassidic Jew from Leningrad. He stood out in his Jewish appearance due to his thick black beard, black eyes, and black eyebrows. He was over fifty years old, of medium height, and had a stout body. Before his arrest, he had worked as a weaver and had been a member of a Hassidic congregation. He was arrested together with many other members of the Hassidic community of Leningrad. I do not know what the official cause for their arrest was.

Maybe they were accused of being American spies; after all, their leader Lubavitch Rebbe lived abroad, in New York.

Kuznetsov arrived at Vorkuta, with all his belongings, straight from Leningrad, and was immediately robbed by the thieves. He was left with only a jacket, which he decided to trade for food. In his naivety, Kuznetsov offered it to a thief with a pleasant face he met in the canteen. The thief put the jacket on, as if to try it. Apparently, the jacket suited him, and Kuznetsov never saw it again.

Horvitz, also a Jew, who worked in the camp administration, appeared from time to time in our barracks. He was a nice-looking young man and was respected by all the prisoners. He was not shy about his Jewishness, and, when Kuznetsov complained to him about the robbery and asked for protection, Horvitz promised to help him. That evening, when all the prisoners in the barracks were lined up for roll call, Horvitz ordered that from now on nobody would touch "the Beard." That was the nickname he gave to Kuznetsov. While he spoke he looked directly at Volodya. Evidently, Horvitz was well aware of Volodya's role in the gang. And it really helped because Kuznetsov was left alone from then on. I had several conversations with Kuznetsov and learned several prayers and psalms from him, one of which was titled "I Will Cast My Sight at the Mountains."

Stalinsky

Stalinsky was an educated and intelligent Russian man, about forty years old. He had been transferred to Vorkuta from Mineral labor camp in Norilsk, also in the Far North of Russia. Stalinsky was a veteran political prisoner. Initially, he'd been convicted to a ten-year term and had already spent seven years in the prison camp. However, his prison term was lengthened by another seventeen years, and now he had twenty more years left in prison. This additional prison term was given to him as a punishment for an anti-Soviet poem he wrote in Norilsk camp. The poem was found in his possession during a search.

Stalinsky was an amateur poet. His poems were written in a shattering impressionist-futurist style and were admired by the prisoners. He was also very fond of the lyrics of Anna Akhmatova and her husband Nikolay Gumilev, both talented Russian poets. Gumilev had been executed in the first years of the Communist Revolution. To this day, I remember Stalinsky reciting a few of his poems very forcefully. He also read us his own poems, among them the one that had caused the extension of his imprisonment. He also told us a lot about his time in Norilsk camp. Prisoners died of hunger there during the war. He had survived because of the extra portions of lentil soup, that, thanks to his connections, he was getting in the canteen. We all licked our lips when he described to us that tasty lentil soup.

Kostia Amarnetov

Kostia Amarnetov was a nice Russian young man. After the war, he had served as an army officer in one of the countries of Eastern Europe that was occupied by Soviet troops. Somehow, he'd managed to get a twenty-five-year prison term, without any fault on his side. He was originally from Tambov, where his family was still living. He was a slender, good-looking, and cordial guy, always clearly shaved. Kostia was able to get along with all sorts of people and the prisoners respected him. Later, I spent several years with him in the 9th Vorkuta camp and got to know him rather well. In barracks 18, Kostia became friendly with my neighbor, the leader of the robber gang Volodya, who in turn treated him well. Kostia, Stalinsky, and Volodya often spent time together.

On the evening of December 31, 1951, we were going to hold a festive dinner to celebrate the New Year. Besides me, our small group consisted of Kostia, Volodya, Stalinsky, and two other prisoners, both stationed at the opposite row of plank beds and one of whom worked in the canteen. He was able to get a large bowl of Russian vinaigrette salad, someone brought sausage, and I contributed a can of sardines. We also had some bread and even a bottle of homemade vodka. However, late in the evening, two or three hours before midnight, I was called for transfer. So I had to bid farewell to the prisoners I had got to know in dreadful barracks 18. To tell the truth, even though I missed the festive New Year's dinner, I was quite happy to get out of that awful place.

1st River Camp

I collected my belongings from the storage and, together with a small group of prisoners, stood next to the camp's entrance gate. It was dark and cold, and we had to wait for a long time for the armed guards. When they arrived, we went outside and walked a short distance to the gate of another camp. That was the first forced labor camp of the River group of camps. The underground coal mine Capitalnaya was part of its territory. Our belongings were searched and we were taken to the hospital barracks for twenty-one-days' quarantine. I spent about four months in the first River prison camp, until the end of April 1952. It was mainly occupied by political prisoners working in the coal mine and was neater and more orderly than the 62nd transfer camp, which was populated by common criminals. Generally, the prison camps for political prisoners differed from those for ordinary criminals. Even though the regime in the political camps was much tougher, life there was much safer; there were no fights, humiliations, or robberies, and political prisoners were usually much nicer.

All six newly arrived prisoners were placed in a single room in the hospital barracks. Everyone was given his own bed. From the first days after our arrival, we were blessed by visits from "fellow countryman." This term in Russian defines a group of people who come from the same area or belong to the same nationality. The most active were representatives of "small" nations, such as Baltic, Caucasus, or Middle Asian states. Every new person in the camp generated a lot of curiosity. For example, if a newly arrived prisoner was originally from Georgia, all the Georgians in the camp wanted to talk to him, help him, learn the latest news about their state, country, or city, get information about mutual friends, relatives, etc.

During the winter, only a few new prisoners arrived in the first River camp, so interest in our arrival was rather considerable. A rumor was launched among the Jewish community of the prison camp that a new Jewish prisoner had just arrived. So the next morning I was visited by a young Jewish man, who offered to help me with food. I was deeply touched by this attention from my Jewish fellow countryman and told him that I still had some food left from the packages that I had received in Abez. At times, prisoners stationed in the hospital barracks also came to see us.

I remember one hospital patient from Ukraine, a Bandera devotee,[1] with fiery eyes and scars on his face. He was hospitalized in our barracks and came to visit one of the newly arrived prisoners in our room, also a Bandera follower. At first, they talked quietly and I did not follow their conversation. Suddenly, the man with scars raised his voice and started swearing and berating "The Mustached Man"—that is what he called Stalin. Never before had I heard such open insults about Stalin, who was regarded as our greatest leader and was admired, loved, and feared by everybody. The scolding went on and on for about half an hour. All the prisoners in the room remained silent, as if their lips were frozen shut. Later, I was told that this prisoner was mentally ill. And really, how could somebody in his right mind dare to say such things about comrade Stalin? But the words of this Ukrainian man were, actually, quite reasonable and logical. It was obvious that he had suffered a lot and that his soul was deeply hurt. He put his whole heart into his speech and his fiery eyes looked very expressive. "Where did this man come from? How come this monster had succeeded in ruining our lives, darkening the blue skies above our heads, and throwing us into this filthy ditch?" That was the crux of his words.

In the hospital barracks, we were given regular prison camp food. We ate gruel soup, porridge, rye bread, and fried codfish. From now on, for the next four years, we ate codfish every day. Sometimes, we were required to do some work, mostly shoveling snow. It was not hard work, but still, prisoners tried to evade it. A popular camp saying was: "Whatever the work, the main thing is not to work." The hospital barracks superintendent was a tough young guy, who made sure that everybody did their fair share of work. The barracks and its surroundings were kept in order. At the end of quarantine, I passed the medical commission and was put in the "Fit for easy work" health category. After that, I got back my regular camp clothes and was transferred to the Black Guardia barracks, where I stayed only several days.

---

1   Stepan Bandera (1909-1959)—the leader and ideologist of Ukrainian ultra-nationalists. During World War II, he was a Nazi collaborator and organized forces fighting against the Soviet army. After the war, his followers were severely persecuted by the Soviet regime.

Black Guardia was the name given to work teams doing hard labor. Our work team mainly shoveled snow in the area around Capitalnaya mine. The Black Guardia barracks was crowded with prisoners, who worked different shifts around the clock, so it was always noisy there. As in the other forced labor camps, the barracks population was a mix of prisoners from Russia, Eastern Ukraine, Lithuania, Latvia, Estonia, etc. There were also several foreign prisoners. One of them was from India. During the war, he had been living in Berlin and collaborating with the Nazis. I also met Kramer, an American Jew. He spoke Russian and was very talkative.

The head of our work team would wake us up at five in the morning. After breakfast in the canteen (the same gruel soup, porridge, code, and rye bread), we would go through the guarded gates to the coal mine territory, collect snow shovels and ice breakers, and clear snow and ice from a designated area. The weather was very cold, my felt boots were old and worn out, and my feet were very cold. Most of my team members felt the same way. The head of our work team was not very strict and allowed us to warm up in an unpopulated office building nearby. The building was in the final stages of construction; it had a roof and a floor and was heated by a furnace. We went there and warmed ourselves in the corridor. Then, we came out, shoveled snow for a relatively short time, and then went back again to warm up. In the evening, we returned the shovels and went back to the camp grounds.

After a few days of shoveling, I was called to the administration building and informed about my transfer to the Technical Control Department of Capitalnaya coal mine. The next day, I was transferred to another barracks and started working in the Technical Control Department . The coal mine operated in three shifts, as did the employees of the two technical control teams. One of the teams worked underground, in the mine; but I was assigned to the second team, aboveground.

On my first day, I was invited to the office of the manager of Capitalnaya coal mine, Priskoka. It turned out that he was a graduate of Moscow Mining University, where I been teaching. I did not remember him, but he knew me, and he even showed me the textbook on coal enrichment I wrote on his office bookshelf. He treated me very well and told me that I was to start working in the Technical Control Department and in the Coal Sorting Department. He also promised that after some time he would invite me again for a talk. However, I never saw him again and later was told that Priskoka had been promoted to head of the Vorkuta Coal Mining Trust.

I worked in the Technical Control Department of Capitalnaya coal mine for about three months. From the Black Guardia barracks, I was moved to barracks 11, which was kept in relatively good shape. The first River camp housed thousands of prisoners living in numerous barracks, and barracks 11, intended for prisoners doing technical work, was clean and neat. So I settled down on an upper plank bed in barracks 11. This plank bed was shown to me by Eduard Haikin. As evident from his family name, Eduard was a Jew, but this fact was also obvious just from a brief look at his face. He was about forty-five, a veteran prisoner serving a twenty-year prison term. In Leningrad, he'd worked as a photographer and was well educated. In the 1st Vorkuta camp, he had served as a camp superintendent, responsible for cleanliness and order on the camp grounds and in the barracks. All barracks superintendents reported to him. Haikin received me very amiably, offered me valuable pieces of advice, and even treated me to breakfast.

All the prisoners in barracks 11 were dressed in fresh uniforms and I was also given a new set of clothes. I also received a new blanket. I was very happy, as prisoners typically only received these items once every four years. I was told that my plank bed had previously been occupied by a prisoner from Austria. At that time, all Austrian prisoners of war were released from forced labor camps and returned to their homeland. I had even met one of them briefly. I'd had a conversation with him in the afternoon and by evening he was gone.

Barracks 11 was very clean. The floor was not only washed daily but was also scrubbed regularly. However, relations between the prisoners were far from friendly. The barracks was divided into two parts, with the entrance in the middle. In my part of the barracks, prisoners chose to stay apart from each other. There were conversations, games of dominoes, chess, or checkers, even jokes, but there was no sense of solidarity. I felt like an alien in the barracks and I have a more vivid recollection of that scrubbed floor than of anyone who lived there. For instance, my neighbor, who resided on the plank bed below mine, was around forty, a veteran prisoner, originally from Poland, who worked as a bookkeeper in one of the camp's offices. He was a pleasant man and we often talked to each other, but he did not impress me at all. He was not coarse. I never heard him swear. On the contrary, he was very polite, boring, and dry and was never interested in discussing things outside of the ordinary life of the prison camp. Food, sleep, clothes, health were the most discussed topics.

Nevertheless, each one of those bookkeepers, accountants, clerks, and other camp bureaucrats had his own soul, his own prison term, and was spending the golden days of his life in a forced labor camp. Likewise, my days were also spent in barracks 11. More precisely, my nights. During the day, I was outside the barracks, working, walking the camp's trails, and talking to other prisoners, many of whom became my friends.

Stein

Among the Jewish prisoners in the 1st River prison camp, only a few knew Hebrew. There was no one with whom I could regularly converse in fluent Hebrew. If I am not mistaken, only Stein, a prisoner from West Germany knew Hebrew. He was much younger than me and we first met during my last days in the camp, so I was able to talk to him only once or twice. Stein was less than thirty years old and was working in the coal mine. He told me that after the war he had overseen the facilities for displaced persons in West Berlin and had been treacherously kidnapped from there by the MGB. He'd been sitting with his wife in a restaurant, while his car was parked outside. He was approached by a West German policeman, who asked about his car and notified him that there was some problem with the car registration. Stein maintained that the registration was in order, but the policeman asked him politely to drive with him to the police station to clarify the issue. Stein asked his wife to wait in the restaurant, went out with the policeman, and they both got into his car. According to Stein, a small section of the way to the police station passed through Berlin's Soviet Zone. While they were driving through it, the car was stopped, and he was arrested by the MGB. Meanwhile, his wife was left in the restaurant, waiting for him. He was sentenced to a twenty-five-year prison term and sent to the forced labor camp in Vorkuta.

The technical offices of the Vorkuta Coal Mining Trust were situated in two locations. While the offices employing civil staff were located outside of the camp in the center of the town of Vorkuta, the technical offices

employing prisoners, more than a hundred of them, were in the industrial area of the 1st River camp. Prisoners were working as engineers,
technicians, bookkeepers, etc. Among them, there were several Jewish
prisoners I got to know: Shkolnik, Kaplinsky, and a few more.

Shkolnik

Shkolnik had been brough to Vorkuta from Odessa. He was a little bit
younger than me and was serving a relatively short five-year prison term.
His work in the camp's technical office matched his profession—building construction engineer. Shkolnik did not stand out in his appearance,
but was unique in his Jewish spirit, knowledge of the Yiddish language,
and friendly way of communication. He had grown up in Odessa at the
beginning of the twentieth century and still remembered some of the
Jewish places there. He was very familiar with the famous hazan[2] Pinhas
Minkowski from the Brodsky synagogue and knew some of his psalms
by heart. We even had an argument regarding the melody of the psalm
"Mikdash Melech," "The Temple of God." Shkolnik tried to convince me
that my version was wrong. So, one dark winter evening, on the snowy
trail of the 1st River prison camp in Vorkuta, I listened to his version of
the psalm.

Reminiscence of Odessa

Yes, we had quite a few walks in the frozen northern gloom. The territory
of the 1st River forced labor camp was quite large and we were able to
find some remote places where we could share our nostalgic memories
of Odessa.

I lived in Odessa from the age of sixteen to nineteen, during the
World War I. It was a time of revolution, unrest, and pogroms, and
during that period my life evolved from youth to maturity. In those years,
I acquired a strong affection for the Hebrew language, religion, history,
and culture. In Odessa, I studied at the Seventh Lublin Gymnasia and
at the Jewish Musical Conservatory, where A. Gordon taught me music

---

2   Hazan or cantor—a Jewish singer who helps to lead the synagogue congregation in
     songful prayer and psalms.

theory and Levin, who had once worked with Yasha Heifetz, was my violin instructor.

I grew up under Odessa's skies, breathed its air, sunbathed on its beaches, and swam in the Black Sea. At night, Odessa's bright stars twinkled down at me, bewildering me, and predicting my bright future. The Brodsky Synagogue, my Hebrew teacher Yosef Klausner, the Jewish Musical Conservatory, the Hebrew journal *HaShiloah*, the Jewish sports club Maccabi—all of them contributed to my Jewish education and self-determination. In Odessa, I was able to see and listen to Jewish celebrities: the writers Mordecai Spector and Jacob Fichman, the attorney Oscar Gruzenberg, the actresses Ester Rachel Kaminska in *Mirele Ephros* and Clara Young in *Pupsik*, and singer Isa Kremer performing Jewish folk songs. That was the world of my youth in Odessa. Experiences and ideas from that period molded me and have remained with me all my life.

And here I was, walking with Shkolnik, an unremarkable man with a tender soul, along the snowy paths of Vorkuta prison camp, shrouded in cold, gloom, and darkness; and in our minds, high above us, shone the blue and sunny skies of Odessa.

Kaplinsky

Kaplinsky was quite different from Shkolnik; he was a small Jewish man, around fifty, very calm and composed. He used to talk slowly, as if weighing every word. As an electrical engineer, he had gained extensive experience at one of Moscow's research organizations and was fairly well known in his field of work. He was managing the electrical department in the camp's technical offices, and even civilian engineers from Vorkuta came to the camp to ask his advice. I do not remember exactly why Kaplinsky had been convicted to ten years in a forced labor camp; probably it was due to some blunder that had happened in his youth. His wife was Russian, two or three years older than him, and they had two daughters.

I spent long hours with Shkolnik and Kaplinsky. Both were good men and they lived together in the same room. Their barracks was planned differently from others and the conditions there were much better. It had a central corridor with separate rooms on both sides. Instead of plank beds, their room had single iron beds. I vividly remember their room. Besides Shkolnik and Kaplinsky, there were four other prisoners, one of them a young Jew from Moscow who worked as a technician. He always kept an open chess board resting on his bed. On the wall above Kaplinsky's bed, there was a photograph of his wife and daughters. One of the daughters was quite pretty. I also noticed that his wife had gray hair.

There was a rumor that, beginning in 1952, prisoners would be paid for their work. Such rumors occupied prisoners' minds and there were many discussions on this topic. Kaplinsky was particularly excited. As the head of the electrical department, he was supposed to receive a substantial salary. He was devoted to his family and hoped that he would be able to help them financially. Kaplinsky was a practical man. He viewed the world very seriously, without imagination, and never spent time on dreams. He was probably not bothered much by doubts and reflections.

Among the Jews of the 1st River prison camp, I also remember Litvakov, a young guy from Moscow. His father was Moshe Litvakov, a well-known Yiddish writer, and an editor at *Der Emes*—"The Truth"— the Yiddish Communist daily newspaper that was shut down in 1938. The same year, Moshe Litvakov was arrested and executed. The young Litvakov had been working as an engineer in the Moscow Dynamo factory, where, as in the Moscow automobile factory, there were systematic arrests of the Jews. I was able to talk to him only once during our walk outside. He did not know much about the work of his father at *Der Emes*. He did not speak Yiddish and was quite distant from Jewish culture. Evidently, this is the fate of many Jewish fathers and mothers in our country. My son and daughters do not speak the language of their nation either. In the Soviet Union, Jewish culture is being destroyed and scattered in the wind.

Capitalnaya Mine Technical Control Department

Meanwhile, I was working every day, except Sunday, in the Technical Control Department of Capitalnaya coal mine. It was a world familiar to me, a world of iron carriages loaded with coal, coal samples for analysis, analytical reports, and technical documents. However, during these three months I did not have a permanent workplace and my job was not properly defined. Eventually, I had found myself a small room with a desk and benches along the walls. This room was used by workers for meetings before and after their shifts. The rest of the time, the room was empty, and I could stay there. The room was without ventilation or windows. It was illuminated by only one weak electrical lamp, so it was always dark there. Coal powder was spread everywhere and the air was quite foggy. Most of the time, I had no assignments, so I just sat on the dusty bench in this murky room.

The head of the Technical Control Department was Sezin, a civilian. He was a young man, who had just graduated from the coal enrichment department of the technical community college in Vorkuta and did not have much experience. I talked to him only several times and he did not impress me at all. The local manager was Sverzev, an old man, about sixty, also a civilian. He was a former prisoner, who had served ten years in Vorkuta prison camp and had worked in the Technical Control Department before his release. He was very effective in overseeing the operation of the department. Besides these two, there were also several civilians, all of them former prisoners. The rest of the team, working above and belowground, were prisoners. The most impressive among them was Kostia Lisovoy, a guy of about thirty from Odessa, who was serving a fifteen-year prison term. He had considerable influence on the civilians and prisoners working in the Technical Control Department . He took care of all the important documentation, preparing the reports and certificates of coal quality, and was in contact with the mine management. Kostia had an assistant, a young and handsome guy, also a prisoner. They both occupied a desk near a window in a large room and their working conditions were not bad at all. I did not meddle in their work and Kostia treated me well. He told me a lot about his life in Odessa during the German occupation. I got that impression that he had worked for the Germans during those years. Sometimes, we drank tea together and once we even drank a bottle of vodka. However, we did not work together. I was not involved in the work of the other team members either. My position and responsibilities were not defined and this situation bothered me a lot. But gradually, I established friendly relations with several of the prisoners who worked above and belowground and had interesting conversations with some of them.

From time to time, while preparing samples for analysis I had to visit the other part of the Technical Control Department . There were two large rooms containing mechanical equipment that crushed coal in order to prepare coal samples in powder form. Most of the work was done manually. The resulting powder samples were sent to the analytical lab. One of the prisoners who worked there was Fedia, a young, pale, and lean Ukrainian guy serving a twenty-year prison term. He was mainly involved in mechanical repair work. I talked to him several times; he was very friendly, but it seemed to me that he felt some guilt deep inside. He told me that during the war he had been drafted by the Germans to serve in a concentration camp, where he'd sorted items belonging to the murdered Jews. A few times he had been involved in packing the hair of executed Jewish women. All the items were meticulously sorted according to their use and degree of wear. Sometimes, they found valuable pieces of gold and jewelry hidden inside clothes. All objects were disinfected, packed in large bags, placed in a large storeroom, and finally transferred to Germany. He said that he had been fired from the concentration camp for attempting to save two young Jewish girls. However, he gave this explanation hastily and after these words there was an awkward silence, as if it was difficult for him to tell me the real reason for his dismissal. It looked as though this thin and pale young man was being pursued by memories and images from the past. Maybe his memory was burning with images of the faces, eyes, and hair of the young Jewish girls, the same hair that he had packed into large bags. Fedia was a simple Ukrainian guy; he had seen what was happening in the concentration camp and had participated in it all. Perhaps he himself had taken part in violating and raping those two young Jewish girls before their murder. Perhaps all this passed before his eyes during that brief moment of silence.

Vlasov was also among the workers in the Technical Control Department , a broad-shouldered young man, less than thirty years old. He was a common criminal and was one of the meanest bullies in the 1st River prison camp. I was told that he had murdered quite a few people before his arrest. Occasionally, he insulted me, calling me "the old kike," and I was quite frightened of him. When drunk, he started quarrels and brawls with other prisoners. Sometimes he caused turmoil in the Technical Control Department offices; and on those occasions I would hear loud shouting, swearing, and the sound of fighting. However, Kostia had some measure of influence on this crude man. Once, three of us even shared a bottle of vodka. That was after we'd been paid our salaries in cash for the first time. But generally, I did my best to avoid Vlasov during my work in the Technical Control Department .

Later, I met Vlasov in the 9th prison camp. To my amusement, he was working there as the head of a construction team. Evidently, he knew how to make prisoners work. His team was exceeding production plans and his name was often displayed on the "Hall of Fame" wall. Instead of a vulgar bully, I saw in front of me a reserved and mannerly man, the entire opposite of the Vlasov I'd known before. I was told that after I left the 1st River prison camp, there had been several arrests among the civil personnel of the Technical Control Department . Among the arrested were Kostia and several other Ukrainian guys. Immediately afterwards, Vlasov had been transferred to the 9th prison camp. Nobody knew the cause of the arrests or Vlasov's role in those arrests.

Sometimes, the office workers entertained themselves by playing with mice. A family of small white mice, with red eyes and long tails, was living in a box on the top of a bookcase in the office. The leader of the mouse family was given a respectable name—Terenty Spiridonovich. He was very much involved in matters related to food and sex. As I mentioned before, prisoners had a strong affection for all kinds of animals. They fed the mice with breadcrumbs and sometimes even cleaned their box to get rid of the bad smell. And the mouse family was thriving and procreating. Kostia was in charge; he even made sure they behaved properly. He once punished one of the females, calling her a "whore," and expelled her from the box. She was having sex with Terenty Spiridonovich immediately after giving birth. In such a situation, Terenty Spiridonovich was not going to miss a chance. The mouse family grew at an exponential rate and Lisovoy gave mouse couple to anyone willing to take them. Sometimes, the guards took them home for their children. I did not like the mice much, personally, mostly because of their red eyes.

Coal Sorting

Finally, I found myself something to do at work. While watching the coal sorting process, I noticed that a certain amount of coal was being thrown away with the tailings. Typically, this coal was in the form of relatively small grains that were very distinct from the large stones the comprised the waste tailings. Thus, it was possible to separate those coal pieces from the tailings using a series of sieves. I told Sverzev about my findings and he took some interest in my idea. He suggested that I collect a sample that weighed several tons from the waste tailings of Capitalnaya coal mine and do a volume analysis of the useful coal in it. I was given a team of prisoners to help me to collect the tailings. I did the volume analysis using sieves and prepared several samples for chemical analysis. The results showed that the amount of coal increased when the size of the tailings fractions was reduced. The concentration of coal reached about 30% in the smallest fractions, which represented about 10% of the total weight of the tailings. Thus, a large amount of wasted coal could be saved by using a very simple enrichment method. I prepared a report and showed it to Sverzev. Calculations showed that my suggestion would add about a million rubles a year to coal production. Sverzev asked me to write a formal report and to submit it to the technical department of Capitalnaya coal mine. I wrote the proposal, adding the names of Sverzev and Lisovoy as authors, even though they had not taken any part in my work.

Several days later, I was called to the office of the chief engineer of Capitalnaya coal mine, who asked me to review the coal sorting process and give him my recommendations for its optimization. At last, I'd been given a serious and interesting assignment. I needed all the documentation on coal sorting, so I started to work in the technical department of the mine.

Capitalnaya coal mine was one of the largest and most organized in Vorkuta. The head of the technical department was Ivan Nikolaevich, an experienced engineer of about fifty-five years old, with a wrinkled face and protruding eyes. He knew the mine very well, was familiar with every part of it, and was highly respected by all the technical staff, which consisted mostly of civilian employees. His instructions were clear and precise. He provided me with the required documents and during the next few days I studied them in a large, well-furnished, and brightly lit office. The working conditions in this office were quite different from those in my dark and dusty room in the Technical Control Department.

The sorting process was managed by Stolyarov, who at the beginning had treated me with some suspicion. Stolyarov was an elderly prisoner, who had spent fifteen years in the camp, since 1937, and was scheduled to be released in three or four months. He had been arrested for anti-Soviet activity, as one of the followers of Leon Trotsky.[3] Stolyarov had been working in the coal sorting department for several years. He was a good administrator, and the sorting process was organized reasonably well.

Getting Paid

The rumors were correct this time. The camp administration started paying prisoners money for their work. I received my first prison camp salary—fifty rubles in cash. The prison store, where we could buy butter, candies, canned food, etc. also began receiving cash. The line was very long, but I stood there and bought some food. It gave me a very pleasant feeling to be able to buy something for my work. Moreover, these cash purchases reduced the financial burden on my wife, who went to great efforts to send me food packages regularly. Shkolnik and Kaplinsky were paid much better, about four hundred rubles a month. However, the camp administration limited the maximum amount of cash given to prisoners to one hundred rubles a month. The rest went into the prisoner's private account and it was possible to send this money home.

In February or March of 1952, all the prisoners were given new numbers to replace the old ones. Everyone had to wear these numbers on the left sleeve and left trouser leg. This process took a long time. The new numbers were drawn by artists using black ink on white patches of material and tailors sewed these "marks of disgrace" to the prisoners' clothes. All the camp tailors and artists were mobilized for this task. Some prisoners, especially those belonging to the camp's "High Society," hired the best artists to draw their numbers in a special artistic way on lovely, white, silk patches. It may sound strange, but sometimes the beautifully drawn artistic number patches that appeared on new peacoats were less pleasing than the crookedly written number patches sewn onto torn and worn-out old clothes. It is only natural for a man, created in God's image, to adapt to any environment, no matter how unpleasant it is. However, abomination and crime can not be embellished by decoration. So man tries to flick a pile of feces from side to side to make it look more aesthetic. But feces remain feces, no matter how one flicks them.

---

3   Leon Trotsky (1879-1940)—Russian Marxist revolutionary, political theorist, and politician. Expelled from the Soviet Union in 1929 due to his conflict with Stalin.

In April 1952, the first signs of spring started to appear and slowly push the gloomy winter away. The spring winds revived our minds, the snow got darker, and my felt boots got wetter. But, most importantly, the everyday darkness was getting brighter. In the Far North, the transition from winter to summer takes much longer than in the south. The northern skies were mostly clouded, and the snow melted little by little in sloppy stages.

Part 13

The 9th Vorkuta Prison Camp

At the beginning of April 1952, I had a meeting with Abram Kreker, a civilian who worked in the coal enrichment laboratory of the Central Coal Research Bureau (CCRB) of the Vorkuta Coal Trust. His position was a laboratory assistant and he was mainly involved in the logistics and housekeeping of the laboratory. Abram came to see me in my dark and dusty room in the Technical Control Department of Capitalnaya coal mine. At that time, I looked up to him. The status of a civilian was much higher than that of a prisoner. Abram was very friendly and informed me that the coal enrichment laboratory was interested in hiring me. But time passed and I almost forgot about this conversation. However, at the end of April, completely unexpectedly, I was given an order to collect my belongings. I was going to be transferred to the 9th Vorkuta prison camp.

It was a bright and sunny day and the snow was melting fast. My things were quite heavy, so Haikin gave me an old sled and I loaded my suitcase and bag onto it. Besides me, there were two other young prisoners. We were escorted by two guards. We went on foot. Our way was long and difficult with ascents and descents. On some parts of our route, the snow was completely gone and it was difficult for me to keep pulling the sled. So at some point I had to put it aside and start carrying my belongings. I got tired and began to lag behind. The other prisoners and the guards did not have luggage and were walking rather fast, so the guards started to rush me. Eventually, the guards ordered the young prisoners to help me carry the suitcase. They did it, but without much enthusiasm.

After arriving at the 9th camp, I went through the usual routine: an interview to establish my identity, a search of my belongings, leaving my luggage in a storage room, and getting a place in the barracks. I was assigned a plank bed in barracks number 62 for prisoners engaged in heavy labor. The next day, I was immediately ordered to shovel snow on the camp's grounds. The snow had mostly turned to ice, and we used heavy metal rods to break it. I did this work for several days and was very tired.

My first days in the 9th camp were not strewn with rose petals. Barracks 62 was a mess and the local canteen was much worse than in the first camp. The canteen was situated in an old and dilapidated barracks and the food there was not tasty. Work teams ate together, one after another, so we had to wait for a long time for our turn. There were seven categories of food ration, depending on the degree of difficulty and the quality of the prisoner's work. The miners, who worked underground were given the best food, which was quite fair. A year later, a new and larger canteen was built in the 9th camp and the food quality improved a lot.

Now I am going to write about a long period of my stay in the 9th prison camp of Vorkuta, lasting more than three years, from the end of April 1952 until the middle of May 1955. The camp was located on the territory of the 8th Coal Mine of the Vorkuta Coal Trust. This mine was about twenty years old, the oldest in the Vorkuta area. The 9th camp had a long history of human misery. Many prisoners had worked, suffered, and perished there. When walking on the camp grounds, I involuntarily imagined my foot stepping on the blood and bones of prisoners buried there.

The Beginning of Coal Enrichment Work

A few days after I arrived at the 9th camp, I was allowed to enter the industrial area of the camp; there, I met with Naum Rodney, the CCRB department head, and Elena Melenevsky, who reported to him, and was one of the managers of the coal enrichment laboratory. They were both civil employees and I treated them as high-ranking officials, with respect.

The Central Coal Research Bureau of the Vorkuta Coal Trust was located outside the camp, but it retained a small building in the camp industrial area, which hosted the laboratory of Professor Georgy Stadnikov.

Rodney and Melenevsky offered me work at the CCRB in my specialty, coal enrichment. Due to the rigid rules of River camp, I was not allowed to work outside the camp in Rudnik Village, where the coal enrichment lab was located. So I had to start working in Stadnikov's lab and they promised me that I would get a place of my own in the camp's industrial area later. My salary would be 1600 rubles a month.

This offer was a real godsend for me. Our meeting was held during the afternoon of a spring day at the end of April. The three of us walked back and forth along the path in the camp industrial area fenced with barbed wire. The skies were covered with clouds and the snow was still present on the ground along our path. Somehow, they did not choose to talk to me inside Stadnikov's lab. As I found out later, relations between Stadnikov and the civil employees of the CCRB, especially Rodney and Parhanov, the CCRB director, were very tense. Among the staff of the CCRB, Stadnikov had warm relations only with Ekaterina Chichikova, who at that time served as chief engineer. This short walk with Rodney and Melenevsky was the beginning of an important period of my life in the prison camp. It lasted four years, until my release and return to Mining University in Moscow, where I had worked before my arrest.

The Laboratory of Professor Stadnikov

Professor Stadnikov was a veteran prisoner, since 1938. He was a world-renowned expert in the field of fuel chemistry and had worked at the Academy of Science. His books on fuel chemistry were widely used by engineers in the Soviet Union and were translated into several European languages. When I first met him, he was seventy-three years old but still very energetic. I spent a long time working together with professor Stadnikov in his laboratory.

The May 1 was a holiday, and I came to see Stadnikov in barracks 1A, where he was stationed. When I told him that I was going to work in his lab, his eyes showed no excitement. He started to describe the situation at the CCRB to me. The most experienced specialist at the CCRB was Evgeniy Prisadsky, a former prisoner who had only been released recently, at the beginning of 1952. Prisadsky had worked at the CCRB since 1948. He was a coal enrichment engineer, and I had met him and his wife before the arrest. They had both worked in the town of Tula as coal enrichment engineers and in 1945 they had come to Moscow to consult with me regarding some professional issues. The wife of Prisadsky, Olga Bazhova, was the daughter of Pavel Bazhov, a well-known writer from the Ural Mountains.

Stadnikov did not rate Prisadsky very highly. According to him, Prisadsky's work at the CCRB was not worth much and I had been brought to the coal enrichment lab to improve the situation. Stadnikov was one of the most educated people I have met in my life. He had a very strong memory and knew English, German, and French well. Stadnikov had a very tough personality and valued solitude. His manner of speech was very sharp, he used strong language, and liked to scoff at people. He respected, and was deeply devoted to, only three or four of his friends and disdained most of the other people around him. Stadnikov maintained strict order in his life and work. He had an electric stove in his lab and prepared his favorite food and ate it at certain hours. There was a small bed in his lab and every day he rested there for an hour or two after breakfast. Nobody dared to bother him during his sleep.

After the holidays, I started work in Stadnikov's laboratory. The subject of his research was the spontaneous ignition of coal. He had developed a new method to prevent ignition, and after his release from the camp published a book on the topic. I was working independently of him on coal enrichment. His lab was equipped with a few pieces of antiquated scientific equipment from the previous century. To avoid interfering in each other's work, the daily schedule of the lab was divided into two shifts. Stadnikov worked with his assistant Nikolay Rozhdestvensky from early the morning until four in the afternoon; and I worked in the lab with another assistant, Georgy Pshenichny, from four in the afternoon until midnight. Both of Stadnikov's assistants were of a rather advanced age, about sixty, and were quite different from each other. Rozhdestvensky had a twenty-five-year prison term and was mostly interested in music. He played violin and in Moscow had been a member of an amateur symphony orchestra. Even in the prison camp he played violin in the prisoners' orchestra. He was rather overweight and quite lazy in his work. His employment in the lab lasted for a relatively short time. He did not get along well with Stadnikov, who could not stand him because of his lack of interest and the poor quality of his work. A couple of months after my arrival, Stadnikov ruthlessly got rid of him.

By contrast, Pshenichny was rather tall, slim, and good-looking, and had been working with Stadnikov for several years. He was very devoted to Stadnikov, who completely trusted him. In his youth, Pshenichny had served as an officer in Wrangel's White Army, which fought the Communists; and after their defeat, he had emigrated to Bulgaria, where he graduated from a local university as a chemist, married, and ran a successful perfumery business. During World War II, he had joined the German army, and after the war was arrested and sentenced to ten years in the prison camp. Both Stadnikov and Pshenichny were openly antisemitic, but I had to work with them for quite some time until I was able to organize a lab of my own.

When I started work at the Central Coal Research Bureau I was transferred to barracks 1A, which was occupied by prisoners working in the camp offices, among them Pshenichny and Stadnikov. Besides double-decker plank beds, there were several beds with mattresses filled with wooden shavings. I was lucky to get one of those. I was given a narrow bed sheet and an old gray blanket with yellow spots. I lived in barracks 1A for two years, until May 1954.

During my first month at CCRB, I was not very busy. I mostly worked on programs for improving the coal enrichment process in the Vorkuta mines. One day, Evgeniy Prisadsky and Ekaterina Chichikova came to see me. We talked for more than an hour about the plans for the next year and our conversation was quite productive. A few days later, Prisadsky gave me a minor assignment, involving the writing of several reports. Only at the end of September 1952 was I given a serious assignment—to evaluate the amount of useful coal that was thrown away at the 8th mine with the waste tailings. I received several prisoners as help and we worked on this project until December. The work was quite difficult: it involved lots of physical labor. The weight of the rock samples was hundreds and even thousands of kilograms, and we had to transfer them to the facilities of the Technical Control Department , which were located a long way from the mine. The rock samples had to be crushed and separated using a series of vibrating industrial sieves with the smallest mesh size of 1 mm. Then, fractions of different sizes had to be weighed and analyzed, and the percentage amount of useful coal in the different fractions calculated. Eventually, the work was successfully completed and I submitted a report.

At the end of 1952, I had a meeting with Prisadsky and Melenevsky to discuss the plans for the following year. Initially, they wanted to give me the rather dull job of writing reports, but I asked them to allow me to set up a laboratory to analyze core samples of rock taken from geological exploration boreholes. Initially, they objected to my suggestion, but I submitted my proposal to Naum Rodney, the CCRB department head, who was responsible for the laboratory of coal enrichment. Relations between Rodney and Prisadsky were quite tense. Maybe that was the reason for his support; and because of his intervention I was given several reports containing technical documentation of the analysis of the mineral core samples performed in Prisadsky's and Melenevsky's laboratory. I examined the reports and found many inconsistencies. Among other things, they had used the wrong analytical methods. On Rodney's advice, I forwarded my findings to Ekaterina Chichikova, and at the beginning of 1953 it was decided to set up a new laboratory at the 8th mine for analyzing mineral cores.

During the spring and summer of 1952, we enjoyed White Nights with fragile illumination and everlasting sunshine. Pshenichny and I would usually finish work at midnight and return from the industrial area to our barracks. The guard on duty, napping in the booth at the gate, would let us in. Next to the gate, there was a large sign: "Mine Workers— Deliver More Coal to the Motherland." Each working team's productivity figures were posted on the bulletin board. There were also lists of prisoners who had letters or parcels from home. I was always anxious to check these lists, but Pshenichny did not care: he did not get any correspondence. We would stroll between the silent rows of whitewashed barracks surrounded by low-rise wooden fences. The camp commander, Colonel Peter Bogaenko, was very strict and cared a lot about the external appearance of the camp grounds. A few green garden beds were next to some of the barracks. In spring, prisoners planted some vegetables and oats, but they never ripened. They were mainly used for feeding the camp animals at the end of summer.

The barrack rows, surrounded by toy fences with green patches of garden beds, stood under the flickering light of the White Night as if we had been carried away to a fairy village in dreamland. But we knew that in those whitewashed barracks, locked up by heavy locks, there were hapless prisoners submerged in a deep sleep on double-decker plank beds after a hard-working day. A heavy stench pervaded the barracks, and the sounds of moaning, snoring, and mumbling could be heard.

Part 14

My Fellow Jewish Prisoners in the 9th Vorkuta Camp

There were at least fifty Jewish prisoners in the 9th camp; about ten of them lived in barracks 1A. I became friendly with many of them, and I still think of them as rays of light in darkness. Our Jewish company included Leonid Kantargy, David Cohen, Meir Gelfond, Yosef Kerler, Volodya Kerzman, Rotenberg, Fayman, Hesin, etc. My task is to remember and describe, even if only briefly, every one of them.

Many meetings with my Jewish friends occurred during the evening hours, while we walked along "Yuden Street" (Jewish Street), the name we gave to the path inside the camp. Evening strolls along Yuden Street were very popular, and not only among Jewish prisoners. It was quite crowded during the pleasant summer nights. Snitching disease was quite common among prisoners, so I often warned my friends about inappropriate chattering in public about politics. So some of my friends even composed a verse about my long walks:

Zvi Preigerzon, a fervent rambler and a Yuden Street regular,
Likes to talk; but should someone simply open his mouth

He immediately screams: "*Oy Gevalt!*[1]
Please, please, please, not a word about politics."

I have already written about Meir Gelfond and Volodya Kerzman, the members of the Eynikeyt Zionist group in Zhmerynka. They were also transferred to the 9th Vorkuta camp and stayed there until they were freed at the end of 1954. However, their civil rights were not reinstated and they were not allowed to live in large cities and continue their education. After numerous efforts and difficulties, Meir was accepted to Karaganda Medical University, where he studied for three years, and then he switched to another university. I taught Meir Hebrew. He was a very diligent student and a quick learner, and very soon began speaking Hebrew. Even though his vocabulary was limited, it was good enough for discussing life in the camp. Meir worked in the camp's medical clinic with Dr. Petrov, who taught him ophthalmology. Petrov was the most experienced ophthalmologist in Vorkuta and was often called to help patients in other camps. In Petrov's absence, Meir replaced him in the clinic and received patients by himself. He was exceptionally smart and talented and, besides Hebrew and ophthalmology, also learned a lot about human nature.

David Cohen

David Cohen was one of the first Jewish prisoners I met. As was the custom among prisoners, he offered me, a newly arrived inmate, some food and sugar. Cohen was from Akkerman, a small town in Bessarabia on the Black Sea. He was thirty-four years old, of short stature, with black hair and eyebrows, a large nose, and smiling gray eyes. He had been sentenced to ten years in 1947 for Zionist activity among the Jewish population of Akkerman during the Romanian administration. Cohen studied at a Jewish gymnasia and knew Hebrew quite well. He did not shy away from speaking Hebrew with me, but preferred to speak Yiddish. To my regret, I was not able to see him very often. In the evenings I was busy in the lab and during the day he worked as an accountant at the mechanical

---

1 *Oy Gevalt*—"Enough already" (Yiddish).

repair factory. Even now, long after his release from the camp, he works as a head accountant at the same factory.

David Cohen was a good-looking and outgoing man. Despite all his love affairs, he was an old bachelor and remains so even today. His stories about his romantic escapades inspired numerous jokes among the prisoners, and David himself used to respond to these jokes with humor. He did not have an ear for music, but liked to sing Yiddish folk songs and melodies. Some of his favorite songs were "Let Us Make Peace" and "Rachel, Shepherdess of Lavan's Herd." His singing was awful. It was simply unbearable to my ears. So I wrote an epigram about him:

> Here comes Cohen David,
> Always happy and upbeat,
> Singing with his deafening voice
> "Let Us Make Peace"

During his youth in Akkerman, David had been a member of Gordonia, a Zionist youth organization founded by Aaron David Gordon, one of the leaders of the Jewish settlement movement in Eretz Yisrael.[2] I am not particularly au fait with Gordon's ideas, but I do recall that they involved the pioneering spirit and hard manual labor of the Jewish youth and the conquest of Eretz Yisrael by establishing kibbutzim[3] and kvutzot.[4] After graduating from gymnasia, David Cohen had been active in the Akkerman Jewish community. When Bessarabia was "liberated" by the Soviet army in 1940, he was not arrested and was able to join his sister and young brother in Moscow, where he worked in a large government construction organization as an accountant. His work was very accurate and efficient, and he always strove to prepare monthly and yearly reports on time. The management treated him well and granted him numerous awards and bonuses.

David Cohen was a kind and decent man. He liked to read books, magazines, and newspapers and actively followed developments in the Soviet Union and elsewhere, and always had something to say about the

---

2   Eretz Yisrael—Land of Israel (Hebrew).
3   Kibbutz—a collective community in Israel, traditionally based on agriculture and industry.
4   Kvutza—a collective settlement intended to remain small and mainly agricultural. Later, this distinction disappeared; most kvutzot became kibbutzim.

various issues that arose. In his private life, he was rather absentminded. Sometimes, he was so deep in thought that he would not respond to someone addressing him, as if he had not heard them. But David was not taciturn; on the contrary, he liked to chat with friends and could tell stories for hours. All his friends loved him. He had a very good memory, easily remembered people, facts, and meetings, and tried to find the funny side in every event. One would often hear laughter and jokes in his company.

Cohen worked as an accountant in the mechanical repair factory and, as an experienced and trusted employee, the management treated him well. On several occasions, he helped Jewish prisoners get transferred to the factory. The mechanical repair Factory was considered a good place to work. The work there was not very hard, the place was warm, and the employees got valuable professional experience. And, indeed, many Jews were employed there. Among them, I recall Bilik, Yellin, Leonid Kantargy, Arkady Shulman, Georgy Grin, Burvitz, Pruzansky, Wittenberg, and Maisel. There were also some other Jewish prisoners, whose names I do not remember. Volodya Kerzman also worked in the factory for a short period of time. There was a general feeling that David Cohen brought Jewish prisoners together. He was a natural community organizer, enjoyed public activity, and was quite successful in this endeavor. If a prisoner asked David to do something to help him, he could be sure that David would do everything in his power to fulfil his request. David Cohen also supported Jewish prisoners with money and food.

David Cohen had a warm Jewish heart. He actively sought out any piece of news about the life of Jews in the Soviet Union and the State of Israel. Every occurrence of antisemitism aroused bitterness and anger in him. If an article about the State of Israel appeared in the newspaper, he was the first to read it. When he read commentaries criticizing or mocking Jews, and there were plenty of them during 1952-1953, he was dismayed. Those days were extremely difficult for Soviet Jews; all Jewish organizations were shut down, the "Doctors' Plot"[5] was looming, and

---

5   The "Doctors Plot," also known as the case of the killer-doctors, was part of an antisemitic campaign in the Soviet Union organized by Stalin. In 1951–1953, a group of predominantly Jewish doctors was accused of a conspiracy to assassinate Soviet leaders. This campaign was accompanied by media publications that condemned Zionism and mocked people with Jewish surnames. Many Jews were dismissed from their jobs and arrested. The antisemitic campaign ended with the death of Stalin.

many innocent Jews were fired from their jobs and arrested. A bunch of desolate Jewish prisoners, locked in a forced labor camp in the Far North, we heard all kinds of news and rumors and energetically discussed them. But even in the Far North, our hearts were warm, our minds blazed, and our souls were wept.

Leonid Kantargy

Leonid (Leibush) Kantargy was also from Bessarabia. He and David Cohen were very close. They used to talk in Yiddish a lot about shared memories and mutual acquaintances from Bessarabia. I met Leibush about a month after my arrival at the 9th camp and soon after he became my favorite person, like Yechezkel Pulerevitch in Karaganda. We were very close during the next three years, and he warmed my heart in the cold Far North. The atmosphere in the camp was very conducive to heartfelt conversations. Almost every evening we walked together along the camp paths talking to each other. From these conversations, I learned a great deal about him and his relatives.

Leonid Kantargy was born in Kishinev. He lived there before arrest and continues to live there now, since his return from Vorkuta. During his youth, until 1940, Bessarabia was under the Romanian government. Like David Cohen, Leonid was a member of Gordonia and belonged to the Maccabi Jewish sports club. He attended a Jewish gymnasia and spoke Hebrew rather well. His written Hebrew was not perfect, but we did not write in Hebrew in the camp because of the frequent searches and fear of being punished by the authorities. Leonid had a large family in Kishinev with numerous aunts, uncles, and other relatives. His family was not wealthy and they often experienced financial difficulties. Leonid was the only son and had several sisters. Before his arrest, he'd worked for the railroad at Romanovka railway station. At the beginning of the war, his family had been able to escape the Germans and evacuate to the eastern part of the Soviet Union. After the war, he'd returned to Kishinev and continued working at the railroad. He told me a lot about those days, about the men and women he'd worked with. Leonid was a good-looking and brave guy, and girls liked him. In 1946, Leonid had been dating a Jewish girl, Bettie, who was studying at the teacher's college. They fell in love, married, and had a daughter, Rita. Leonid showed me a picture of her. She was very beautiful, with large black eyes widely open to the word. I almost fell in love with her.

In 1950, Leonid was accused of helping Jewish youth illegally escape the Soviet Union and was sentenced to ten years in prison. I do not know if Leonid was involved in smuggling Jews, but during the first years after the war many Jewish boys and girls were able to cross the border with Romania, and from there move to Eretz Israel. The illegal border crossings occurred in the Chernivtsi region, a former Romanian territory, occupied by the Soviet army in 1940. It was facilitated by a group of Zionist youth with connections to a Romanian Zionist organization which operated openly in Romania during that time.

Marriage prevented Leonid from going to Eretz Israel. Bettie did not possess a Zionist spirit. At the end of 1946, before the birth of Rita, the young couple moved to Chernivtsi, where Leonid's sister lived. On November 7 of the same year, disaster struck. A large group of Jews crossing the border was arrested by the Soviet authorities. After that, the border was strictly guarded and there were no more illegal crossings. Soon after Leonid's arrest, his wife left their daughter Rita with Leonid's mother and went to Tashkent where another sister of Leonid lived. There, she continued to study at the local university's teachers college. Leonid's daughter Rita stayed at Leonid's sister's in Chernivtsi. Leonid's father died soon after his arrest and his mother is still alive.

After his arrival at Vorkuta's 9th camp, Leonid was placed in the first category of health and was sent to work as a miner in the 8th coal mine, where he labored for several months. The 8th mine was known for its lack of order and equipment. The work there was mostly manual and particularly hard. The coal mining tunnels were far removed from the central shaft, the ceiling mounts were insufficient, and serious accidents—sometimes deadly—often occurred. Later, Leonid suffered from an irregular heartbeat and was downgraded to the second category of health, which prohibited work belowground. Back in Kishinev, Leonid learned the woodcarving trade from his neighbor. He was very handy and could operate woodcarving equipment. Because of these skills, Leonid was transferred to the mechanical repair factory, where he started working as an engraver at the electrical department. He was also engaged in rubber vulcanization, and became an expert in this area. Besides engraving and vulcanization, Leonid also learned the locksmith trade. He was able to operate various types of equipment and gained a lot of experience at the mechanical repair factory, where he continued working until his release from the camp. Now, in Kishinev, he continues to work in the mechanical factory and thanks to his skills, handiness, and energy earns a good salary.

Leonid did not look like a Jew, but his Jewishness was obvious as soon as he opened his mouth. He had a very strong Jewish accent. He stretched sounds and his speech sounded a bit metallic. His laugh was marvelous; it also had a hint of metal, as if it was simultaneously a laugh and cry. Leonid had a very pleasant tenor voice; it sounded like silver bells. As a southerner, he did not like being outside the barracks during the severe northern weather. There were evenings when I was walking back and forth along Yuden Street waiting for him and he would not come. He liked to sing and had a perfect ear for music, so we used to sing a lot together. During our walks, he taught me many Hebrew and Yiddish songs, which became my prayers. I admired his soul, his songs, his stories, and his laughter. Some of them were just melodies without words.

When we met, Leonid was thirty-two years old. He was of medium height, slender, and broad-shouldered. His eyes were very large, black as coal, with long lashes. His body was always tanned, but his face was skinny and yellowish, as if it belonged to an unhealthy person. However, Leonid was the healthiest among us. He was a natural sportsman and played soccer. Leonid was one of the best players in the mechanical repair factory soccer team and at times we made fun of it. One of the rhymes went like this:

> A Jewish guy, Kantargy Leonid,
> Kicks the ball at the soccer field;
> He is now the soccer champ
> Of Vorkuta prison camp.

Soccer games were the most popular events in the camp's life. During summer, a soccer field was set up inside the camp territory and there were several teams, representing different groups of prisoners—such as miners, mechanical repair factory workers, construction workers, etc. From 1953, the soccer games were also held between teams from different camps. Each team had its own uniform in a distinct color and with large black numbers on the back. After the referee's whistle, the half-naked prisoners with numbers on their backs ran after each other and kicked the ball. When the teams were strong and the weather was good, many spectators gathered around the soccer field. Some of them even brought chairs and benches from their barracks. There was an improvised score-board too. As in any sport, the teams and star players had devoted fans, and there were even commentators who analyzed the games. Every goal scored was accompanied by shouting, applause, and sometimes hats were even thrown enthusiastically into the air. But when the spectators got frustrated with their teams, there were loud whistles and curses were directed at the unlucky players. The camp's commanding officer, Colonel Peter Bogaenko, and his staff also came to watch important games.

Yosef Kerler

Yosef Kerler was born in 1918 in Haisyn, a small Jewish town in the Vinnitsa region of Ukraine. His father was a small merchant, but had to close his shop during the Communist regime, and his family struggled financially. When Yosef was twelve, they moved to a Jewish collective farm in Crimea, where everyone spoke Yiddish and Jewish life blossomed. The flavor of the Jewish way of life in a small town had stayed in Yosef's heart since the days of his youth. He spoke Yiddish and enjoyed Jewish songs and melodies. He began writing poetry and songs in Yiddish; he would pour his soul into them. At the age of eighteen, he moved to Moscow and studied at the Yiddish Drama School of the Moscow State Jewish Theater. One of his instructors was Solomon Mikhoels. Yosef Kerler was a good-looking and brave young man. At the beginning of the war, he enlisted in the Red Army and was wounded in battle. His face was injured and his teeth were broken and replaced with dentures. Following a long recovery, he was discharged from the army and in 1944 joined the Yiddish Theater. He was warmly welcomed there and soon resumed writing and publishing articles and poems in *Eynikeyt*, the newspaper of the Jewish Anti-Fascist Committee. Writing Yiddish poetry became his life's purpose. Kerler started working at the information department of the Jewish Anti-Fascist Committee headed by Lozovsky. The committee had connections all over the world and Yosef's poems were published abroad.

Kerler played an important role in Yiddish poetry, theater, and journalism and contributed to Yiddish culture in the Soviet Union. He was a member of the Union of Soviet Writer and became well acquainted with Jewish poets, writers, artists, actors, and singers. But all of this came to a bitter end. With the launch of the antisemitic campaign, Yosef Kerler's whole world was ruthlessly crashed. Solomon Mikhoels was murdered and the other members of the Jewish Anti-Fascist Committee were either executed or arrested. The Jewish Theater and Yiddish publications were shut down. In 1950, Kerler was arrested and sentenced to ten years for "anti-Soviet nationalistic activity."

And here in Vorkuta 9th camp, I met him, dressed in a peacoat with a number on his back, padded pants, and a prisoner's hat. His life in the camp was not strewn with rose petals. He did not have a profession that was useful in the prison camp and was sent to work in the coal mine. Later, he was transferred to a work team doing hard manual labor aboveground, which was a tough job in the harsh northern weather. Eventually, he got a job in a work team that maintained the steam boilers and the network of steam heating pipes. He was stoking the steam boilers, which was also hard work, but at least it allowed him to stay warm in winter. When his work team was downsized, he was one of the first to go and got a job in a pigsty. Pigs were raised in our camp and were fed leftovers from the canteen. This was in 1953-1954. By that time, prisoners were getting paid and there was no longer a lack of nutrition in the camp. Soup, porridge, and sometimes even bread and salted fish, were good for fattening a pig. Pigs were held in one of the old barracks. It was a pig paradise and there were rumors among prisoners that some of the pigs raised there belonged to camp officials.

I visited the pigs' barracks several times with Leonid Kantargy, who was a close friend of Kerler. Yosef Kerler adjusted well to the work there. Besides the strong and unpleasant stench of pigs, life in the pigs' barracks was pretty good. Furnaces warmed the place and Yosef was even able to cook potatoes. So there we were, the three of us, sitting at a table eating fried potatoes and discussing world affairs. One could hear the loud snoring of the pigs, bright electric lamps lit the space, and the pigs rested comfortably in stalls to the left and right of the central corridor.

However, the pig paradise did not last long; Yosef was soon laid off again. I do not remember the exact reason for his discharge. The administration might have begun to question his pig-raising skills and found an expert. After his expulsion from paradise, Kerler, this former member of the Union of Soviet Writers did ordinary work for a while, but he soon found a job as a sanitation worker. This work was not very pleasant, but it allowed him to have two free days after each day of work, which was quite convenient to him. He used his free time to compose poems and songs. Kerler joked that Vladimir Mayakovsky[6] had been a sanitation worker of the revolution and that he was a sanitation worker of the counterrevolution.

But Kerler's Jewish luck did not last long. He was sacked from this cushy job as well. After some time, he started working for Dinaburg, who was responsible for the horses and transport in the camp. Yosef lived in the barracks housing the stable hands and coachmen. There, he started studying the Hebrew language with Leonid Kantargy. More precisely, he began learning Hebrew from Leonid. Somehow, they got hold of a Hebrew textbook. It was already 1955. The barracks were small, crowded, and filled with smoke and the voices of coachmen. Yosef and Leonid sat at a small and dirty table and learned to talk and write Hebrew. There was something sacred in this scene. If I were an artist, I would paint a picture of them.

Even in the harsh conditions of the prison camp, Yosef Kerler remained a true Yiddish poet and writer. He worked tirelessly and was able to compose many beautiful poems, stories, and songs. He showed me some of them and I even composed music to one of his rhymes:

When I drink a glass of vodka
Everything becomes bright and shiny;
So I throw away the empty bottle and burst into dance.

But rhymes were not the essence of his creative work; the essence was found in his poems and stories filled with humor and irony. Despite his ordeals and torments in the prison camp, he never gave up and always maintained an elevated mood. He looked around him with observant

---

6   Vladimir Mayakovsky—famous Russian poet of the Communist Revolution. He wrote in his dramatic poem "At the Top of My Voice": "I, a latrine cleaner / And water carrier, / By the revolution mobilized and drafted, / Went off to the front / From the aristocratic gardens."

eyes full of irony and was very good at dead-on and funny portrayals of the people around him. To the three of our friends, Rotenberg, Hesin, and Fayman, he gave the nickname "the stinky troika" and he called another prisoner by the nickname "the old adulterer." I really liked to listen to his low and slightly husky voice, especially when he was making fun of people and their manners. Now, Yosef Kerler lives in Moscow. He and his wife visited us last week. After release from the prison camp, he had his rights reinstated and is very active in writing Yiddish poetry.

Rotenberg

I have already mentioned the three friends Rotenberg, Hesin, and Fayman, "the stinky troika." This trio had only a few things in common; they were all of an advanced age, had disabled status, were quite intelligent, and talked a lot. However, they were quite different from each other in every other respect. Rotenberg was the most prominent and talkative of the trio. He had been a metallurgical engineer and before his arrest had served as a high-ranking executive of the Communist Party—a secretary of one of the regional party committees. He behaved as if he was a very important person and the prisoners gave him the nickname "The District Secretary." Like Kerler, he was originally from Haisyn, but his self-image was quite different. Kerler managed to preserve the innocent spirit of this small provincial Jewish town, whereas Rotenberg had lost his Jewish identity. He had left Haisyn long before Kerler and become a completely assimilated man of the world. Rotenberg looked old, was very tall, and had a broad face and large straight nose. He was suffering from high blood pressure and was given the health category of a disabled person, and did not have to work. He always carried a bottle of nitroglycerin with him and took a few drops of this medicine every time he had chest pain.

Rotenberg liked to talk and was a skilled speaker. In his company, one could only hear his loud voice; Rotenberg would not allow anybody else to open his mouth. If you asked him a question he would deliver a long and convincing speech the topic. And the manner of his speech was very sincere, as if he was speaking from a podium. It is not my intention to criticize Rotenberg; he was quite intellectual and had seen and experienced a lot in his life. While in the prison camp he learned of the death of his wife and two sons in Leningrad. His only remaining family was his sister, who was trying very hard to get him out of the camp.

When a law regarding the release of disabled prisoners was issued, Rotenberg hoped to be released under it. The decision partially depended on Colonel Bogaenko, the commanding officer of the camp. Rotenberg was very good at communing with the camp authorities and tried to persuade him to approve his release. Bogaenko promised to help, but did nothing in the event. Rotenberg, with the assistance of his sister, wrote numerous complaints to the Attorney General, the Supreme Court, and the leaders of the Communist Party; but he got a negative reply every time. This lasted until 1955 when political prisoners began to be released in large numbers.

So Rotenberg felt unfairly treated. He became a desperate and unhappy person. The "District Secretary" looked like an unfortunate man, unfortunate because of his imprisonment, old age, sickness, and the death of his relatives. I remember him walking around the camp and complaining to anybody ready to listen to him about his unjust fate. But he would have been better keeping himself quiet. Rotenberg did not realize that his complaints looked ridiculous in the eyes of other miserable prisoners, who'd had their own share of injustice. In a camp, one needed to avoid self-pity and, instead, see oneself and others with a measure of irony while cultivating a simple and practical attitude towards events and people. And if your heart is about to be crushed, let it be crushed in silence. Hide your tears from others. Let your soul fly far away from the prison camp, people, thoughts, and yearnings. And here you are: calm, alone in the whole silent world, without a sound or rustle.

Hesin

The second member of the "the stinky troika" was Hesin, a Jewish man from Moscow, also a former member of the Communist Party. He was the youngest of three, about fifty years old. He had a solid body, elongated face, and black eyes. Hesin's appearance and behavior indicated that he had seen better times. He even wore prison camp clothes with dignity. Before the arrest, he had been an influential person, the head of the state office for the copyright protection of literature and art. The office was in a tall building opposite the Tretyakov Art Gallery in Moscow and employed a large number of lawyers, clerks, and accountants. All Soviet writers, poets, composers, and artists were connected to his office. Hesin was well known by them and had met many of the famous authors. He said he was personally acquainted with Maxim Gorky, Alexander Kuprin, Vladimir Mayakovsky, Mikhail Sholokhov, Isaak Dunaevsky, and Matvey Blanter. On many occasions, he had been invited to the office of Vyacheslav Molotov, who at that time served as a head of the Soviet government.

His arrest had come unexpectedly and was without any rational cause. One would assume that the "District Secretary" in the twenties or thirties might have been somehow involved with one of the rival factions of the Soviet Communist Party, but Hesin was completely innocent. Hesin was not reckless in such matters and his prudence always allowed him to stay on the right side of the road. We talked a lot about his affairs. I suspect that he got eight years in prison camp simply because of his high position. A plausible cause for his arrest was that he preferred to hire Jewish employees, but Hesin firmly denied it. Hesin's denial was believable; he did not have a drop of Jewish nationalism in him and even in the prison camp shunned Jewish matters. He also had disabled status due to high blood pressure, but he worked a few hours a day in the camp's administration office.

If Rutenberg was the most talkative man in the trio, Hesin was a listener. He listened very attentively, but not like a silent listener who concurs with everything. He would respond with an objection or his own opinion on world affairs, and he did so in a very reserved manner, without being excited. He had a pleasant voice and showed intelligence, understanding, and irony in the matters he chose to discuss. He was very precise and was clean and orderly. His plank bed was on the bottom level and always neatly made. I met Hesin's wife when she came to visit him in the camp. She was a pleasant and good-looking woman, quite beautiful then. The gray hair under her kerchief testified to the difficult time she was going through, like many other Jewish women in those years.

Solomon Fayman

Now I am going to describe Solomon Fayman, the third member of the trio. He was a pleasant old Jewish man of short stature, always with a cane in his hand. Like other members of "the stinky troika," he spoke an elegant Russian. Fayman was more than sixty years old and suffered from heart disease. During his time in the camp he was hospitalized several times because of heart attacks. Despite being disabled, old, and sick, he had to work. Fayman belonged to a group of Jewish prisoners from the Stalin Automobile Factory in Moscow. Their files were stamped with the inscription "Only hard labor." Initially, this old man was sent to work belowground inside the mine, then he was transferred to a work team operating above the ground. His team worked on coal enrichment, the kind of labor that requires strong hands and young eyes, and Fayman was weak and old.

In his youth, Fayman had been a hairdresser and a make-up artist at one of the Moscow theaters. He was a pleasant and friendly person and knew how to organize a good party with delicious food. These abilities prevailed over his hairdresser skills, and he moved into the food and hospitality business. Before his arrest, he had served as the canteen manager at the Stalin Automobile Factory. During the antisemitic campaign, he was accused of giving preferential treatment to Jewish personnel in food distribution. The factory employed many Jewish engineers and managers; all of them were accused of sabotage. Such dreadful indictments were directed at Soviet Jews in those days.

So, despite his bad health and old age, Solomon Fayman had been sent to this northern prison camp. I remember him sitting with a cane in his hand together with Rotenberg and Hesin on the bench next to his barracks. The three of them would discuss various issues, the news, and rumors, small and large—from things related to everyday life in the camp to global world affairs. In these conversations, Fayman's voice was not the weakest one or, God forbid, suppressed. The main speaker of the trio was always Rotenberg and the second was Hesin, but Fayman did not hide his head in the sand. He was a chatterer of the first category and enjoyed telling his own stories.

At times, I met Fayman in the industrial area of the camp, where we both worked. I liked talking to him. Fayman would talk in his pleasant voice about his work in the mine and camp affairs. He was always optimistic, tried to find a positive side in every piece of news, and hoped for the disabled prisoners' early release. He told me that the members of his working team respected him and were gave him easy assignments. He was getting paid for his work and, in addition to the food parcels that his wife was sending him from home, was able to buy some food on his own. I remember him shaking my hand with his tiny soft hand and encouraging me: "Do not worry, Zvi, everything will be good, soon we will be home." And this small man, dressed in worn-out prison clothes, who was being held in a prison camp without any fault on his side, slowly moved away from me, leaning on his cane. Even though he was old, sick, and had to work hard, despite all this, Fayman was self-assured, believed in a higher justice, and did not stop hoping to return home, to be like ordinary people. And in the end, after his release from the camp, he succeeded in going back home and reuniting with his wife.

Have sympathy for aging, decrepit, and gradually fading people. If anybody in this world is worth compassion and mercy, they are, with their bald heads, wrinkles, and false teeth. My heart is with them, with those old people who still try to drink from the vast ocean of life, but who cannot quench their thirst out of helplessness. The world is constantly changing, and with each passing year they get close to death, to silent infinity. And here, on this spinning globe, the blue sky will remain, and the rivers will continue to flow. New people will be born, will grow, learn, and strive to achieve their mission in life, and everlasting love will not be erased from their hearts. They will drink their portion of happiness and, later, their time to wither and fade will arrive, the time of old age.

Shaya Bilik

Another Jewish prisoner in the 9th camp was Shaya Bilik, who spent three years with me in Vorkuta. We did not become close friends, but had warm and cordial relations. Bilik was about my age, maybe two or three years younger. He was of rather short stature, with broad shoulders; his most distinctive feature was his baldness, as his head was always cleanly shaved. Bilik was a mechanical engineer and before his arrest had worked as a scientist for one of the aviation research organizations.

Bilik had been arrested because of his membership of the HeHalutz[7] Zionist organization during the days of his youth. His name was found in the records of one of the HeHalutz conferences held in the twenties. Later, Bilik graduated from one of the Moscow universities and devoted himself entirely to research. He defended his PhD thesis and published numerous scientific papers. Even though Bilik had given up his membership a long time ago, the MGB had not forgotten the mistakes of his youth. He had been sentenced to eight years and imprisoned in the 9th Vorkuta camp, where he was a head in the mechanical design department of the mechanical repair factory. His department employed several engineers, one of whom was from Austria.

I met Bilik many times and had long conversations with him. I tried to talk to him in Hebrew; he still remembered a bit from his youth. He was a very serious-minded man and spoke in a low and hoarse voice; his laughter could only be heard on very rare occasions. Both of us had a common weakness; we liked to discuss the gossip and rumors that were plentiful in the camp. Such gossip, along with other things, sweetened prisoners' lives. I must confess that I sometimes even enjoyed inventing and spreading my own rumors. Every time we met, Bilik began with the question: "So, what's new?" To start, I usually recounted gossip that I'd heard from other prisoners, most of it cooked up too, but I would then add some of my own. After that, we would discuss and analyze all of this "news" seriously. As a scientist, he possessed an analytical brain and used its full power to prove that a rumor was false. He vigorously looked for logical inconsistencies and contradictions. I enjoyed such conversations. Every one of them was an exercise in sharpening my brain and scrubbing away mental rust.

But Bilik was not a "dry" person; he had a warm Jewish heart. He was often upset by the unfairness around us and liked to help other prisoners. He did this mostly by comforting and calming, rather than by providing actual help. Bilik became close friends with David Cohen; they spent long hours together, discussing and analyzing various issues. In his efforts to find work for Jewish prisoners, Bilik was the adviser and Cohen did the actual work. Shaya Bilik had another distinctive quality.

---

7   HeHalutz (The Pioneer)—Zionist youth movement that trained young people for agricultural settlements in the Land of Israel.

He deeply feared the camp's snitches. Therefore, he often talked in a whisper, in a restrained manner, looking around him, even when meeting people one-on-one. I am quite certain that such behavior would only have increased the suspicions of any real snitches had they been nearby.

During his time in the camp, Bilik invented a new method of removing rafters, strengthening the ceilings of the shafts in the coal mine. Usually, after all the coal was extracted from a shaft, the wooden rafters holding up the shaft's ceiling would be manually removed and reused. As a result, the shaft would collapse, which was quite dangerous and caused numerous injuries. Bilik suggested removing the rafters using a special pulling machine, with the operator at a safe distance. According to Bilik, if his method was used in every coal mine in the Soviet Union it would save numerous human lives and a huge amount of money. The invention was of enormous interest to the mine administration. A mock-up of a mine shaft was built next to my laboratory and on a summer evening in 1953 Bilik's machine was used to pull the rafters out of it. Bilik directed the experiment and many prisoners, along with the camp administration, were present during the demonstration. I was also there. The demonstration was not completely successful, but it produced some encouraging results.

Mordechai Shenkar

Reb Mordechai Shenkar, an orthodox religious man, was a notable person among us. For quite a long time I had not met such a true and devoted believer in our fickle world. He was originally from Berdichev, about fifty years old, pleasant-looking, with an upright and tall body, a highly conspicuous curved nose, and a protruding shaved chin. His hair was graying, but there was no sign of baldness. He was an experienced accountant and had worked in this profession all his life. During the war, he had been evacuated with his wife to the eastern part of the Soviet Union. However, his parents and twelve other relatives, who stayed in Berdichev, had been murdered by the Nazis. After the war, his family moved to Lvov and lived there until his arrest. He had been working as the chief accountant of one of the local government agencies.

After the war, during 1945-1946, Jews who lived in the parts of Poland annexed by the Soviet Union in 1939 were allowed to return to Poland. Many of them passed through Lvov on their way to Poland. Apparently, among them were local Jews, who had obtained fake documents or bribed the Soviet officials. Shenkar had not been involved in such activity but was blessed with a warm heart and hosted Jewish families on their way to Poland. His home turned into an illegal hostel, and his wife took care of the guests her husband brought from the synagogue. Reb Mordechai had been arrested in 1950, together with about forty other Jews from Lvov and Leningrad. His accusation was somehow connected with a group of Leningrad Hassids. Apparently, a woman who stayed at his place in Lvov had snitched on him and, as a result, he was given ten years in a prison camp.

Reb Mordechai believed in God with all his heart and soul. He prayed regularly, three times a day, and observed the Jewish holidays. He fasted according to the Jewish calendar and, most importantly of all, during his entire time in the prison camp only ate kosher food. In camp conditions, such strict devotion to religion was tantamount to heroism. Employed as an accountant, he abstained from writing on Shabbat and did it in such a way that the people working with him did not even notice. For hours, he would sit at his desk moving the beads on an abacus and did not write. His coworkers were convinced that he was busy verifying calculations. Every Sunday, I asked him if he had written the previous day and he would answer me, "Praise God—the Creator of the Universe, I managed to avoid writing." The three obligatory daily "Eighteen Prayers"[8] were particularly challenging for Reb Mordechai; they had to be recited while standing on one's feet. It was especially difficult to perform this task during work hours in the overcrowded camp without getting attention from the camp authorities, who forbade any manifestation of religiosity in the camp.

Despite all the obstacles, Reb Mordechai prayed several times every day. Besides daily Shaharit, Mincha, and Ma'ariv prayers, he also recited psalms, which he knew by heart, most often the Song of Ascents. During the dark northern evenings, he searched for a secluded place to recite Ma'ariv—the evening prayer—and he often found such place by

---

8 The "Eighteen Prayers" (Tefilat Shemoneh Esreh) or "The Standing Prayer" (Tefilat HaAmidah) is the central prayer of the Jewish liturgy at each of three prayer services on a typical weekday: morning (Shacharit), afternoon (Mincha), and evening (Ma'ariv). The prayer is recited while standing and preferably facing Jerusalem.

the soccer field that was used as the garbage yard during the winter. But even the garbage yard was not secluded enough; it was used by prisoners for their evening walks and I often saw members of different religious groups gathering there for prayers. My heart ached when I watched Reb Mordechai Shenkar praying by the soccer field. He swayed back and forth and whispered the words of a prayer. It was very cold and it would have been much easier for him to recite his prayers while walking; but he stood where he was and lifted his eyes to the sky. After he was done with his prayer, I approached him with two of my Jewish friends and announced in a ceremonial voice: "Reb Mordechai, on behalf of this place and the audience present here and above us in heaven, you are permitted to recite the 'Eighteen Prayers' during your walk." I do not know if my suggestion contradicted Jewish tradition; I only wanted to make life easier for my fellow Jewish compatriot and friend. But Reb Mordechai was not looking for comfort; he continued to pray while standing. In this respect, he really was a holy man.

Eating kosher food was also a sacred act in the reality of the prison camp. He did not eat in the camp's canteen and only took bread from there. He had his own pan and prepared barley soup by himself. He was receiving some kosher food from home and on Passover would even get matzos. Obviously, despite all his caution and care, it was impossible to adhere to all God's Mitzvahs,[9] but the difficulties of the prison camp also served to his benefit. They gave him strength and made him resilient. He prayed to God with all his heart and gained God's forgiveness and compassion. Prayers softened his heart and gave him a measure of self-confidence. Many others lacked such a strong kernel and felt helpless at moments of hardship. The heavens above Reb Mordechai were bright. Almighty God was there, on his royal throne. It was to Him that Reb Mordechai sang his Song of Ascents. He knew that his prayers were reaching the heavens and that redemption would come from there.

I spent many hours talking to Reb Mordechai. He spoke Yiddish and Hebrew with a Berdichev assent, which reminded me of my childhood in Shepetovka fifty years before, at the beginning of the century. Initially,

---

9   Mitzvah—a commandment to be performed as a religious duty. The Jewish law numbers 613 different Mitzvahs.

his Hebrew was not very fluent, but it improved a lot over time. At the end of 1954, Shenkar's wife came to visit and brought him a small book of prayers that made Reb Mordechai very happy. I borrowed the book for a few days and learned Song of Songs by heart. To me, this wonderful gem was a rare and valuable gift. Every day I recited the psalm and each time I discovered new golden nuggets in it. Reb Mordechai also learned Song of Songs by heart and during our evening walks we recited it together and enjoyed its beautiful poetry. Reb Mordechai also taught me the Song of Ascents, and by reciting it we revealed its beauty. Even though Reb Mordechai lacked an ear for music, he enjoyed listening to Hebrew and Yiddish songs. He often asked me to sing him the psalms "Mikdash Melech" and "Avinu Malkeinu."

Reb Mordechai was a man of charity and spent a significant part of his camp wages on it. He also collected money for charity purposes from other prisoners. If a prisoner got sick or was hospitalized, Reb Mordechai was the first to visit him and attend to his needs. He was always in good spirits, especially on Saturdays and holidays. And if in the middle of the twentieth century, in a northern prison camp, in snowstorms, ice, darkness, and extreme cold, there was a man like Reb Mordechai, it signifies the strength of the human mind and proves that belief in God is one of mankind's greatest virtues. We all respected and liked Reb Mordechai and composed a verse about him.

> Reb Mordechai lived peacefully in Lvov.
> Suddenly the butchers came with their grim faces
> And arrested our Reb Mordechai.
> The days and years are passing by
> And Reb Mordechai is still in prison.
> We pray to God to relive his bitter lot.
> God, have mercy on this Hebrew man!
> And our Reb Mordechai is alive,
> Alive and well is our Reb Mordechai.

Perhaps I can conclude my short sketch of Reb Mordechai with the following image, which is deeply carved into my heart. It was on the holiday of Purim[10] in 1953. It was snowing heavily. Three of us, Reb Mordechai, Leibush Kantargy, and I were standing in the middle of Yuden Street and watching the heavy snowflakes fall under the light of the streetlamp. Reb Mordechai was in high spirits and full of enthusiasm and excitement. We were talking about past and present Hamans and about the redemption that, we hoped, was close. In a prison camp, one always strives to restrain one's feelings, but that evening Reb Mordechai was not able to hold his emotions back. He embraced us and with tears in his eyes showered us with kisses, the kisses of a brother and mentor. That evening I saw Reb Mordechai as a symbol of our future redemption.

Leonid Aronov

Before his arrest, professor of metallurgy Leonid Aronov was employed as a department head at Moscow University of Steel and Alloys, located next to Mining University, where I was working. However, I had never encountered him before our meeting in Vorkuta. Leonid was older than me by three or four years. He was tall, solidly built, pleasant-looking, and had gleaming eyes. We did not become close friends, but I enjoyed having friendly conversations with him. Aronov had a medical problem with his bladder and was granted a disabled status, so he did not have to work in the camp. His prison term was fifteen years, and one of the articles of his conviction was treason.

According to him, the reason of his arrest was a casual encounter with Solomon Mikhoels, the famous Yiddish actor and chairman of the Anti-Fascist Committee. It had been in 1946. Mikhoels's nephew, who was studying in his department, was an inept and lazy student and was going to be expelled. Aronov knew about the student's family connection. He called Mikhoels on the phone and described the situation. Mikhoels was very concerned about the future of his nephew and suggested coming to the university to meet Aronov. But Aronov thought that Mikhoels was too busy and suggested that he would come to see

---

10 Purim is a Jewish holiday, which commemorates the saving of the Jewish people from Haman. According to the Book of Esther, Haman was a high-ranking minister of the Persian king Ahasuerus, who was planning to kill all the Jews in the Persian Empire. His plot was foiled by Queen Esther, the Jews were saved, and Haman was severely punished.

Mikhoels at the theater. When they met, they initially talked about the student and Mikhoels promised to help in bringing his behavior to order. Then they discussed Jewish issues. Mikhoels, who was one of the editors of *Eynikeyt*, the Yiddish newspaper published by the Jewish Anti-Fascist Committee, asked for his help in promoting the newspaper. He also suggested that Aronov approach his Jewish fellow workers and ask them to contribute articles about their work at the university. Mikhoels promised that articles written in Russian would be translated into Yiddish. Aronov assured Mikhoels of his help and conveyed Mikhoels's request to several Jewish professors working at the university. He also mentioned these conversations to the head of the university's Communist Party committee, who in turn reported him to the MGB.

A few years later, during the time of the "Doctors' Plot" and the antisemitic campaign deployed by the Soviet government, when Mikhoels was murdered and accused of treason, the case had been revived and professor Aronov was accused of subversion and Jewish nationalistic activity. His conviction involved the confiscation of property; so Aronov was worried about his mother, who lived with him and, despite her poor financial situation, was sending him food parcels. His mother died during his time in the prison camp and Aronov looked like a lonely and sick old man. But his spirit was not broken. Even though he was a leading specialist in electro-metallurgy, he did not want to help the authorities and had no intention of taking part in technical work in the camp. He liked to play chess, but was often losing to other players. We had long and sincere conversations during our walks. He possessed a sharp mind, common sense, and liked to analyze the news and tell stories based on his life experiences.

Shmuel Ferdman

I became close with Shmuel Ferdman, a small man of about fifty, with a large prominent nose. When I met him in 1952, his hair was still black, but over time it turned gray. His neck was always bent, as if he was expecting a disaster. During his youth in Ukraine, he had studied at a yeshiva, got some Zionist education, and gleaned a lot from Jewish wisdom. Before the war, he had moved to the Far East, where he'd worked hard and later served in the Red Army. But something from his Jewish upbringing remained with him. He told me that for a long time he had been trying to recall a Hebrew song from his youth, and had eventually managed to do that. He recited the song to me and I learned it by heart.

After the war, he moved to Zhytomyr, Ukraine, where he worked as an accountant in one of the local restaurants. Ferdman was a bachelor and rented a room in the house belonging to a Jewish widow, whose husband had been killed in a war. They become close and he helped her with housework and raising of her small daughter. However, this relationship was doomed to failure. He knew Hebrew and sometimes visited his Jewish friend's house, where they listened to radio translations from Israel together with several other people. One of those people turned out to be an MGB informer. After the radio broadcasts, they would talk and discuss the news coming from Israel and, of course, the main instigator and participant in these discussions was the informer. In 1950 they all, except for the snitch, were arrested. Ferdman was given a prison term of twenty-five years. Besides listening to Israeli radio, he was also accused of treason. He may have compounded his fate while talking to the judge during his hearing. When asked if he would like to emigrate to Israel, he had naively answered that he would not mind, given proper permission from the authorities.

Life in the prison camp was very hard for Shmuel Ferdman. He did not get any letters or food parcels from home. He sent a letter to the Jewish widow from Zhytomyr and asked her about the belongings that he had left in her house, but received only a short and dry letter in response, with no trace of hope or compassion. At his initial medical examination, he hadn't complained about his health, and even though his age allowed him to be released from the hard labor, he was given the first category of health and assigned to a working team doing hard labor. Initially, he worked in the quarry, digging and loading stones used for construction. One of the stones fell and hurt his face and he was put in hospital. After that, for more than two years, he worked in the bathing house of the coal mine, where he established friendly relations with the other team members. Eventually, his health worsened and he was granted a disabled status. But this only came about in 1954, when significant changes took place in the prison camp. During the day, Ferdman mostly stayed in the barracks, reading books, and dreaming of Israel. Only rarely was I able to meet him outside and have a conversation with him. He had a rather naive voice, and his soul was also naive and innocent. He was a simple man, treated people with respect, and everybody liked him.

Menachem Levi

Menachem Levy was an experienced mechanical engineer, and before his arrest had worked at one of Moscow's research institutes. He was older than me by two or three years. Despite his chubby body, he walked with a proudly raised head and comported himself with self-respect. He was originally from Lodz, Poland, and had come to Russia in the twenties. As a young man, he shared Communist ideals and dreamed of taking part in building a new technologically advanced country. He married a Russian girl, had a son, and advanced on the road towards assimilation. However, a love of Jewish culture and tradition did not leave his heart. When the State of Israel was established after the war, Menachem began attending a Moscow synagogue, where he met an informer, Sasha Gordon, the same Sasha Gordon who was behind my arrest. And like all Gordon's victims, he had been sentenced to ten years of prison without any fault on his side. Once in the prison camp, he had become very critical of the Soviet government and; during our conversations did not hide his views. He was very smart, had a sharp tongue, and was quite disillusioned about his former beliefs.

In the camp, he was initially given the "Fit for work" health category and dug ditches, shoveled snow, etc. Then he was transferred to the Mechanical Repair Factory and was eventually given disabled status. Menachem remembered some Hebrew from his youth and sometimes we conversed in this language. I once recited Song of Songs to him and he became very excited and asked me to write it down for him. I did not do it out of caution, but I still regret not fulfilling his wish, as if I deprived this dear man of a small drop of consolation. However, he later obtained a copied Hebrew text of the Song of Songs with a Russian translation. I met Menachem Levi in 1956, after our release, in the Moscow Lenin Library. He was reading Hebrew books. He told me that his sister was living in Israel and that he had petitioned the government to let him join her. I eventually learned that he had been allowed to repatriate to Poland and from there to Israel.

Boris Dinaburg

Boris Dinaburg was one of the first Jewish prisoners I met in the 9th camp. He was about thirty-five years old and was stationed in barracks number 1, where I lived for the first two years in the prison camp. Throughout his time in the camp, he oversaw the stables and transportation and was one of the high-ranking prisoners. Boris was a veterinarian by education; he fought in the war with the Germans and was a member of the Communist Party. His first wife had been murdered by the Nazis. After the war, he married for a second time and had two sons. Before his arrest, he had managed a large stud farm in the Kirov's region. Dinaburg was a strong and practical man and had always been able to take care of himself. But his luck came to end. He had a quarrel with a local MGB officer and had once even kicked him out of his office. This heroic act resulted in a twenty-five-year prison term.

The transportation of goods in the camp was done by carts drawn by bulls. The stables contained about fifteen young bulls, several horses, and one mechanical truck. Dinaburg was responsible for the animals' health and food, and managed the stable workers and coachmen. He had very good organizational skills and worked in direct contact with the camp's administration. In 1953, he suggested building new stables. Even though he was not a construction engineer, he helped with the design and for the next year managed the construction work and arranged all the required manpower and construction materials. The new stables housed both the animals and coachmen. Dinaburg had his own office, where his prisoner friends often gathered to chat. He liked to tell stories about animals and did so in a very animated manner.

Dinaburg had a pleasant appearance, a golden mustache, and a strong voice. He liked to talk a lot and would not avoid any conversational topic. He had valuable skills—not only in raising bulls and horses, but also in human relations. He was a good and smart man, and behind his burly appearance and loud voice hid a sensitive man who understood the needs and suffering of others. He was not particularly expressive about his Jewishness, but was ready to help a Jewish prisoner in need. I was not particularly close to Dinaburg. Initially, I thought that he looked down on other people. But my first impression was wrong. His loud voice, rough manners, and bossy behavior was a kind of armor, a means of survival in the prison camp.

Michail Shulman

Michail Shulman was a younger brother of the well-known singer of Yiddish folk songs, Zinovy Shulman, who I met in the Karaganda transfer camp. It was Michail's second arrest. He had used to be a member of the Communist Party and served as the first manager of the Red Army Ensemble of Song and Dance. The first time he'd been arrested was in 1937, and he'd spent two years in a mental hospital and then ten years in Kolyma prison camp. His second arrest was in 1950. This time, he only got a five-year term. His brother Zinovy told me that Michail had behaved dishonorably during his interrogation. However, Michail did not want to talk about it and I felt that there was no love lost between the two brothers.

Before his arrival to the 9th camp, Michail had tried, to commit suicide by cutting his veins with a razor, and survived by pure chance. After his recovery in the hospital, he was punished by spending time in prison that had an especially severe regime.

Everyone in the Shulman family had a gift for music, and Michail was also very talented. He remembered the melodies of many Jewish songs and, during our walks along the Yuden Street, often sang me psalms that he'd learned from famous performers back in Odessa. Since my youth, I have had a weakness for Jewish folk songs, melodies, and psalms and I loved listening to his singing. His brother, Zinovy, was very picky about things related to singing and rarely performed; but Michail enjoyed singing and I heard a lot of Jewish songs from him. He also liked to tell stories and was a decent and sincere man. In the camp, he performed at the club and directed prisoners' performances and concerts.

In 1953, after the death of Stalin, there was a general amnesty for prisoners with a prison term of five years or less, and Michael was released from the camp. However, he was not allowed to return home and had to stay in Vorkuta, where he found work in a local theater.

Sasha Eisorovich

Sasha Eisorovich was thirty-six years old when I first met him. He was working as an X-ray technician in the camp's hospital. His prison term of seven years ended in March of 1954. Sasha's background was in radio electronics; he was very handy and could assemble a radio receiver by himself. Sasha had been arrested while serving in the army, and even though he talked a lot, he never mentioned the reason for his arrest.

Sasha was of medium height, with a head full of black hair. He chain-smoked a pipe and was always unshaven. Dark stubble appeared on his face immediately after shaving. He was a smart man with original thoughts and a sharp tongue. He argued with his boss, Doctor Grushevsky, also a Jew, who was the chief radiologist and a surgeon in the hospital. Sasha always described Grushevsky in a bitter and insulting way. They had to work together, but hated each other. Sasha had not received a Jewish education. His father was a veteran of the Communist Party and Sasha had been raised on Russian culture. However, in the camp, he became friendly with Jewish prisoners and began showing an interest in Jewish culture and tradition; he even started to learn Yiddish. His friends were Leonid Kantargy, Yosef Kerler, and Meir Hefner, who also worked in the hospital, as well as George Grin, also an electronics engineer.

As I have mentioned before, one of my technical inventions in the camp was a coal enrichment machine that used X-rays. Kummer and Eisorovich helped me with this work. Kummer did the mechanical part and Sasha the electronic part. We called the machine an ARS—an automated roentgen separator. In the course of our work on this invention, we had many meetings and Sasha made an impression on me as a talented engineer. Sasha was also responsible for the stage lights during performances and concerts at the prison camp club. The club performances were very popular among the prisoners. It could accommodate about 250 people and the camp population was more than ten times that. So each performance was repeated several times for different groups of prisoners. Tickets for the first performance were always distributed among the camp administration, mine workers who'd excelled in their work, and members of the camp's "High Society." Then the performance was repeated for other groups of prisoners: miners, workers at the mechanical repair factory, construction workers, teams employed aboveground, etc. Before the performance, there was usually an official meeting, held by the camp commander and his officers, where technical and administrative issues related to specific groups of prisoners were discussed.

Sasha was often busy and it was quite difficult to catch him for a talk. In addition to his work in the hospital, he spent long hours at the club. He became an expert in stage lighting and after his release was hired as a stage electrician in Vorkuta's theater. Like Michail Shulman, he was not permitted to leave Vorkuta, so they both worked in the local theater.

George Grin

George Grin, a friend of Sasha Eisorovich, was about the same age as Sasha and was also an electronics engineer. He'd moved to the Soviet Union from the USA with his Communist parents in the thirties and his whole family had been given Soviet citizenship. George was tall, with thick black hair, wore glasses, and had a classic Jewish appearance. He had received a good education and was well versed in Western and Russian literature. Before his arrest, George had worked as an interpreter at the American embassy in Moscow. He was accused of spying and was convicted to a twenty-five-year prison term. His sister was also arrested and given a ten-year term.

George was working underground inside the mine and was responsible for replacing the electric lamps in the shafts. All of our efforts to move him to a more comfortable job were unsuccessful. After the release of Sasha Eisorovich, we all hoped that Grin would replace him as an X-ray technician, but Grushevsky was against it, and the job was given to another prisoner from a Baltic republic. It was only in 1955 that he was able to get a job in the mechanical repair factory. I enjoyed talking to George and appreciated his extensive knowledge and intellect.

I encountered many Jewish and gentile prisoners during my time in the 9th camp. In this diary, I have described only a few of them in detail, those I got to know more closely. Obviously, there were many, many others, and I can't write about everyone. Each one had his own life, his own story.

Part 15

Work on Coal Enrichment. Fresh Winds

The New Laboratory

In February of 1953, the Central Coal Research Bureau (CCRB) leased a small building on the territory of the 8th mine, which was intended for my laboratory. I was given permission to hire an assistant and chose Roman Kummer, a German prisoner. Abram Kreker, who I mentioned earlier, was responsible for the logistics and administrative aspects of the lab's operation. At the beginning, the building was empty, but slowly, with Kreker's help, we outfitted it with the minimum required equipment. We had to do everything with our own hands. Kummer turned out to be very inventive and made everything with his "golden hands," from a large box for coal storage, located outside the lab, to a rheostat for the small sorting machine. If all Germans are like him, Germany is indeed a talented nation. We had to bring drinking water from a well located three or four hundred meters from the lab, which was somewhat inconvenient. The water was quite good, even though it smelled slightly of hydrogen sulfide. However, the smell disappeared after some time and I enjoyed drinking this fresh water. The regular tap water for the lab's operations was brought from a workshop that was located about two hundred meters from the lab; but this water was unsuitable for drinking.

After all the equipment was installed, we received the first mineral core samples. The main steps in our analysis involved crushing the mineral cores, separation of the material into different fractions according to particle size (using sieves) and specific gravity (using solutions of zinc chloride of different concentrations), and the flotation separation of powder fractions with a particle size of less than one millimeter. In the beginning, the chemical analysis of samples was done by Pshenichny, Stadnikov's chemical assistant. Later, we hired another German prisoner, Ernest Virth, who began doing chemical analysis in our lab.

Kummer was thirty-six years old, lean, and tall, with a bald head. Before working with me, Kummer was employed at hard labor, so working in the lab was a huge relief for him. He was a very talented mechanical engineer and was very efficient in doing lab work, writing records, and making drawings. And he did everything with amazing speed. I got to know him rather well during our two years working together. I respected him as an engineer, but did not like him because of his views. He did not hide his affection for Konrad Adenauer, the chancellor of West Germany, and even for Hitler, and often expressed hostility towards the Soviet Union and the Jews. Before his arrest, he had worked in the engineering department of an artificial rubber plant in Leipzig, East Germany. One of the engineers he worked with ran away to West Germany and the police came to search his workplace. After the search, Kummer called the engineer's wife, informed her about the search, and warned her to throw away "all the garbage." The phone call had been intercepted and was used as the reason for his arrest. He had been accused of spying and sentenced to twenty-five years. He was deported to Vorkuta forced labor camp, while his wife and children remained in Germany.

Virth was about twenty years old and had a twenty-five-year prison term. Before his arrest, he had been studying at Leipzig University, where he was a member of an anti-Soviet student group. He was tall and wore glasses. He was very friendly with Kummer and other German prisoners, especially with Jan and Hans Mattis, who often visited our lab. Jan was a professional singer and was a member of the famous Tirol Choir; and Hans was a housekeeper in barracks number 17, where I lived later on. Kummer and Virth were also stationed in barracks number 17. Hans

Mattis was a pleasant-looking young man. In his broken Russian, he told me a lot about his life in Germany. He'd been a wealthy businessman, the owner of a photo studio network with branches in both parts of Germany. The Communist government in East Germany was not going to tolerate his success, so he had been accused of spying and sentenced to twenty-five years in prison. There were more than a hundred German prisoners in the 9th camp. Most of them were doing hard labor. However, I preferred not to make friends with the German or Lithuanian prisoners. Even though there were many decent people among them, they all seemed quite odd to me, with their foreign language and alien mentality.

In April 1953, Kreker brought a young woman to the lab, Luisa Putatova, who was going to work with me as a technician. Even though she was only twenty-one, she was already married and was breastfeeding a baby; she was therefore permitted to work reduced hours. She was a Russian girl from the town of Kalinin and had just graduated from Vorkuta Community College, with a specialization in coal enrichment. While in college, she had met her future husband, Volodya, who had been studying electromechanics. Volodya was older than her by one year. Luisa was a pleasant woman, of short stature, with blond hair, blue eyes, and a soft childish voice. She said that she'd been given the uncommon first name of Luisa because, at the time of her birth, her older sister had been reading the novel *The Headless Horseman* by Mayne Reid and was very fond of the main character of the book, Louise Poindexter.

Luisa's arrival brought a pleasant change to our work environment. After spending long years in a prison camp inhabited by men, it was our first encounter with a member of the female sex. The younger workers were particularly taken with her. At first, she seemed lazy and would spend most of her time chatting, but eventually Luisa turned out to be a useful assistant. She was instrumental in helping with the process of flotation separation, which required the presence of two people. She learned the procedures quite well and was able to make calculations using an ancient arithmometer that was older than her by a considerable number of years.

Meanwhile, life in the camp went on. In spring and summer, the days dragged on forever. In winter, darkness, cold, and heavy snowstorms reigned. My days were quite monotonous; every morning after roll call I passed through the prison camp gate on my way to the lab. The workday lasted for eleven to twelve hours and every night I came back to the camp through the same gate and heard the new stories and rumors that had surfaced during the day. Twice a day, I ate in the camp canteen and always had an aluminum spoon tucked in my pocket. But most of all, I enjoyed evening walks with my friends, usually with Leibush Kantargy, along Yuden Street.

At times, I read novels, but not as often as nowadays. Every day, I "prayed," i.e., sang and recited the Jewish songs and psalms in Hebrew and Yiddish that I'd scheduled the day. At times, I received letters or parcels from home. Such days were like holidays to me. We went to the lab even on Sundays and holidays. It was much more pleasant being in the quiet lab than in the overcrowded and noisy camp barracks. On Sundays, we did not work; we just sat there, reading technical books provided by the Central Coal Research Bureau. We even received technical periodicals that were published abroad. Once, in the German magazine *Glukauf Mining Report* I noticed a translation of one of my papers on coal enrichment, which had originally been published in 1948 in the Soviet journal *Coal*. Kummer and I were also busy working on inventions.

Fresh Winds

After the death of Stalin in March 1953, fresh winds began to blow and changes started to happen in the prison camp system. First, there was a general amnesty for prisoners whose prison term was five years or less. However, this amnesty was largely for nonpolitical prisoners; it was mainly for common criminals and thieves, as the prison terms of the political prisoners were typically eight years and above. Then, there was an amnesty for young prisoners, who'd committed their crimes before the age of eighteen. Next in line were prisoners who's completed two-thirds of their prison term. All releases were subjected to the decision of the regional court, and in the beginning the number of released political prisoners was quite small. The camp administration fed us with false explanations and promises, e.g., they told us that in Vorkuta there was only one law court and that it was overloaded with petitions from all the Vorkuta prison camps. This uncertainty created a fertile atmosphere for rumors and speculation. Everyone had his own theories, based on his word view and personality.

The prisoners from the Baltic republics were confident that they would be returning home first. The Jews also had their hopes. Immediately after the death of Stalin, prisoners that had been arrested during the antisemitic "Doctors' Plot" campaign were released and their accusations quashed. The Russian woman doctor, who'd given false testimony against the well-known Jewish physicians, was demoted and all of her awards were taken away. The fall of Beria in June 1953 also contributed to optimistic feelings. But life in the 9th camp continued as usual and, besides hopes and rumors, nothing changed in the camp's routine.

In July 1953, there was a prisoner strike. For several days, the coal mining was disrupted. The prisoners demanded that the camp administration implement the government decree regarding the release of young prisoners, who'd committed their crimes under the age of eighteen, as well as those who had served two-thirds of their prison term. Such cases had to be decided by the regional court, but the months passed, and the court did not convene. When the strike began, the camp commander, Colonel Bogaenko, took drastic measures. He doubled the number of soldiers guarding the camp perimeter and armed the guards on the watchtowers with automatic rifles. He also shut down the entrance to the camp and reduced the food ration. The only member of the camp administration who was allowed to enter the prison camp was the medical officer in charge of the hospital. After a week of the strike, a large group of high-ranking officials from Moscow, including State Attorney Rudenko and Commander of Internal Troops Maslennikov, came to the camp. All the prisoners were called for a meeting. They were allowed to voice their concerns. About twenty prisoners took the opportunity to speak. Bogaenko, who really was a despicable man, was accused of numerous violations of the law. The officials promised to take care of the prisoners' demands. Their only stipulation was the resumption of mining operations. The very next day, the regional court was held in the camp, the release of prisoners got underway, and the strike was over.

During 1954, many changes occurred in the life of prisoners. The 9th camp's strict regime was revoked it and became like the prison camps for common criminals. The number patches on the back of our clothes were removed. We were permitted to wear civilian clothes and take photographs. Unrestricted postal correspondence and visits from close relatives were allowed. At first, visits were limited to three or four hours, in the presence of guards, but from May 1954 unguarded visits by relatives were extended to a week and even longer.

By pure chance, I was the first who was permitted a long family visit. My wife came to see me on May 4 and stayed for eight days. We were allocated a room in the guards' barracks, which was furnished with tableware and bedclothes. At that time, I did not have permission to go outside the camp, but my wife was free to come and go.

The gradual release of political prisoners also began in 1954, and everyone felt a ray of hope in his heart. Prisoners from foreign countries, such as Germany, Austria, Poland, and Yugoslavia were released in an organized manner. Some prisoners were released after a positive response to their petitions. Some of my friends, Shaya Bilik, Meir Gelfond, Volodya Kerzman, Stadnikov, and Sasha Eisorovich were released in 1954. But many Jewish prisoners remained in the camp until 1955 and even later.

By the end of 1954, the Germans working with me, Kummer and Virth, together with Jan and Hans Mattis were sent back to Germany. In barracks 17, where I lived at the time, there were a lot of empty plank beds and I started to feel sad. Of course, lack of space is bad for sanitation, but it also creates a warm feeling because of people's closeness.

In 1954, several groups of actors who were prisoners were allowed to give performances in the Vorkuta camps. The artistic groups included musicians, singers, and actors from all the camps. They also featured woman actors, who created a huge wave of excitement among the prisoners. The free tickets to these performances were grabbed like hotcakes. The audience greeted the artists with excitement. Particularly popular was the clarinet player Vasily Bender and a young Russian girl who performed lyric songs that touched the hearts of the prisoners. The concerts raised our spirits and gave us a feeling of hope. Outside the club, hundreds of prisoners who were not able to get tickets to the performance were waiting: they were just hoping to have a look at the women actresses, as they left the club building.

In October of 1954, I spent three weeks in hospital because of thrombophlebitis in my right leg. While in hospital, I lay with my leg raised up. After that, I began walking with a cane, and I kept using it until my release. My cane was just a knobbed stick, painted in brown.

In the fall of 1954, the Central Coal Research Bureau of the Vorkuta Coal Trust was transformed into the Vorkuta branch of the All-Union

Coal Research Institute, whose headquarters were in Moscow. For a few months, I continued to work on the analysis of mineral cores, but at the end of the year this task was given to another entity belonging to the geological office and my lab was transformed into a flotation laboratory. Olga Bazhova, the wife of Evgeniy Prisadsky, was appointed as a lab manager. My work in the lab was progressing very slowly. After the release of my German assistants, Kummer and Virth, I'd had to hire new ones. They were decent people, but lacked motivation. They behaved according to the Russian saying: "Wherever you work—avoid work." Luisa came to the lab each day, but she mostly chatted and flirted with the young prisoners who were attracted to our lab because of her. Laughter and chatterer continued throughout the day in the lab.

In February 1955, the first group of common criminals was brought into our camp. The objective was to replace the political prisoners who were being released. The camp territory was subdivided into two zones, one for political prisoners and another for common criminals. The real intentions of the camp administration were not clear, as one could pass freely from one zone to another. Immediately after the arrival of the common criminals, incidents started to occur. Thefts, fights, swearing, and confrontations between the common criminals and political prisoners became commonplace. The barracks occupied by the common criminals quickly became neglected and turned into dirty garbage bins. The common criminals refused to work and mainly played cards during the day.

The newly arrived common criminals were given new clothes. Immediately, a market for clothes grew up, and political prisoners who had money were able to buy new peacoats or shoes for a relatively small amount of money.

With the arrival of the common criminals, we were transferred from barracks 17 to barracks number 43. But soon, the common criminals started entering barracks 43 too, and I had to ask Dinaburg to shelter me in the stable barracks. The living area was part of the stables. It was mostly occupied by the coachmen and the prisoners who took care of the bulls and horses. The barracks were rather dirty and the people there were uncouth, but quite decent. The Jews were represented by Dinaburg and Yosef Kerler, who was a member of one of Dinaburg's working teams. Leonid Kantargy often came to visit us. Kerler and Kantargy were studying Hebrew; they'd somehow obtained a textbook with pictures. I loved them both with all my heart.

Many political prisoners were released during those days. I remember the day when a coachman, who occupied the plank bed above me, received the news about his release. By pure chance, in our conversation the morning of the same day I mentioned his upcoming release. In the evening, when I returned to the barracks from work, the man rushed to hug me and offered to treat me to all his food. A rumor spread that I was a prophet and that anyone who lived next to me was going to be released. And, in fact, while I was stationed in barracks 43 all my neighbors did get released one by one—so I began believing the notion myself.

From February to May 1955, a large number of common criminals arrived in the 9th camp. Life in the camp became difficult and walks along Yuden Street and even club visits became dangerous. Once, someone stole my glasses when I was at the club. I was perplexed. Why a young thief need them? Maybe he was just practicing his trade? I put notices on the canteen wall and bulletin board and promised to pay for their return; but no one responded.

I once again moved to barracks 11, which had previously been occupied by common criminals. The barracks had been cleaned and repurposed for political prisoners. In one of the three rooms of the barracks, we arranged a Jewish corner, where my neighbors were Mordechai Shenkar, David Cohen, Hesin, Izkovich, and Mitelman.

The Rudnik Laboratory and Transfer to the 40th Prison Camp

At the end of 1954, I was permitted to stay outside of the prison camp without escort from six in the morning until ten in the evening. So I began going on both short and long trips outside the camp. I often visited the large and well-equipped Coal Enrichment Laboratory in Rudnik Village. At the beginning of 1955, the management of the All-Union Coal Research Institute decided to move my lab to Rudnik. So, in April 1955, with the help of Abram Kreker, all the furniture and equipment from the small building in the industrial area of the 8th mine where I'd worked for more than two years, was loaded onto a carriage and moved to the main lab in Rudnik Village.

With the arrival of spring, the speed of release of political prisoners increased. Many prisoners were permitted to work and live outside of the camp territory. But many Jewish prisoners in the 9th camp remained. Hesin and Rotenberg received negative replies to their petitions, Solomon Fayman was put in hospital after a heart attack, Samuel Ferdman was given disabled status and relieved from work in the mine's bathhouse, Menachem Levi, who had disabled status, kept playing chess most of the time. Once, he received a parcel from his sister in Israel. We all looked at the precious things from Israel that were inside and our hearts melted. Boris Dinaburg's prison term was reduced from twenty-five to ten years. I often spent time with Leonid Kantargy. We sang melancholy Hebrew songs together. Reb Mordechai Shenkar kept praying regularly; he loudly recited psalms and talked to God:

> I will raise my eyes to the mountains in the distance
> And my voice will be heard as a scream, as the prayer of a man,
> And my heart will discover where my help come from.

The snow was gradually melting, but in the Far North it took a long time. The camp territory turned into a dirty swamp. But the White Nights were coming; the skies became brighter and clearer. The fresh winds of spring inspired us to dream about freedom.

Yes, fresh winds were blowing, but my body still ached on the upper plank bed of barracks 11 in the 9th camp. The days were getting longer and longer and the nights shorter and shorter. During the day, I worked in the Rudnik laboratory. Many decent people were also employed there, most of them former or current prisoners. Peter Bezsilko, Viktor Profestis, Semen Dolzenko, Sarah Weissman. Evgeni Prisadsky, Elena Melenevsky, and Abram Kreker also worked there. My assistants were Luisa Putatova, who'd come with me from the old lab, and Maria Stezenko, a very nice woman, and a very good coworker, who had moved to Vorkuta with her son to be close to her husband, who was serving time in the forced labor camp. In the lab, a room was set up for me to live in, if I was permitted to live outside of the camp. The head of the Vorkuta branch of the All-Union Coal Research Institute wrote several letters to the camp administration asking them to let me live outside, as was previously done for Stadnikov.

But the camp commander Bogaenko refused to let me go without any reasonable explanation.

I spent the May Day holiday in the 9th camp, under the authority of Bogaenko. He was an ill-bred and cruel man. Sometimes, he pretended to care about a prisoner; but he was actually a ruthless and greedy tyrant. It is quite possible that at the bottom of his soul he realized the horrific role of an executioner that he was playing. The whole forced labor camp system was designed to destroy human dignity in both the prisoners and the camp administration. Every officer in the prison camp administration had to be an executioner, otherwise he could not keep the job.

In the middle of May 1955, I was ordered to collect my belongings for transfer. I was able to say goodbye to all my friends in the 9th camp. And again, with a suitcase in my hand and a knapsack on my back, I headed to the 40th prison camp together with several other prisoners. Our way was not very long, only a few kilometers.

Barracks 34 in the 40th prison camp was mostly empty and very dirty. For several days, I was not able to go to my job in Rudnik. My authorization to work outside the camp was effective only in the 9th camp. I had to call Prisadsky, and he arranged new permission for me. The route from the 40th camp to the Rudnik laboratory was about four to five kilometers. It ran mostly through the tundra, partly along the railway tracks. The spring days were very bright. Early each morning, I left the camp through a checkpoint, crossing the territory of the coal mine and entered the tundra. On my right was the prison camp's cemetery. Many simple crosses with blurry inscriptions. The name of the prisoner, his year of birth, and year of death. I see the name of a Jewish prisoner, who I've heard about before. I leave this sad place and continue along the railway tracks. On my left, the Vorkuta river is flowing quietly. The tundra is blooming. Here and there, I can even see small flowers. I continue along the barbed wire fence of the 9th camp, where I have lived for the last three years. Behind this fence, in bitter winter snowstorms, we have suffered, spoken Hebrew, sung songs, and dreamt about the future. Then, I turn left and go down the steep slope towards Rudnik Village, where the Coal Enrichment Laboratory is located.

It is still early, about seven in the morning. The working day starts at eight, and my coworkers have not arrived yet. The cleaning lady, Maria Ivanovna, is opening the door; she works the night shift. She likes to talk, and every morning I have to listen to her stories about the hard work she does and problems with her family. But the bell is ringing and Semen Dolzenko enters the building. He is Ukrainian, a former prisoner, who has served ten years in the camp; and after his release married a young woman, Nina, who once worked in the lab. Sometimes she visits him in the lab with a baby girl in her hands. Then Profestis arrives, a Lithuanian, around fifty. He's already served his ten-year prison term, but his wife is still imprisoned somewhere in Siberia. And here comes another Lithuanian, Victor Kazimirovich, a tall and pleasant man of about forty. He used to be a Catholic pastor and had also served ten years in the camp. I've had many conversations with Victor Kazimirovich. He knew Bible very well and could even recite few lines from the Old Testament in the Hebrew language: "In the beginning, God created . . ." He was very intelligent, understood the human soul deeply, and continued to perform confession, even in the prison camp.

The time is almost eight. Abram Kreker, Peter Bezsilko, and Vania Sinushin are arriving. I've mentioned the name Abram Kreker several times. He helped me a lot during my stay in the 9th camp. He was never imprisoned, but was deported to Vorkuta during the war. There, he married a local woman and they had four daughters. He was responsible the lab's housekeeping and the delivery of coal samples from the mine. I respected Abram Kreker because of his good attitude towards prisoners.

Peter Bezsilko was about thirty, a former prisoner. He was the most active and experienced assistant in the lab and was studying at university by way of a remote learning program. He was originally from Western Ukraine. When the Soviet army arrived in his hometown in 1939, his family ran away to Poland. During the war, he was sent to work in Germany and afterwards returned to Ukraine, where he was arrested as a deserter. He worked in the lab during his imprisonment and continued to work there after his release.

Vania Sinushin was released after serving ten years in the prison camp. He was a talented guy, a close friend of Peter, and was also studying remotely at university. The lab managers, Prisadsky and Melenevsky, respected both of them and relied on their work.

Then Evgeni Prisadsky, Elena Melenevsky, and Sarah Weissman enter the building. The last to arrive is Luisa; this pretty and talkative girl always appears at the last possible moment.

Work in the lab continues until five or six in the evening. It is time for me to return to the 40th camp. And here I am, walking back along the same path. Along the barbed wire fence of the 9th camp, the railway tracks, the Vorkuta river, and the cemetery. The guard opens the gate, and I enter the 40th camp.

Thank God there were many Jews in the 40th camp as well. Some of them lived in barracks 18, where I was stationed. One of the Jewish prisoners was Levin, a veteran prisoner, who I first met in the Abez prison camp four years ago. He had grown a bit older but, as before, he liked to read newspapers and discuss recent news while walking outside the barracks with his fellow Jewish prisoners.

David Yoffis, from Riga, was a fluent Hebrew speaker. He was forty-four years old, but looked much younger than his age. Yoffis was tall and healthy, with glittering raven-black hair that partially covered his forehead. Before his arrest, he'd served as the principal of a school for technical education. His wife, a music teacher, was barely making ends meet in Riga, where she lived with their two children. She often sent him letters full of love and compassion. In the camp, he worked in the planning office of the 40th mine. I enjoyed talking Hebrew with him during our evening walks. He loved the Hebrew language as much as I did and had solid opinions on many subjects.

And here I am, walking with Yoffis on the grounds of the 40th camp, along the rows of white barracks. The late evening is very quiet, the gray-blue sky is spread out above our heads, and the guards on the watchtowers do not take their eyes off us. The muted words of Hebrew can be heard in this northern part of the world. Yoffis is telling me stories about his life in Riga before the Soviet occupation. Riga used to be one of the main Jewish towns. Then, we talk about literature and review recent world news and the future that awaits us. Yoffis was an innate optimist and was hoping for our early release. He foresaw that in a year we would all be free, and not just released from the camp, but with our rights fully reinstated. And, as it happened, his predictions were right.

In 1955 there was a reorganization of the Soviet prison camp system. Now there were the following types of regimes in prison camps and prisoner statuses, starting with the harshest:

—penalty camps
—high-security camps

—medium-security camps

—low-security camps

—prisoners with permission to live outside the camp

—prisoners released without the right to live outside Vorkuta

—prisoners released but restricted to living outside large cities

—prisoners released without restrictions—full reinstatement of rights

Up to 1953, the camps where I was held—Karaganda Sand camp, Inta camp, Abez Mineral camp, and Vorkuta River camp—were all defined as high-security prison camps. In 1953, the name of River camp was changed to Vorkuta camp and its status was reclassified as a medium-security camp. Life in the 9th Vorkuta camp, where I was until May 1955, became unbearable after the arrival of the common criminals. At that time, the 40th camp was still occupied by political prisoners, and life there was safer. But soon after my arrival, it was subdivided into three zones: one for common criminals; another with medium security for political prisoners; and a third one with low security for political prisoners.

After the fence dividing the camp territory was completed, I was transferred to low-security zone. It was a big relief. I was able to leave and enter the camp territory at any time and, besides Rudnik Village, where I worked, I was able to go to the town of Vorkuta and its surroundings on any day of the year. However, David Yoffis remained in the medium-security zone, where the canteen, the store, the hospital, and the bathhouse were located, so I went there to see him almost every evening.

New transfer! It was announced that all elderly and disabled prisoners were going to be transferred from the 40th camp to Abez. Many of my fellow Jewish prisoners, including me, were on the list. I went to the camp commander, Pavlov, and asked to be taken off the list because of my work in the coal enrichment laboratory. With great displeasure, he allowed me to stay. It was very sad to part with my friends who were destined for transfer.

The management of the Rudnik laboratory had asked Pavlov to permit me to live outside of the camp several times. But Pavlov had a negative opinion of me, and each time he rejected their request. So I continued walking an hour each way, back and forth on foot, to my work during the whole summer, until September. But I do not look at this period with regret. I was doing interesting work in the lab, and I regularly met with my old friends Leonid Kantargy, Reb Shenkar, Yosef Kerler, and David Cohen, as well as with my new ones.

In summer, prisoners were allowed to build homes outside the camp. Building materials were supplied by the mine authorities. In a short time, about ten new barracks appeared along the road leading to the camp. Each evening, after the end of the official workday, one would see prisoners working on the construction. The banging and sawing could be heard from afar. All this construction was being done in the middle of the silent tundra, and the water of the Vorkuta river slowly flowed to faraway places.

In the fall of 1955, Leonid Kantargy was released from the camp. Initially, he did not get a permit to leave Vorkuta and had to stay in the area, so he continued working at the mechanical repair factory; but he was paid full salary and temporarily lived with David Cohen. Permission to leave Vorkuta arrived from Moscow two or three months later. One day it arrived, and Leonid left for Chernivtsi. I was happy for him, but was a little sad too. I loved Leonid with all my heart; he was like a ray of sunshine in the darkness. Soon, a letter from Leonid arrived. He wrote about his warm reception form his family and friends. Later, he moved from Chernivtsi to Kishinev, the town of his youth, and began working there at a local mechanical factory. His wife and daughter joined him there. When I was released from the camp, he sent me a congratulation letter. After that, our correspondence stopped.

One by one, our friends were leaving us and moving to the wide world far beyond Vorkuta. I continued living in the 40th camp's low-security zone and working in the Rudnik lab. In the evenings, I would meet David Yoffis, who was at last transferred to the low-security regime zone. We would speak Hebrew and sing Hebrew songs. One day, Yoffis was granted freedom with the full reinstatement in his rights. He told me that his wife had traveled from Riga to Moscow and personally submitted a petition for his release to the Central Prosecutor's Office. After two or three days, David Yoffis left for Riga. Before his departure, he assured me again about my upcoming release.

The camp commander, Pavlov, continued to refuse to allow me to live outside the camp. However, in August I received an official patent for my invention, which I'd submitted with Andrey Usov back in Karaganda.

The patent was awarded to me by Pavlov. This time, he was more friendly and promised to help me. A few days later, I found my name on the list of prisoners allowed to live outside the camp. In the Rudnik laboratory, there was already a room ready for me to live in. Abram Kreker had done his best again and the room was freshly painted and furnished with a desk, chairs, a bed, a mattress, and linens. I soon moved to my room in the laboratory.

In the coal enrichment laboratory, I continued working with my assistants Luisa Putatova and Maria Stezenko. Luisa, as always, was quite lazy and liked to chat a lot. However, Maria turned out to be a very valuable coworker. She was still waiting for her husband to be released from the camp. During that time, I was also working with Sergey Furmansky. The old man had finally got his formal release from the prison camp, but not full reinstatement in his rights; and he had to stay in Vorkuta. However, his employment status was above mine. We would meet in Rudnik's canteen every afternoon. The food there was quite good, fresh, and tasty, the waitresses wore white aprons and smiled at us. Once a week, I had to check in at the camp. So on certain days I had to go all the way to the 40th camp. The fall was at full strength. The days became shorter, the tundra turned yellow; it often rained and the water of the Vorkuta river turned gray. Again, I found myself walking next to the snow barriers along the railroad, the cemetery, the barbed wire fences, and the camp watchtowers.

In the middle of September 1955, I was invited to the camp's medical commission. There was a rumor that the commission was going to certify the release of disabled prisoners from the camp. And indeed, a month later I was given my release papers, according to the government decree of 3 September 1955 pertaining to the release of disabled prisoners. However, it was only a partial release. I was still forbidden to live outside Vorkuta. But it was a huge change in my status. My position at the All-Union Coal Research Institute was officially upgraded to senior researcher and group leader, and my salary increased significantly. Now my status was equal to that of Sergey Furmansky. Parhanov, the head of the Vorkuta office, gave me his full-hearted congratulations. The lab's work was conducted in two shifts, from eight in the morning until midnight. Viktor Kazimirovich, a former priest, worked the second shift, and I often had long conversations with him. At night, all the workers went home and I was left alone in the large building. All the doors and windows were tightly locked to prevent theft by the common criminals who worked in the neighboring cement plant. However, after midnight, the cleaning lady, Maria Ivanovna, would enter the building.

The Home of Haim and Nehama Solz

Haim and Nehama Solz lived in Rudnik Village with their daughter Sarah. Haim was working as a chemist in the analytical laboratory of the geological organization, Nehama was doing housekeeping, and Sarah was in the second or third grade at primary school. Both Haim and Nehama knew Hebrew. Before the Soviet occupation of 1940, they'd lived in Kovno, Lithuania, and had been married there in 1939. When I first met them, at the beginning of 1955, Haim was about forty years old. He was tall and good-looking, with brown hair and fiery eyes. Back in Kovno, he had been a yeshiva student and a member of a Jewish Zionist organization. During the war, he served in the Soviet army. However, in 1946 Haim was arrested for Zionist nationalistic activity and convicted to seven years in a forced labor camp and three more years in exile. After his release in 1953, Nehama and Sarah, who had been exiled to the eastern part of the Soviet Union, joined him in Vorkuta.

Nehama was a very pleasant Jewish Lithuanian woman. She was somewhat younger than Haim, a bit plump, had a lovely face, and wore glasses. When I first met her, she was in the first months of pregnancy, and in the fall of 1955 she gave birth to their son Reuven. The Solz family lived in a small house on Rudnichnaya Street. I had spent the happiest days of my life in Vorkuta in this house,

A Jewish atmosphere reigned in the Solz house. It really was a Jewish house in the Far North of the Soviet Union. Haim and Nehama warmly welcomed all Jewish prisoners. Every one of us, after spending long years in overcrowded and dirty barracks, felt himself at home in their house; this sweetened the bitterness of the Far North. When given a pass to be outside the prison camp, each one of us found his way to this warm place. I often met my friends there—Yosef Kerler, Leonid Kantargy, David Cohen, and later Mordechai Shenkar, who was the last to get a pass. Reb Shenkar became a frequent visitor at their place, and with Nehamas's help often cooked kosher food.

In the Solz's house, I become acquainted with many other Jewish families who lived in Vorkuta. Among them were Boris and Klara Urman, Avraham and Athalia Bandes, Ida Putik, Isai and Rita Haichik, Yasha and Lina Moshkovich. All of them had been arrested because of their Jewish roots and many of them were accused of Zionist activity. At first, I was worried about informers, and out of caution only visited the Solz family occasionally. But when I got to know everyone, I started to trust them; besides, we never had anti-Soviet conversations. Some of Solz's friends were trying to emigrate to Israel and eventually achieved their goal. The Bandes, Haichik, and Moshkovich families got permission to leave the Soviet Union for Poland, and from there they went to Israel. All those dear people, most of whom I am unlikely to see again, will stay forever in my memory.

Nehama was very hospitable; we were always welcome in her house. Sarah, Solz's daughter, liked to sing the Hebrew song "It's not a Miracle if There Are Such Beautiful Nights" and her parents were delighted to hear her singing. I spent many hours in the Solz's house and every visit there was like a holiday for me. We also met at the Urman's several times, as well as the Haichik's and Bandes's houses. Even though not everyone understood Hebrew, we tried to speak in it as much as possible. We sang Hebrew and Yiddish songs and celebrated Jewish holidays. What can I say? It was such a pleasure; maybe it was even more pleasant than it is now?

The summer of 1955 was especially hot. The Vorkuta river became warm enough for bathing and swimming. I also got into the water several times during my walks to the lab in Rudnik Village and back. There is no greater pleasure than to jump into cold water. I remember one day in July when the Solz family and several of our friends spent an afternoon on the banks of the Vorkuta river. It was a beautiful day, a southern day in the Far North. We talked a lot, joked, jumped into the water, and sunbathed until our skin was burned.

We often celebrated Jewish holidays at the Solz house. Everybody, apart from Reb Shenkar, enjoyed drinking. And when we got quite drunk, we cheered our hearts by singing. Leibush Kantargy would begin with his pleasant and soulful voice. I would follow him. Kerler, Bandes, Urman, and Nehama Solz also joined the choir. The problem arose when David Cohen added his voice. It was a disaster. He could even ruin the well-known Jewish folk song "Hava Nagila." David liked to entertain his audience, especially when he was a bit drunk.

Abram Bandes was a former member of Beitar, from Lithuania. He was a pleasant-looking man, slightly over thirty, with a proudly held head full of dark curly hair. Both he and his wife Athalia spoke fluent Hebrew and it was a great pleasure to talk to them. I was especially fond of Athalia, a short-sighted woman, who was marvelous at singing Jewish songs and would waggle her head from side to side the way small children do. Avraham also had a good ear for music. Sarah, Solz's daughter, enjoyed playing with Avraham. When he entered the room, she would immediately jump on his lap and start a friendly fight with him.

Yosef Urman was originally from Chernovtsy. Later, he and his wife Klara moved to Moscow, where he worked as a teacher. Klara was also very pleasant and intelligent. They did not have kids. Yosef had been arrested in Moscow, accused of Zionist activity, and had served time in Vorkuta forced labor camp. Klara had joined him in Vorkuta after his release. Yosef was about forty, with a bald head. He was fluent in Hebrew and enjoyed singing Jewish songs. He had seen a lot during his life and I loved talking to him.

In the Solz house, I also met the married couple Yasha and Lina Moshkovich. Yasha was over thirty, originally from Poland, a devoted Jewish man. He liked to sing, in his hoarse voice, a song about the Warsaw ghetto, which deeply touched our hearts. After completing his prison term, he married a nurse, Lina. Lina was not young; she had come to Vorkuta from the Caucasus to find a husband and had caught Yasha in her net. One of Yasha's songs about the Warsaw ghetto, sung in his hoarse voice, still rings in my ears.

I should also mention another member of our company, Moshe Teif, a Yiddish poet from Minsk, who fought in the war and was released after serving his second prison term. Moshe was about fifty and sported a goatee. He often recited his charming lyrics and we all enjoyed his deep voice. He was corresponding with a middle-aged unmarried Jewish woman from Moscow, who he never met. It was a pen pal love affair, and she was helping him with petitions for his release and sending him food parcels. After the reinstatement of his rights, he went to see her in Moscow, but their meeting did not go well, and she became very upset.

Nehama tried her luck at matchmaking. She knew an unmarried woman in Vilnius and attempted to connect her and David Cohen, who was a bachelor. The woman sent him a picture. Her face was very pretty and we all worked hard to soften David's heart. Somebody even helped him to write a suitable reply, which was not an easy endeavor. But all our efforts were in vain. David remains a bachelor until this very day.

Sometimes, our company was joined by Ida Putik, a woman from Bessarabia, who was serving a prison term for her Zionist activity. She was not that young or pretty, but was like a sister to us. She was living in a women's camp with a low-security regime and worked at the brick factory. Everyone tried to support her and find her a husband. David Cohen was the obvious candidate, and Ida hoped to get the attention of this fickle guy. They were both Zionists from Bessarabia and, had experienced a lot in their lives, and even had many mutual acquaintances. She was courted by other bachelors, but only had eyes for David. But again, David couldn't make a decision, and the match never happened. Ida was very disappointed. I was told that after I departed from Vorkuta, Ida Putik married Semen Fish, a former prisoner from Poland, and together they were able to leave the Soviet Union for Israel.

Mazal Tov! In October of 1955, Nehama Solz gave birth to a son, Reuven. His birth coincided with the Simchat Tora[1] holiday. A large party was held at the house of Haim and Nechama. There were toasts for the newborn and it was a joyful holiday. I wrote comic verses in Yiddish for the occasion. We drank a lot and sang our songs. It all was very pleasant and delightful.

In November 1955, my wife came to visit me for a second time. This time, we stayed in my room in the lab. She stayed with me for about a month and had to adjust to life in the laboratory and the harsh Vorkuta weather. Before long, she got to know, and became friends with, Haim and Nehama Solz and all my Jewish buddies. She was welcomed by everybody and became a part of our company. But it was already winter, and the polar nights, cold, and snow ruled life in Vorkuta with their full force. The laboratory was on low land, and to get to the Solz's house we had to climb a steep and icy slope. For a while, our journey was aided by

---

1 Simchat Torah (Rejoicing of the Torah)—a Jewish holiday that celebrates the conclusion of the annual cycle of Torah readings and the beginning of a new cycle.

steps that were cut into the ice covering the slope. But when a new layer of snow buried the steps, my wife, God bless her and let her live a long life, who was not exactly a mountain climber, had a hard time getting up the slope. We climbed uphill and slid back down many times, which was actually quite fun. At the beginning of December, she traveled back to Moscow.

Part 16

Release from Vorkuta Prison Camp

Later, in December of 1955, Haim Solz brought me a telegram from my wife. She informed me of an important telegram that was waiting for me at the post office. I immediately went to the post office, and in the second telegram there was a formal notification by the State Prosecution Office about the full reinstatement of my rights, dated December 12, 1955. It was total rehabilitation. My imprisonment had lasted six years, nine months, and twelve days. The management of the All-Union Coal Research Institute received the news about my rehabilitation with great compassion. All the years that I had spent in the forced labor prison camp were redefined as the years of work in the Far North, and my salary, which was already quite high, was doubled. I now got ten thousand rubles a month. I also submitted an application to the local social security office for my retirement pension. As a mine employee, after the age of fifty I was eligible to receive both—the regular salary and the state pension.

After becoming a free man, I threw a party at Haim's and Nehama's house. I invited all my Jewish friends, most of them former or current prisoners. I bought all the food and wine in the local store with the help of the store manager, who was married to one of the former Jewish prisoners from Azerbaijan. The party was very joyful; we ate and drank a lot. There were many toasts and speeches. The party continued with the singing of Yiddish and Hebrew songs. We felt like brothers; we were all united by past and present suffering, and by hopes for a better future. I cannot help thinking about the hospitable house of Haim and Nehama Solz, about my friends who were jailed by a tyrannical government for no reason. Even though their lives were ruined, a spirit of friendship united us and turned our company into a closely knit brotherhood.

My wife wanted me to return to Moscow immediately, but I felt an obligation to finish my scientific projects at the lab and prepare the final report. I was working very hard, days and nights. I had to process a large amount of data and my assistants helped me a lot. Eventually, the report was ready. It was verified, typed up by the typist, and bound into two voluminous books. The first one contained text and the second one contained tables and attachments. At the beginning of February 1956, our team, including Prisadsky and the other managers from the Vorkuta office of the All-Union Coal Research Institute, traveled to Moscow to submit the report. However, I still had to return to Vorkuta to receive my pension documents. My journey on the passenger train was very pleasant. The service was quite decent. The radio played nice melodies and songs, and dinner was served in a separate restaurant carriage. How different it was from prisoner transfer in an overcrowded Stolypin carriage.

At Moscow train station, I was welcomed by my wife, children, and some of my close friends. Our reunion was very warm and convivial. While waiting for the taxi, we were standing in front of the train station and talking loudly with excitement. Suddenly, a stranger of about forty approached us and shouted, "You dirty Kikes, get out of here!" That was how Moscow greeted me after seven years of absence. That kind of abuse was not very common in Moscow. Maybe the man was just drunk, but his insult is imprinted on my heart forever.

And there I was, at home in Moscow, where my family had lived since the thirties. We had a festive party attended by my extended family and many friends—more than thirty people. Among our guests was my daughter Nina and her husband German Lipovetsky. They had married during my absence. German's mother and grandparents were also in attendance. Professor Ilya Verhovsky, the department head of Moscow Mining University, where I had worked before my arrest, was also present. There was an abundance of food and drink. I was very excited to see this crowd of people; all of them were very close to my heart. There were many toasts in my honor, and we sang joyful Jewish songs. After the party, my wife and I received numerous invitations; so we were very busy, going from one friend or relative to another, for many evenings after my return.

During the working day, I went to the main office of the All-Union Coal Research Institute, located in Panki, a suburb of Moscow. There, I met Prisadsky, Parhanov, Starostin, and other members of the Vorkuta branch. The presentation of our reports was going to be held at the Central Institute for Coal Enrichment, also located in Panki. But the days passed, and the presentation was delayed and delayed. Eventually, the meeting was held, and I presented not only my report but also the entire Vorkuta laboratory report for 1955. There were several remarks by the reviewers, but they were mainly concerned about the work done by Prisadsky. Eventually, all our reports were approved.

At the beginning of March 1956, I returned to Vorkuta and was given my pension documents. From the beginning of January 1956, in an addition to my salary, I started to receive 2500 rubles. But my luck did not last long. In October the same year, the law changed and my pension addition was suspended.

I remained in Vorkuta until March 20. The management of the All-Union Coal Research Institute tried to convince me to stay for another year and continue receiving my very high northern salary. But I was not willing to stay there, even for such a large amount of money. Besides, I had been offered my previous position as a professor at Moscow Mining University. So I bid farewell to Vorkuta and to all my dear friends who remained there: Haim and Nehama Solz, Reb Shenkar, David Cohen, Yosef Kerler, Sasha Eisorovich, Yakov Moshkovich and his wife, and many, many others. I also said goodbye to my coworkers at the Rudnik laboratory, to my assistants Luisa and Maria, Prisadsky, Melenevsky, Kreker, Furmansky, and Parhanov.

The day of my departure was very sunny, and bright snow sparkled all around us. It was cold, but very pleasant. Vorkuta train station looked neat and clean. The trains' noises were accompanied by blasts of steam. I stood on the platform with the friends who came to see me off. We exchanged memories and jokes. And then, the last call and the train was leaving. My train ride back to Moscow was very joyful. I bid farewell to the prison camp surrounded by barbed wire fences and the guard towers standing along the railway tracks.

Shalom to Vorkuta. Shalom to my memoirs.

Moscow
April 28, 1957–February 18, 1958

Images

A page from Zvi Preigerzon's memoirs.

The Preigerzon family, 1949. Binyamin, Nina, Lea, Athalia, and Zvi.

Zvi Preigerzon in Lubyanka prison, 1949.

Zvi Preigerzon in Karaganda prison camp, 1951. Drawing by prisoner artist Bokov.

Zvi Preigerzon (bottom left) and his coworkers, Vorkuta 1954.

Zvi Preigerzon and Luisa Putatova, Vorkuta 1955.

Zvi Preigerzon before his release, Vorkuta 1955.

Zvi Preigerzon, 1968.

Nina, Binyamin, Lea, and Athalia at Zvi Preigerzon's grave, Kibbutz Shfaim, Israel, 1979.

The Solz family, Vorkuta 1954. Haim, Sonia, and Nehama.

Meir Baazov before his arrest.

Zvi Plotkin before his arrest.

Yosef Kerler.

Aron Kricheli.

Members of the Eynikeyt Zionist group, Vorkuta 1954. Top row, from left to right: A. Polonsky, A. Band, Y. Miller, and David Cohen. Bottom row, from left to right: Volodya Kerzman, Michail Spivak, and Meir Gelfond.

Alexander Khodorkovsky.

Michail Spivak.

Meir Gelfond.

Yechezkel Pulerevitch and his wife in Kaunas.

Reb Mordechai Shenkar in Israel.

Leonid (Leibush) Kantargy after his release from prison camp, 1955.

Motl Grubian, Yiddish poet.

Shmuel Halkin, Yiddish poet.

Index

www.ingramcontent.com/pod-product-compliance
Lightning Source LLC
Chambersburg PA
CBHW020530270326
41927CB00006B/516